To Wilma, Darrick,
Marc, and Michael

Demystifying
Social Deviance

Demystifying Social Deviance

Stuart L. Hills
Professor of Sociology
St. Lawrence University

McGraw-Hill Book Company

New York St. Louis San Francisco Auckland Bogotá Düsseldorf
Johannesburg London Madrid Mexico Montreal New Delhi
Panama Paris São Paulo Singapore Sydney Tokyo Toronto

1 2 3 4 5 6 7 8 9 0   KPKP   7 8 3 2 1 0 9

Library of Congress Cataloging in Publication Data

Hills, Stuart L
  Demystifying social deviance.

  Includes index.
  1. Deviant behavior. 2. Conformity. 3. Social control. 4. Social structure. 5. United States—Moral conditions. I. Title.
HM291.H527   301.6'2   79-9788
ISBN 0-07-028917-4

This book was set in Times Roman by Automated Composition Service, Inc.
The editors were Richard R. Wright and Barry Benjamin;
the cover was designed by Mark Wieboldt;
the production supervisor was Donna Piligra.
Kingsport Press, Inc., was printer and binder.

Contents

1

SOCIAL DEVIANCE IN MODERN SOCIETY

2

STUDIES IN DEVIANCE AND CONFORMITY

Preface

Central to the perspective of this book is the conviction that deviance is in large measure a social creation—a dynamic product of human judgments and the particular social and cultural patterns that characterize a society. The kinds of behavior socially condemned as deviant are tremendously variable; and particularly in modern pluralistic societies, both the conceptions and the social control of deviance become the frequent object of moral and political struggles.

The introduction briefly describes this broadly conceived interactionist-conflict perspective around which much of the text is oriented. This sociological perspective, which perhaps is best characterized as humanistic, frames the study of deviant behavior around these parameters: the meanings people impute to social behavior, the significance of shared and conflicting values, the distribution of power, and the structure of economic, legal, and political arrangements in the society. Every theoretical orientation, of course, carries with it a variety of implicit biases, especially when filtered through the research lens of flesh-and-blood sociologists. Any approach to the study of social behavior implies a point of view, assumptions as to what is worth studying and from what particular vantage points and value orientations. The guiding perspective in this book is no exception. Whatever else may have inadvertently colored our sociological observations, the tone of the analysis throughout the text clearly supports (I hope) the values of individual dignity and self-determination and the creation of a more humane and just society.

Chapters 1 and 2 develop this humanistic sociological perspective further, focusing particularly on the ways in which established groups attempt to conceal the relativistic, changing, and ambiguous nature of deviant social phenomena. Despite the mystifying rhetoric of moral absolutism, sometimes cloaked in scientific and medical garb, I believe that the most disturbing features of social deviance are not usually the result of any pathological condition lodged in the individual but a human adaptation to particular social values and beliefs, divergent interests and life-styles, and situational strains created by sometimes oppressive social institutions. Indeed, many of the most culturally approved social arrangements in society that shape conforming behavior also help produce many of the troubling problems that upset and anger many Americans.

Each of the five chapters that make up Part Two of the book explores in greater depth this close interrelationship between deviance and conventionality. Although each chapter contains a wealth of information, there is no attempt to "cover the field" for each topic. Instead, each chapter is written from a particular thematic point of view that I think readers will find more interesting. Implicit in the analysis is the assumption that deviant social behavior and the reactions to it grow out of the basic culture, social structure, and deep social changes transforming modern American life. By focusing on such important but diverse problem areas as rape, organized crime, psychoactive drugs, drunken behavior, and homosexuality, we can reach a deeper understanding of the humanly manufactured character of social deviance that may at the very least suggest the possibilities for the creation of a society more responsive to human needs and diverse values. The book concludes with a brief epilogue on the future of deviance and diversity in America.

Although this book is primarily designed as a short text or supplementary reading for college courses in social deviance, social problems, and criminology, the treatment of the issues in these studies hopefully will prove useful to a wider reading audience, one concerned with exploring the complexities of disturbing social phenomena.

Chapters 1 and 2 draw upon a few pages of material previously appearing in two earlier articles of mine: "Absolutist and Relativist Views of Social Deviance: Toward a Humanistic Perspective," *Humanity & Society*, **1** (Summer 1977) and "The Mystification of Social Deviance," *Crime & Delinquency*, **23** (October 1977). Part of Chapter 4 incorporates a few sections from the chapter "The Cosa Nostra and Organized Crime," in my book *Crime, Power, and Morality*, Chandler Publishing Company, Scranton, Pa., 1971. Chapter 5 includes selected excerpts from my article, "Drugs and the Medicalization of Human Problems," *Journal of Drug Education*, vol. 7 (4), © 1977, Baywood Publishing Co., Inc. Appreciation is extended to the journal editors and publishers for permission to adapt these materials.

This book was written during my sabbatical leave, and I am grateful to St. Lawrence University for providing me with financial support and this opportunity. To those authors whose basic research and theoretical perspectives I have utilized so liberally I owe a rich debt, acknowledged only imperfectly through footnote citations. I am also deeply grateful to Joan Mousaw and Gwen Clookey who typed most of the manuscript and to Barry Dank, Bruce Johnson, Charles McCaghy, and Richard Troiden for their constructive comments on earlier drafts of the book. Finally, special thanks go to Lyle Linder for his enthusiastic support in the conception of this project and to McGraw-Hill editors Richard Wright and Barry Benjamin for their devotion in guiding the book through the editorial and production process.

Stuart L. Hills

Introduction

Until very recently, one major question dominated the study of social deviance: *Why* does a person become a prostitute, a political radical, burglarize safes for a living, sniff cocaine, inject heroin into his veins, "drop out" of society without working, practice satanic witchcraft, make love to someone of the same sex, or act in other kinds of deviant or criminal ways? Implicit in much of this inquiry were several typical assumptions: (1) that such deviant behavior is self-evidently undesirable and intrinsically harmful, consistently condemned by all normal, well-adjusted people in society; (2) that persons who engage in such behavior are *essentially* different from other ordinary citizens—a small fringe group of deviants: immoral, dangerous, abnormal, or sick (popularly viewed as whores, crooks, dope fiends, hippies, commies, perverts, weirdos, faggots); and (3) that a satisfactory explanation for the actions of such *kinds* of people can be discovered only through study of the distinctive biological or psychological disorders presumed characteristic of deviants or the disturbed social environments (deprived, disorganized, or pathological) in which they are reared—the basic root causes that allegedly compel such persons to act out and persist in their unconventional behavior.

Many sociologists, however, have begun to question these and other related assumptions of the conventional wisdom, indeed, to challenge the adequacy of the very way of formulating the fundamental question—Why do they do it?—that has oriented the vast bulk of scientific research and popular discussion in this field. Increasingly they have insisted that the following kinds of questions are equally important to achieve a fuller understanding of the complexities of social deviance:

1   Why are certain kinds of behavior considered deviant in the first place? What functions do such conceptions serve for various individuals and groups in society?

2   By what processes does a person come to feel and act like a deviant? What maintains his or her deviance at the present time?

3   Why are certain individuals or groups singled out and branded as deviants while others engaged in similar activity are not?

4   How does the societal reaction to persons considered deviant affect their commitment to deviant life-styles and identities? What are the consequences of the social control of deviance for the larger society?

5   Why do certain kinds of deviant roles in a society emerge, persist, and subsequently change? How are these changes related to the culture, structure, and dynamics of the society?

Although some aspects of these questions have a rich heritage in sociology, only recently have they prompted sociologists to strike out in new research directions. Perhaps one of the most fruitful lessons learned from this growing research is the importance of grounding analysis of deviant behavior in the social meanings, human values, and economic, political, legal, and social arrangements in the society. Rather than being freakish, alien, pathological, genetically fated, or biologically aberrant, many of the most disturbing aspects of deviant behavior represent a response to the cherished values, beliefs, deeply ingrained institutional practices, and often repressive features of our civilization. Deviance and conformity are but two sides of the same coin: the conventional configurations of American life that help shape conforming behavior also help produce much of what most troubles us. The integral relationship between deviance and conventionality, however, is frequently obscured by the mystifying rhetoric of moral absolutism and the pronouncements of medical and social science.

The purpose of this book is to sensitize the reader to some of these *deviance-creating and mystifying processes* in modern complex societies. Part One explores particularly the ways in which dominant groups attempt to conceal the humanly constructed character of activities and persons thought of as deviant or normal, thereby masking the conflict of interests, competing values, and mainsprings of power in society. Part Two examines in greater depth the implications of this humanistic sociological perspective for the understanding of five problem areas in American life: *rape, organized crime, psychoactive drugs, drinking behavior,* and *homosexuality.* Central to the analysis of each of these topics is the conviction that such perplexing social behavior grows out of the very culture and structure of the society.

The sociological perspective that guides our inquiry takes as its starting point the somewhat ironical observation that in a very real sense society manufactures, *creates* through social condemnation, deviance. Deviance is not a property *inherent* in any activity but something which is *conferred* upon it by human judgement. Deviants are not objective, raw phenomena "out there" in nature—furtive creatures floating around in the universe external to and independent of human observers—but arbitrary, artificial, socially constructed categories of persons. Therefore, deviants are relative to a given society, social setting, and the ability of certain powerful, well-organized minority or majority groups to make their social rules and conceptions of deviancy the dominant, controlling ones.

From this theoretical view, full-blown deviancy is not usually a suddenly occurring phenomenon—nor preordained by the wrong chromosomes, personality traits, or neighborhood residence—but the emergent *outcome* of social interaction. The acquisition of most deviant roles and the commitment to deviant identities typically involve *developmental processes* of action and reaction, response and counterresponse, through which behavior and personal attributes take on social significance. Through informal or formal interaction with other individuals and organizations (such as relatives, friends, peers, teachers, employers, psychiatrists, police, prison and hospital officials), some rule-breakers may be labeled as deviants. They may come to acquire deviant self-images, to drift into deviant life-styles, and to experience stigmatizing, harsh or punishing modes of social control (even if sometimes masked by a vocabulary of "therapy" and "treatment").

Occasionally, these social processes of defining, labeling, and treating others as deviant may function in unintended but self-fulfilling ways to engulf the person in a deviant role, impelling that person to live in a kind of internal exile within society. Escalation to a deviant self-identity, however, does not necessarily result only from official, dramatic acts of *public* labeling, as in arrest and the degrading ceremonies of court trials or entrance into a prison or an asylum. From the mass media, from jokes, from the mundane, everyday events of social life—from all the informal and amorphous processes of socialization—the growing awareness of the general public contempt felt toward people "like one's self" (frequently the case for undeclared homosexuals) may constrain persons to label themselves as in some manner deviant and to organize their life partly around the consequences of this *symbolic* (rather than publicly affixed) *stigma* they experience.

Yet this emphasis on symbolic interaction also reminds us that humans are not simply passive, inert objects on which external social forces deterministically exert their influence. Men and women need not be mere pawns of fate, totally victimized by genes, labels, or social circumstances. Instead, through *self-initiated* reflection and collective action humans can shape to some degree their identity and experience.

A full understanding of deviance, then, must not only include analysis from the perspective of the powerful or the majority—and their formal social-control agents—but also take into account the subjective *meanings* that persons considered deviant impute to the social forces which impinge upon them—*their* assessment of the situation, *their* interpretation of social reality. The investigator must try to understand how such persons *experience* the mainlining of heroin, furtive sexual encounters in a public rest room, blasting open a safe, sexual assault on a date, or "corrective rehabilitation" in a 6- by 9-ft cage; how they label themselves and their behavior, even when their social transgressions go undetected; how they seek to manipulate the impressions others have of them, to negotiate or neutralize derogatory labels and social penalties; how they—like all of us—attempt to enhance, protect, or dramatize their most prized possession: their self-conception. Such sensitivity to the deviant's perspective will necessitate an examination of their social world: its imagery, argot, life-styles, taken-for-granted beliefs, subterranean values. What kinds of symbiotic relations exist with more conventional, "respectable" worlds? How do thieves, homosexuals, and heroin addicts cope with the existential problems of managing their lives—meeting their needs and desires, relating interpersonally to others (both hip and square), and maintaining themselves psychologically in a society that often brands them as social outcasts?

Since conceptions of deviance and normality will vary among groups with different values, beliefs, and life-styles, such stigmatizing designations as criminal, sick, insane, subversive, and dangerous are also *political* actions— often backed by coercive legal sanctions: death, imprisonment, enforced hospitalization, police harassment, job disqualification. In modern pluralistic societies, acts of labeling, therefore, frequently become the focus of social conflict and struggle between the individual or small, loosely organized, less powerful groups and the established, dominant groups. Conceptions of deviance (such as psychedelic drug use, homosexuality, rape, abortion, pornography, communal living, sexual freedom) may become the basis of moral crusades and countercrusades, of liberation movements and countercultures contesting the proper moral and legal status of the disputed deviant activity as well as the most just and effective method of social control (including simply being left alone to pursue "alternative" life-styles). And because the outcome of such crusades is often *symbolic* of the social and political dominance of certain groups—their ideals, life-styles, interests, versions of reality—many kinds of partisans of repression or support of the behavior in question are drawn into these struggles. The participants include not only militant deviant groups and their organized moral adversaries but also scientists, psychiatrists, and others whose expertise, credibility, and influence are mobilized as strategems to discredit opposing views.

Part One

Social Deviance in Modern Society

Chapter 1

The Mystification of Social Deviance

When most contemporary sociologists speak of social deviance they are simply referring to socially condemned behavior: violations of the established social rules and customs that prevail in a community or society, particularly actions that anger and upset the powerful or the majority and which elicit attempts to punish, correct, or isolate individuals engaged in such personally discreditable activity.

In practice, however, the determination of what kinds of behavior, belief, or personal attributes comprise deviant activity, who should be treated as a deviant, and in terms of whose social rules is a complex question. The degree of consensus regarding what is immoral, abnormal, or even criminal may be highly variable. Different individuals and groups may hold radically divergent views as to the nature of conformity, morality, and normality, indeed, as to the very essence of social reality: conceptions of what *is* and what *ought* to be. Especially in a rapidly changing, heterogeneous, complex society, conflicting conceptions of deviance may prevail.

For example, who is more deviant in contemporary America: a nineteen-year-old boy scout or a recreational pot-smoker at an Ivy League university?

A twenty-nine-year-old unmarried traditional virgin or a militant women's liberationist? A New York City legislator who tries to ban the film *Last Tango in Paris* as "evil, obscene and pornographic" or an upstate rural New York minister who condemns *The Grapes of Wrath*, assigned as reading in a high school English class, as "the work of the devil"? A Wall Street stockbroker who dabbles in the occult and witchcraft or a middle-class, suburban house-wife who worships a fifteen-year-old oriental guru? A Harlem janitor who plays the illegal numbers game at the corner candy store or the Baptist who censures her atheist neighbors as sinful for their Saturday night poker games? A Mississippi man who insists he has boarded a space ship manned with strange creatures from another planet or the members of a mystic cult in New Jersey who flee to a mountaintop to await the imminent end of the world? A General Electric vice president who conspires with other corporate officials to fix prices or an executive who refuses to do so? A San Francisco college girl who enjoys oral-genital sex with her boy friend or her roommate who contends that such behavior is disgusting and abnormal? A man who burglarizes a psychiatrist's office in the name of national security or a Catholic priest who spills blood over draft files to protest pilots' "roasting babies alive" by bombing Vietnamese villages?

Most readers would have difficulty in answering these questions with assurance. Nevertheless, many groups and individuals, including some scientists and psychiatrists, define deviance as departure from an absolute set of values. Only a minority of persons view deviance as man-made, shifting, and frequently ambiguous.

ABSOLUTIST AND RELATIVIST VIEWS OF DEVIANCE

In both the popular and scientific histories of social deviance, two basic ways of looking at the subject stand out: the *relativist* and the *absolutist*. Each of these views pervades the vast writings on social deviance, influencing the definition of deviance, research topics, assumptions as to the causes and characteristics of deviants, interpretation of research findings and current events, and policies of social control.[1]

The *absolutist* perspective is shared by the largest and most influential segments of the public. According to this view, fundamental human behavior may be classified as *inherently* proper or, conversely, self-evidently immoral, evil, and abnormal. The absolutist believes that most persons agree on the basic goals that people should pursue; he believes in an invariable set of fundamental values and in a general social good that transcends the mundane interests of individuals and groups in society. For the absolutist, no normal, decent, psychologically well-balanced person would seek to join a deviant group or participate in a deviant life-style. Consider this letter to the editor from an irate citizen protesting the discussion of homosexual literary themes by an avowed homosexual teacher in a college English class:

> Homosexuality is one of the most vile blasphemies against God. . . . [I]t is not society that is sick, it is those whose life-styles debase the sacred purpose of the sex act. Homosexuality is not part of "the total human experience" which a healthy, well-balanced human being can ever accept. The practice of homosexuality is an abomination of the natural order. . . . It is not love; it is undisciplined lust, drawing man down to the level of animals. . . .[2]

The *relativist* position, held in some manner by many contemporary sociologists, sharply challenges this view. Relativists view complex societies as dynamic, a mosaic of groups with different values and interests who sometimes agree and cooperate on some issues but frequently conflict and struggle to realize their own interests and ends. Deviance is seen as being in large measure a matter of human evaluation and differential power. Thus the nature of deviance will vary significantly among different groups and subcultures within a society as well as between societies. As Jerry Simmons observes, an astonishing variety of human actions and characteristics have been considered deviant:

> If we went back through history and assembled together all of the people who have been condemned by their contemporaries, the range [would include] the Plains Indian youth who was unable to see visions, the big-breasted Chinese girl, the early Christian skulking in the Roman catacombs, the Arab who liked alcohol instead of hashish, the Polynesian girl who didn't enjoy sex, and the medieval man who indulged himself by bathing frequently.[3]

For relativists, deviance is not inherently "unnatural" nor is it intrinsic to any particular act, belief, or human attribute. Instead, deviance is socially *created* by collective human judgments. Deviance, like beauty, lies largely in the eyes of the beholder and is relative to particular social standards and particular social settings. As Thomas Szasz points out, it is not by their behavior but by the traditional sexual double standard that men are labeled "virile" and women "nymphomaniacs." If people appear to be talking to God while kneeling at an altar, they are thought to be praying; however, if they insist that God has been talking to them, they are described as schizophrenic and we try to "cure" them of their "mental illness."[4] Similarly, the concrete act of injecting heroin into a vein is not inherently deviant. It is obviously acceptable for a doctor to inject a narcotic drug into a patient. Only when the drug is administered in a manner publicly forbidden does this action become deviant. The deviant nature of the act varies with the situations in which it is appropriate to supply drugs. Thus, in one situation, a person may continue to live as an ordinary citizen; in another, he may be treated as a criminal.

Further, the degree of harm or danger of specific acts to the welfare of others is not, according to the relativist, necessarily a decisive factor in the application of a stigmatizing label or in the severity of punishment. Is the husband who violently rapes his resisting, estranged wife in their home less dangerous than the twenty-six-year-old Kentucky mountaineer jailed in Chicago on statutory rape charges for having consensual sexual inter-course with a sixteen-year-old girl? In the former case, the police may refuse to take any action (the courts have a long-standing aversion to public inter-ference in family disputes). In the latter, the man's justification that "she was willing" and that back home "if they're big enough they're old enough" is no legal defense. In another instance, the operators of a coal company whose evasion of the federal mine-safety laws was partly responsible for the deaths of seventy-eight coal miners in an explosion were merely ad-monished by the federal mine inspectors to begin complying with the law. But a twenty-one-year-old Massachusetts Institute of Technology senior was sentenced in a Boston courtroom to five years in prison for the sale of marijuana to his college friends. Former Vice Presient Spiro Agnew, charged with extorting thousands of dollars in kickbacks from building contractors seeking preferential treatment, "copped a plea" and was convicted only of income tax evasion and given a three-year informal probation. George Jackson, black and eighteen years old, was sentenced to prison for from one year to life for stealing $70 from a gas station. Szasz makes the point nicely:

> Policemen receive bribes; politicians receive campaign contributions. Mari-juana and heroin are sold by pushers; cigarettes and alcohol are sold by business-men. Mental patients who use the courts to regain their liberty are trouble-makers; psychiatrists who use the courts to deprive patients of their liberty are therapists.[5]

Deviance, then, is simply human behavior, beliefs, or attributes that elicit social condemnation by others in particular social situations. Kai Erikson succinctly expresses this relativist view: "Deviance is not a property *inherent* in certain forms of behavior; it is a property *conferred upon* these forms by the audiences which directly or indirectly witness them."[6]

Not all views of deviance, however, gain an equal public hearing or have an equal social impact on those persons considered deviant. Those groups dominating the key positions in our major institutions in the com-munity and in society as a whole—the mass media, legislatures, government agencies, schools, corporations, the military, crime control agencies, and so forth—are best situated to disseminate information and make far-reaching policy decisions. These "social audiences" have effectively legitimated their versions of morality and immorality in the community or larger society and are supported by the law in their conceptions of wrong-doing. Repressive measures are potentially applicable (though selectively administered) to all those individuals and groups whose activity or existence threatens the dominant, controlling views of deviance. To challenge openly certain social norms is to risk becoming an outsider, a deviant who is "in" but not "of" the community. For example, in many small communities the outspoken atheist becomes an outsider—a heretic. The cocaine user or the homosexual may view others with disdain, but each risks arrest, imprisonment, public disgrace, and economic discrimination.

The sense of alienation and estrangement from the larger community that many deviants experience is caused not only by the threat of arrest and retribution from official agencies but more fundamentally by the day-to-day indignities—the insults, the stares, the frowns, the jokes, "the shushed conversations which engender the sense that you are a stranger in a strange land."[7] A young black with a white girl friend in a small Midwestern town vividly describes this sense of isolation:

> When this white chick and I first started making it I felt like I'd been plunked down in the middle of Russia, like I was a spy. . . . After we were sleeping together I hated to show up for work even, and I finally quit. I had this feeling that everybody was looking. And there was no place for us to go. . . . We were just sitting having coffee one day and a couple of football guys come over and ask her, "Is he bothering you?" One of her roommates called up the school and turned her in to her parents and the dean. Then they all wanted her to go see a psychiatrist. We just quit going out anywhere together. We even had to split up to buy a pack of cigarettes. A patrol car stopped us one night and a cop told me I'd better hurry up and suck her out cause he was putting a curfew on us. She crying and crying and me getting mean, things you just never known about. I know who that cop is. Maybe I'll kill him someday.[8]

To understand further the nature of these deviance-creating and judging processes, we shall examine first four major features of the absolutist view that are central to the whole process of deviance imputation and control: the nature of deviance stereotypes, the alleged pathology of deviancy, the sense of moral indignation, and the evil-causes-evil contention.

DEVIANCE STEREOTYPES

In essence, most deviants are different kinds of persons from ordinary citizens in the eyes of the absolutist. Deviant labels tend to be *essentializing* labels. The attribute or behavioral act that is singled out as the basic reason for application of the label is seen as pervasive and essential to the person's entire character. To label someone as a deviant—a thief, a sex fiend, a junkie, a nut, a queer, a prostitute, a radical—is to assign one to a kind of "master status," seen as the essence of the person's personality.[9] "To call a person 'mad' or 'criminal' is to imply that he is different in kind from ordinary people and that there are no areas of his personality that are not affected by his 'problem.'"[10] From the vantage point of the distant viewer, the unsavory deviant characteristic becomes the basis for interpreting the deviant's total identity. The knowledge that a person has presumably been involved in some deviant activity may overshadow other bits of information the viewer may have of him, weaken any interest in obtaining such information, or lead to a reinterpretation of previous information about him. Many deviant roles appear to have this built-in primacy, informing others of "the kind of person" one is dealing with. As Albert Cohen puts it:

> It is one thing to commit a deviant act—e.g., acts of lying, stealing, homosexual intercourse, narcotics use, drinking to excess, unfair competition. It is quite another thing to be charged and invested with a deviant character—i.e., to be socially defined as a liar, a thief, a homosexual, a dope fiend, a drunk, a chisler, a sinner, a criminal . . . a hoodlum . . . and so on. It is to be assigned to a role, to a special type or category of persons. The label—the name of the role—does more than signify one who has committed such-and-such a deviant act. Each label evokes a characteristic imagery. It suggests someone who is *normally* or habitually given to certain kinds of deviance; who may be *expected* to behave in this way; who is literally a bundle of odious or sinister qualities. It activates sentiments and calls out responses in others: rejection, contempt, suspicion, withdrawal, fear, hatred.[11]

These one-dimensional views of the deviant, of course, tend to ignore the perceptible differences that do exist among those falling into the same deviant category, emphasizing certain selected characteristics to the exclusion of others. Such stereotypical conceptions obscure the tremendous variability in the actual personalities, beliefs, self-concepts, idiosyncratic attributes, and life-styles among persons assigned these cardboard-cutout deviant identities. That deviants, too, may have fallen arches, hold ultra-patriotic beliefs, suffer from boredom, worry about taxes, inflation, and growing old, or share with ordinary citizens many similar negative stereotypes regarding other kinds of deviants is seldom apparent to the absolutist, who sometimes would consider deviants to be almost another species of humanity.

The prevalence of emotionally laden and powerful stereotypical imagery is particularly evident in the area of drug use. In the United States the use of illicit mood-altering substances is assumed to play a *radically* different role in the lives of drug users than is the case for legal drug users. All aspects of the life of the illicit drug user may be seen as centering around the use of this demoniac, forbidden substance. For many conventional Americans, the LSD, cocaine or even marijuana user is enslaved, possessed, or dominated by the drug: "stoned," "high," "hopped up," or "tripping out" many of his waking hours, crowding out other normal, important, highly valued activities. Thus, insurance companies will frequently discontinue or refuse to sell policies to known marijuana users. For conventional older Americans to read that someone "smokes dope" is to invoke a much more vivid, distinct, stereotypical picture than with "he drinks." For instance, news stories frequently portray some young person found in possession of illegal drugs as "on drugs." As Erich Goode incisively notes:

> This is typically not used to refer to being under the influence, but to the entire panorama of use from sporadic to "chronic." Thus, if a person is found in possession of an ounce of marijuana, he or she is said to be "on" marijuana. However, the same phrase is not used for alcohol; one is described as "on" alcohol only if one is under the influence, or an alcoholic. Obviously, there is more powerful stereotyping machinery for illegal drugs than for legal.[12]

Similarly, the label "addict" in the United States typically conjures up a picture of a strung-out, dirty, furtive, lower-class street junkie—but does not readily bring to mind the millions of middle-class alcohol- and barbiturate-addicted housewives. Nor does it convey a mental picture of the thousands of clean-shaven, affluent, hardworking physicians, stethoscopes dangling from their necks, who are currently addicted to narcotics, perhaps the occupational group with a higher rate of addiction than almost any other in American society. "Doctor junkies" or "dope-fiend surgeons" do not fit smoothly into the conventional stereotype. To try to accommodate too many exceptions and qualifications might threaten the whole edifice of dogmatic assumptions, half-truths, and misinformation which frequently serve to legitimate the absolutist's moral view and often hostile treatment of illegal drug users. So, too, with the stereotypes of most other deviants: complexity, ambiguity, facts that do not coincide with these oversimplified, homogeneous mental pictures—all such inconvenient phenomena tend to be selectively ignored, reinterpreted, or rejected, thereby helping to bolster such conventional images of deviance.

Serving to heighten the sense of moral righteousness and outrage that pervade the absolutist view is the tendency to associate the deviant activity or the deviant with the most *extreme* and *exaggerated* aspects of these phenomena. Thus, the use of the methedrine drug ("speed") by the Charles Manson "hippie family" may be mentioned in the same breath with their bloody killings of Sharon Tate and her Hollywood friends. The smoking of hashish by soldiers in Vietnam may be prominently associated in the absolutist's mind with the My Lai massacres. This tendency is particularly encouraged by newspaper accounts which regularly link the person's past involvement in deviance with incidents in which he is subsequently involved.

Thomas Scheff cites this example from a news item: "*A former mental patient* grabbed a policeman's revolver and began shooting at 15 persons in the receiving room of City Hospital No. 2 Thursday."[13] Such connections between previous mental hospitalization and acts of violence are frequently made in the mass media, despite the well-documented fact that violence rates among former mental patients are lower than in the general population. Scheff observes that a news item such as this is practically inconceivable: "Mrs. Ralph Jones, an ex-mental patient, was elected president of the Fairview Home and Garden Society at their meeting last Thursday." These and other ordinary kinds of activities *do* occur regularly in the lives of "former mental patients." Yet such selective references in the news media serve not only to perpetuate the stereotype that persons treated for psychiatric problems are especially prone to violence but also to obscure and distort the ways in which "ex-mental patients" adjust to everyday social life.

This public identity of deviance with its most extreme, radical, and atypical forms is common in many different spheres of deviancy. Older adult male homosexuals, for instance, may be viewed as having a special yen for the seduction of barely pubescent young boys; marijuana becomes a "stepping stone" to heroin use or "psychotic" episodes; militant radicals are dangerous crackpots who will use any means to achieve their goals, including arson-bombing; married "swingers" prefer sadomasochistic sexual orgies, and so on. It is partly through such exaggerated imagery that intense fear of deviants and hostility toward deviant activity is created and maintained.

Of course, stereotypical conceptions of some deviants are occasionally subject to modification when the viewer has extended opportunities to interact with a member of that stigmatized category, especially in face-to-face, intimate, diversified situations and roles. For example, more complex, varied, and somewhat positive elements are likely to pervade the image of the village "eccentric," seen as a bit strange but otherwise harmless and cheerful; the office stenographer, rumored to be a lesbian, but who is also good company at coffee breaks, an efficient typist, and a staunch Republican; the small-town lawyer, who everyone knows is an alcoholic but when sober can be counted on to give you reliable legal advice, a good game of tennis, and a sizable donation to the Little League; or the small-town physician who provides aging addict-patients with maintenance doses of narcotics. However, for most citizens, such firsthand extensive encounters with different kinds of *known* deviants are rare because the deviance may be concealed. And such occasional discrepant evidence may be defined as "an exception" that does little to discredit conventional stereotypes. The conventional assumptions thus persist and solidify—reinforced by titillating, sensational images in television, movies, magazines, and mass-circulation newspapers, by jokes, literature, song, and story, and by all the distorted information communicated through the everyday informal socialization processes.

Indeed, those deviance stereotypes which convey intense feelings of moral indignation may become so pervasive as to become almost a requisite or test of in-group membership. When most members of one's clique, group or local community share those highly charged stereotypical beliefs and sentiments, the lone individual who would publicly question or challenge the view of his friends and neighbors risks ridicule or social ostracism. Where the pressures for social conformity are strong, a phenomenon of *pluralistic ignorance* may occur. The person who does harbor some private reservations or doubts about the correctness or fairness of the conventional stereotypes assumes that these publicly expressed beliefs and feelings are shared privately by all his associates. Reluctant to expose his own divergent attitudes, he remains in ignorance of the similarly divergent views that may also privately prevail among some of his fellow in-group members.

In our increasingly segregated, impersonal, urban societies, the distant, unconventional stranger thus becomes transmuted into that one-dimensional deviant, to be dealt with by bureaucratic social-control agents: the police, FBI, probation officers, wardens, social workers, hospital officials, and institutional psychiatrists. When a person has been stamped successfully as a bona fide deviant—as basically immoral, evil, degenerate, dangerous, or sick—such labels frequently set in motion efforts to exclude that person from full participation in the community. Others may deny him certain privileges, courtesies, options, and freedoms normally accorded members in good standing, or exile her physically or symbolically to the margins of the community. Feelings arise in the community that "something ought to be done" about the deviant—exterminate, punish, harass, humiliate, cure, convert, or segregate him. It is frequently these very coercive conditions under which many deviants must manage their lives that provide the apparent "evidence" to confirm and strengthen the initial stereotypes, thereby often providing, in a self-fulfilling kind of way, some descriptive value to selected aspects of this distorted and exaggerated imagery.

THE PATHOLOGY OF DIVERSITY AND DISSENT

For the absolutist, deviant activity is not merely an alternative, possibly valuable way of functioning in society.[14] There is no provision for *multiple* conceptions of social reality, no allowance that some groups might legitimately find the conventional demands for conformity oppressive, unfulfilling, often dehumanizing. The possibility that alternative life-styles might be personally meaningful is almost inconceivable. Instead, the refusal by some persons to embrace the Puritan work ethic or the nuclear family, to defer gratification until the "proper occasions" or to repress bisexual or "promiscuous" sexual feelings is considered automatically undesirable. Such deviant behavior is viewed as personally satisfying only to persons who are "sick," "disturbed," or "abnormal." No one would otherwise choose to engage in extramarital sexual adventures in which several married couples participate together, join a radically militant political group, make oral-genital love with persons of the same sex, get "high" on psychedelic drugs, dance naked before an appreciative audience, prefer food stamps to IBM, or go to bed with an acquaintance for fun or money.

For many citizens, such departures from conventional expectations may trigger strong feelings of anger. One sociologist tells of his conversation with a British woman about the attempt by some hippies to occupy a deserted building in downtown London. In response to his question of why she found this rather harmless activity so disgusting and upsetting, she replied in an angry tone: "It's shocking and shameful, wasting their lives like that. They should be taken and whipped with the rod."[15]

Clearly, in the view of the absolutist, deviancy is not something in which a healthy, well-adjusted person would engage but is, rather, a malfunction comparable to malignant cells in an organism, to be eliminated, treated, or contained. The source of this pathological condition may be located in the individual's own makeup or in the social environment, and the condition itself may be described in genetic terms as mental illness, maladjustment, undersocialization, social disorganization, and so on. Whatever the mode of explanation, the absolutist sees as valid only the conventional norms and values and customary ways of behavior. These become synonymous with *reality*, and forms of deviance are diseases in the body of society.

Deviancy is explained by the absolutist as a product of either *internal coercion*—enslavement to inner compulsions, a weak ego, a pathological or dependent personality, inadequate socialization, an unharnessed libido— or *external constraint*, the corruption of the innocent and immature by other disturbed persons (e.g., drug users seduced by the syndicate drug pusher). Free choice and preference thus become illusory freedoms. To depart from the norm is to exhibit some form of disturbance.

Thus, drug use may not be simply pleasurable activity but must necessarily reflect a deep-seated personality flaw. Indulgence in illegal mood-altering substances is prima facie evidence of an "abnormal" or "inadequate" personality, an "escape from reality," a "rebellion against authority," a "deep-seated dread of intimacy," a "defective superego," and so on. In 1970, Dr. Robert Baird testified at a government crime committee hearing:

> Anyone who smokes marijuana . . . already has a mental problem. They are taking it to escape reality, to get high. . . . I do not care what euphemism you want to employ, they are mentally ill.[16]

In order for the absolutist to discredit the deviant activity effectively, the alleged pleasures of the condemned act must be seen as inauthentic or as dangerous and insidious. The state of euphoria experienced by some drug users was defined by one writer as "an artificial, exaggerated sense of pleasure and well-being." The contention that marijuana is fun is countered by the specter of a greased path to more evil kinds of pleasure:

> If . . . the main reason for smoking pot is pure fun, does it not follow that sniffing, then injecting heroin might be the most fun of all? After experiencing the much-touted delights of marijuana, wouldn't a person, at the very least be tempted to try the greater glories of the big H? It seems likely.[17]

In Russia, political liberals who openly criticize the ruling regime have been declared "mentally ill" and are incarcerated in psychiatric prison hospitals for their treasonous views. Inmates are medically "treated" for their political "delusions." Allegations of persecution by the KGB or "anti-Soviet agitation" may be diagnosed as a symptom of paranoia or "sluggish schizophrenia." Patients who do not respond to "therapy" have been labeled incurable madmen and dosed with depressant drugs that turn the political dissident into a human vegetable.[18] The use of such pathological labels, however, is not restricted only to political dissent. Many government officials are concerned about the increasingly casual attitude toward premarital sex among Russian teen-agers who view it as a "physical necessity" rather than as an expression of "true love." One Soviet scholar comments on the *pathology* of passionate sex outside the sanctified context of love and marriage:

> Any fashion in love with a light-hearted attitude toward sexual intercourse, female promiscuity or a male insolence, I consider pathological. A psychologically and physically healthy person would never let passion into this sacred sanctum of life.[19]

In some Communist countries, even religious activity is frequently associated with mental illness. According to an Associated Press news story from Prague, the Communist party paper, *Pravda*, has warned Czechoslovak parents:

> . . . religion constitutes a grave hazard for the mental health of children. Religion interferes with sound and harmonious emotional development . . . it impedes social adaptability, creating the conditions for the emergence of delinquency. By burdening the nervous system, it leads to psychical disorders. It brings up individuals with an undermined will and stands in the way of the development of firm moral sentiments. . . . It weakens the will to learn, leading to lower grades.[20]

And religious agitators may be dealt with severely. In 1973, a news release out of Communist Albania reported that a Roman Catholic priest had been sentenced to death for "secretly baptizing a child." As Thomas Szasz ob-

serves, apparently many Albanians feel that a "pusher" of holy water de-
serves such a fate, just as for many Americans, importers of heroin are also
"pushers" who deserve to die. This view of religion is as integral a part of
their cultural values and laws as is our attitude toward "dangerous drugs."
Szasz notes: ". . . we warn travelers not to bring narcotics into the United
States; the Russians warn travelers not to bring Bibles into the U.S.S.R."[21]

The relativist would contend that in a complex society there are many
ways of being human, many viable, worthwhile ways of securing joy and
self-esteem, of coping with the dilemmas, tragedies, and problems of life.
Moreover, rather than necessarily being "undersocialized" or reared in a
"disorganized" or "pathological" social setting, one may simply be socialized to *different* standards, expectations, or ideals. For example, to come
of age as a young man in a lower-class, big-city ghetto neighborhood may
expose a person to a set of demands and life-styles which *permit*, and sometimes *require*, behavior often radically different from that found in a small,
middle-class farm town in Iowa. In Harlem or the South Bronx, a well-
dressed, stylish pimp, an operator of a flourishing illegal numbers game, or
a courageous, daring "stand-up cat" may frequently serve as models of success to admire and emulate, rather than to condemn and pity as victims of
deep-seated personality inadequacies.[22]

While the relativist might concur in the importance of some stress-
provoking psychological disturbance in a given individual's life, he or she
is likely to view the precise relationship of that disturbance to subsequent
involvement in deviant behavior as exceedingly complex and problematic.
For instance, the psychological characteristics associated with some proportion of those persons assigned to the deviant category may often be as
much the *effect of the societal reactions* to that deviant's actions as they are
the initial causes of it. Thus, for example, the stressful conditions under
which many lower-class heroin addicts in New York City must secure their
outlawed drugs—hustling and stealing to scrounge up enough money to
pay the black-market prices, dodging narcotics police, worrying about
dwindling drug supplies, informers, and busts, getting ripped off by preda-
tors—may all contribute to the addict's sense of paranoia or personal insecurity. These realistic personal reactions to social stress are then sometimes
cited as evidence of the deep-seated personality flaws presumed responsible
in the first place for the drug user's addiction.[23]

The relativist might agree with the absolutist that in many instances
the *initial* acts of the person considered deviant may be precipitated in important ways by some psychological or social strain. Yet the common preoccupation with the significance of distant, often obscure, earlier life experiences often deflects attention away from the importance of *present* social
forces and processes, which may transform the initial deviant acts into
persistent deviant roles, "careers," and self-concepts. How, the relativist

might ask, do current associations, situations, and social reactions help *initiate, maintain,* or *shape* deviant life styles and identities, which the individual may come to embrace, learn to live with, and from which he may find it difficult to extricate himself ("once a junkie, always a junkie")? How does the person himself feel about and *subjectively* experience his activity? Is it valid always to assume that the meanings the deviant assigns to his or her activity are irrelevant to an understanding of that person's behavior— mere rationalizations or delusions which mask the "real" hidden inner forces that compel the deviant to behave as he or she does? In short, *do* we know that the person really smokes hashish because he was fixated at the oral stage of childhood development? That the call girl is simply the inevitable product of a weak, unloving, ineffectual mother? That the militant gay liberationist is but the preordained victim of personality flaws formed during the early years of life or hormonal deficiencies laid down at birth? That former Vice President Spiro Agnew extorted kickbacks because of an inadequate personality? That the Watergate burglars suffered from parental neglect?

Is it not possible, for example, that the decision by a seventeen-year-old unskilled black male in New York City to make $100 a day selling drugs is an exciting and *rational* choice in view of the prospects of dead-end, monotonous jobs such as parking cars, mopping floors, or pushing a hand truck for $80 a week? Is it not possible that the mugging of an old lady by a young Puerto Rican high school dropout is at least partly a prepolitical response to the alienation and powerlessness he experiences daily in his life? Do not many street crimes in white neighborhoods adjacent to our inner-city ghettos perhaps represent a primitive lashing out at the symbols of authority and oppression (albeit a protest that is individualistic and often misdirected, victimizing others equally oppressed), a striking back at a racist society that bombards the predator with the rhetoric of equal opportunity but denies him genuine chances for achieving significant economic and social advancement and a meaningful life?[24]

In short, for a more complete explanation of deviance, the relativist would insist that the absolutist approach—which typically locates the "real" causes of deviancy only in deep-seated, flawed characteristics of the individual "wrongdoer" or in his pathological and asocial childhood experience—is inadequate. The impact of current social forces, involvement in specific subcultures, conflicting definitions of deviance; the stigmatizing treatment of persons as deviants and the interacting responses, choices, and subjective interpretations of these so-categorized and labeled; the oppressive moral attitudes and restricted opportunity structures imposed by the dominant groups on the poor, powerless, and marginal members of the society—*all* are equally important to a fuller understanding of the complexities of these troubling phenomena.

MORAL INDIGNATION

The vehemence with which citizens have deplored deviant values, such as the hippie values of sexual expressiveness and spontaneity, may thinly disguise their own unfulfilled desires and fantasies, their own nagging doubts about the adequacy of their lives. Deviant impulses such as these—in themselves and in others—must be vigorously suppressed. As Philip Slater observes, "The peculiarly exaggerated hostility that hippies tend to arouse suggests that the life they strive for is highly seductive to middle-class Americans."[25] Thus, the basis for moral indignation is frequently the dual fascination and repulsion that often coexist in the minds of those who would fervently condemn moral transgressions from the dominant social norms.

As many observers have noted, significant segments of the conforming public are to some degree *ambivalent* about illicit and unconventional pleasures. Their feelings are sometimes bound up in a complex tangle of conflicting values, desires, fears, fantasies, and guilt. These ambivalent conformists who defer gratification, who at considerable psychic cost deny or inhibit impulses toward forbidden pleasures (such as escape, spontaneity, adventure, uninhibited sex, disdain for work, physical aggression, excitement, autonomy, etc.), thus often react with righteous hostility toward persons who appear to flout the officially sanctioned moral codes and rules. The vivid stereotypes of the sexual "swinger" indulging in undiluted hedonism, the hippie "living in idleness," the expensively dressed black pimp effortlessly living off the "hustle" of his stable of white whores, the psychedelic drug user continually "tripping out" in a dreamy state of euphoria—all such deviants are frequently viewed as unjustly rewarded, irresponsible persons who have not *earned* their pleasures through productive, legitimate hard work and compliance with the social rules. Especially where the "victimless" deviant act (e.g., illicit sex, psychedelic drugs, gambling, pornography) does not appear to threaten directly the life, possessions, or immediate welfare of conventional citizens, the outpouring of moral indignation may be triggered by the suspicion that the wicked are *undeservedly* realizing the pleasures and rewards secretly desired by the virtuous. Richard Blum nicely describes this fascination-repulsion relationship in regard to illicit drugs:

> Pharmaceutical materials do not dispense themselves and the illicit drugs are rarely given away, let alone forced on people. Consequently, the menace lies within the person, for there would be no drug threat without a drug attraction. Psychoanalytic observations on alcoholics suggest the presence of simultaneous repulsion and attraction in compulsive ingestion. The amount of public interest in stories about druggies suggests the same drug attraction and repulsion in ordinary citizens. "Fascination" is the better term since it implies witchcraft and enchantment. People are fascinated by drugs—because they are

attracted to the states and conditions drugs are said to produce. That is another side to the fear of being disrupted; it is the desire for release, for escape, for magic, and for ecstatic joys. That is the derivation of the menace in drugs—their representation as keys to forbidden kingdoms inside ourselves. The dreadful in the drug is the *dreadful* in ourselves.[26]

Moreover, it is this very ambivalence that the mass media exploit, first titillating the public's sensibilities and then reaffirming its prejudices and upholding the public morality by condemnation and symbolic punishment of the deviant. Television, movies, and the tabloids use these distant and misperceived deviant outsiders as a kind of lurid projection screen—as scapegoats through which the collective fears, frustrations and forbidden impulses of the conforming public are vicariously expressed and, perhaps, partly neutralized. By portraying deviants as immoral persons invariably coming to a bad end, as "innocents" who have been corrupted by the wicked but who may be "saved," as "sick" persons in need of "treatment," or as persons whose actions are basically meaningless or contain their own built-in horrors (LSD leads to madness, illicit sex to venereal disease, homosexuality to neurosis), the mass media thus reinforce, legitimate, and partly create the images and myths of a basically consensual and just society.[27]

THE EVIL-CAUSES-EVIL ASSUMPTION

For the absolutist who would sternly condemn deviant behavior, such morally repugnant phenomena must be the result of some other equally despicable condition lodged in the individual or in a sector of the society. As noted, there is little overt recognition that a well-adjusted person in full control of his faculties might freely choose to participate in deviant activity. Any positive meaning the rule-breaker might assign to his actions is generally ignored and stripped of any significance. Evil conditions presumably have evil antecedents. Thus the search for the basic causes of deviance has ranged from possession by the devil to XYY chromosomes; from psychopathic personalities and schizophrenia to coercion by the Sicilian Mafia; from poverty and alcoholic parents to permissiveness, matrifocal families, and disorganized slums. Yet whatever the specific alleged cause, all these explanations have in common a conviction that the evil phenomena of deviance must be the result of some other obviously undesirable condition, which all decent citizens would agree should be eliminated or prevented, and that such sordid and sinful conditions can produce only evil consequences.

However, the proponent of the absolutist ideology is unlikely to perceive that "good" may also sometimes lead to "evil," that *often much of what he considers deplorable may have its origins partly in things he con-*

siders admirable. That is, his own cherished values and esteemed goals may play a major part in the occurrence of socially harmful activity. Thus, for example, the culturally sanctified drive for profit and gain in American society may precipitate deleterious consequences. In a nation in which a $45,000-a-year account executive feels inadequate because his associates receive $65,000 in salary—affording a more prestigious residential address and life-style—a gnawing, persistent sense of *relative deprivation* is not uncommon. This extreme cultural emphasis on individual pecuniary success—an emphasis that encourages traditional Americans to assign status and success in large measure on the basis of the visible symbols of luxury, wealth, and material comfort—severely weakens the restraining influence of social norms that channel the attainment of such cultural goals through legally permissible paths. One such socially injurious consequence is pervasive "white-collar crime."

The preoccupation in the mass media, however, with the conventional "street crimes" of robbery, burglary and assault—commonly viewed as the product of disturbed lower-class blacks, Puerto Ricans, Chicanos, and others reared in disorganized slum environments—serves to obscure the serious consequences of the massive criminality of respectable middle- and upper-class citizens in the course of their *legitimate* business and professional occupations. Spurred on in large measure by the relentless effort to achieve these culturally sanctioned individual success goals of financial gain and status, corporate officials may conspire to rig prices illegally, robbing the public of millions of dollars. Vice presidents of pharmaceutical firms may knowingly market drugs with dangerous side effects, yet fail to inform physicians or the Food and Drug Administration. Bankers may juggle the books to cover up their embezzlement. Such white-collar lawbreakers also include contractors who intentionally use defective building materials to enhance profits; prominent government officials who barter their political influence for private gain; physicians who perform "ghost surgery," padding the bills of medicare patients; stockbrokers who peddle fraudulent securities; businessmen who drive the poor and gullible to despair in home-improvement frauds; and industrialists who criminally pollute rivers and beaches, endangering health and despoiling the countryside. Only rarely, however, do these and other kinds of respectable and powerful occupational offenders come to occupy the deviant status of "criminal" and experience stigmatizing and punitive sanctions. Consider, for example, these two cases recently called for sentencing on the same day before a U.S. District Judge in Manhattan's Federal Court:

> The first was *United States* v. *Velasquez*. A twenty-two-year-old Puerto Rican woman with two children, five and four years old, pleaded guilty to aiding in the theft of part of a group of welfare checks amounting to a total of $2,086.

The woman had come to New York only a few years before, could not speak English and was on welfare herself. She was living with her husband in Brownsville, a poverty-stricken section of Brooklyn. Her husband was a diabetic and she provided insulin for him. She had no prior criminal record. The judgment of the court: imprisonment for eighteen months.

The next case was *United States* v. *Delatorre*. An educated white-collar defendant pleaded guilty to commercial bribery and extortion in the amount of $23,000, as well as prejury and [inducing another to commit] perjury. The judge went out of his way to point out, along with other considerations, that the defendant had two young children and no prior criminal record. The judgment of the court: a suspended sentence.[28]

In American society, the economic costs of such pervasive and diverse occupational crimes dwarf in magnitude the financial losses from conventional burglars and robbers. And the consequence of these low-visibility occupational crimes and society's often ambivalent and feeble response to them, many criminologists would contend, seriously threaten the welfare of the nation's economy, endanger the safety and health of the public, erode confidence in the integrity and credibility of our political leaders, and challenge the legitimacy of the entire criminal-justice system. Even "mass homicide" may not be treated as a crime when perpetrated by powerful and wealthy corporate officials. No one, for example, was ever arrested, prosecuted, or convicted for the manufacture of this airplane with known structural defects:

On March 3, 1974, a Turkish Airlines DC-10 jet liner crashed nine minutes after taking off from the Paris airport. At least 246 people were killed. The causes of the crash were a faulty baggage door and a weak cabin floor. The manufacturers of the plane—McDonnell Douglas Aircraft—knew about these weaknesses, which had caused a similar (but non-fatal) accident in Canada two years before. No one was even indicted, much less imprisoned, for this crime. The only question was how much of the loot which McDonnell Douglas picked up by cutting corners in design and production would have to be paid out in civil damages.[29]

The cultural obsession with attaining the accoutrements and symbols of economic success—luxurious homes in suburbia, horse riding lessons, prestigious colleges, and the "right marriages"—may not only "turn off" some of the children reared in these more affluent families but also widen and intensify the conflict between parents and their offspring. Many upper-middle class parents are puzzled and angered when their adolescent children come to disdain and reject the pursuit of these success-oriented life styles as superficial, joyless, "plastic," and dull. Such rejection is particularly grating for parents who feel they have "sacrificed most of their lives"—given their children "everything money can buy"—to provide these culturally blessed material comforts and opportunities. A high school girl in Maryland who prefers the excitement of LSD says:

> My mother wanted me to take riding lessons or to go out and do something with the other girls at the high school. I don't know what she wanted me to do with them. Talk about our shampoos maybe. Or how we were choosing a college where we could get married off fast to some eligible boy. She wanted me to go out on dates with these dumb, well-behaved kids that she approved of. Go to a movie, make out in the car, go get a hamburger. Who the hell does she think I am? Work hard in school so you can get into a good college, go to a good college so you can marry an ambitious nurd who will sell insurance and buy you a nice house in the suburbs so you can wash dishes and buy furniture and play bridge with the girls on alternate Tuesdays, so that when you've done this for fifty years and you die, everybody will say "She was nice" or something like that. Jesus Christ, I can't take any more of her shit. Isn't it normal to want to have a little adventure? A little excitement for a change? Taking acid is a fuck of a lot *more* normal than doing nothing.[30]

The traditional evil-causes-evil mode of explanation also obscures the socially valuable, *positive* functions which deviance may perform for many conventional groups in the society. Under certain conditions, such socially defined evil may enhance or help maintain the vitality and effectiveness of cherished social institutions and safeguard the welfare of their participants. For instance, some deviant activity often provides a kind of "safety valve," serving to protect the general public from behavior that it might construe as injurious and offensive to its sensibilities. As Cohen observes, "A certain amount of deviance, disparaged but not rigorously repressed, may perform a 'safety valve' function by preventing the excessive accumulation of discontent and by taking some of the strain off the legitimate order."[31] Thus, the easy accessibility to pornographic films, pictures, and literary materials—"smut and filth" in the absolutist rhetoric—although in itself not apt to cause persons to engage in direct sexual crimes against others, may, however, function as a substitute outlet, draining off harmlessly the tensions of some persons (lumped together under the pejorative label of "sexual perverts") who might otherwise engage in some kinds of concrete offensive actions against others.

Although the empirical evidence to verify such relationships is still inadequate, recent studies in Denmark suggest such a linkage.[32] According to criminologist Berl Kutchinsky, the open sale of hard-core pornography in that country is largely responsible for a drastic *reduction* from 1959 to 1970 in certain sex crimes against both women and children. While the frequency of rape (which amounts to about four percent of Danish sex offenses) has apparently remained the same, "exhibitionism" declined 66 percent, "physical indecency" 56 percent, and the number of "peeping" (voyeurism) cases fell from 99 to 5. Sex crimes against children (child molesting) declined to 69 percent, with 60 percent of the drop occurring between 1965 and 1969 when hardcore pornography became *legally* available (first in written form and later pictorial and film pornography). During the ten-year period surveyed, Kutchinsky notes, the greatest decrease in sex offenses against women coincided with the legalization of pornographic materials, and the accessibility of pornography depicting children coincided with a similar decline in sex offenses committed against them. Part of the decrease in exhibitionism and indecency may reflect increasing tolerance for more trivial sexual acts, leading to changing attitudes toward reporting them by either the public or the police. But according to Kutchinsky, this was not a factor in peeping and child molesting. Rather, he concluded, the sufficient sexual satisfaction obtained through the use of erotic pornographic materials, combined with masturbation, was the major factor responsible for the reduction in a large number of these offenses.

In a somewhat related fashion, the prostitute may also serve to satisfy the needs of the sexually frustrated, thereby serving to protect traditional feminine virtue and, in addition, helping to safeguard conventional marital and family institutions.[33] The brazen street hooker, adorned in wig and bright hot-pants beckoning the wayward husband whose wife may be frigid or ill; the sophisticated call girl who provides an outlet for the man whose spouse is unable to accommodate his desire ("disgusting and animallike") for more sexual variety in their lovemaking repertoire; the "massage parlor" employee who services the sexual wants of the lonely stranger, the ugly, the deformed, the soldier—all such illicit services, vehemently condemned by many moralists, help meet the needs of many different individuals and groups in society. As a latent consequence—an unintended by-product—of such deviancy, the level of discontent and tension that might otherwise build up and fester in a repressive society is likely to diminish, and the more respectable "good" woman may be protected from the hassles, indignities, and demands for sexual favors. Without some mechanism to siphon off the frustration generated by the inability of large numbers of persons to satisfy their sexual desires "legitimately," many of the social rules and values supported by the conventional family institutional patterns conceivably might crumble. This dilemma is especially likely to exist in a male-dominated society in which the potentially available sexual outlets for men are restricted through the stringent emphasis on female chastity, the ban on adultery, and strictures against masturbation.

Prostitutes, of course, are not unaware of some of these positive contributions, and occasionally cite them as justification for this illicit sexual activity (thereby helping to preserve their self-respect, and partially neutralizing in their own eyes the negative public image). Consider the sentiments of these call girls:

> We girls see, like I guess you call them perverts of some sort, you know little freaky people and if they didn't have girls to come to like us that are able to

handle them and make it a nice thing, there would be so many rapes and . . . nutty people really.

I could say that a prostitute has held more marriages together as part of their profession than any other divorce counselor.

I don't regret doing it because I feel I help people. . . . They come over for companionship, someone to talk to. . . . They talk about sex. . . . A lot of them have problems.[34]

Because of the heavy stigmatization of the prostitute and the impersonal, commercial nature of the transaction, however, such fleeting sexual encounters do not seriously threaten to divert the loyalty, affection, and resources of the errant husband away from his family (as might an intimate emotional entanglement with an extramarital lover). Devaluing this transient relationship, in which sex is merely a commodity for purchase—condemning and degrading the prostitute as unfit to be seen with in public— allows people to feel that the marital bounds of solidarity, the status and security of the wife, and the other familial obligations of conventional marriage are not seriously put in jeopardy. Nor is this highly impersonal, tainted sexual encounter with the prostitute (in an earlier era, literally fenced off in red-light districts out of sight of more respectable citizens) likely to weaken significantly the desire of the single man to form a more durable, intimate, and socially respectable marital relationship.

Ironically, it is perhaps the very increase in "permissive sexual norms"— the much-heralded "sexual revolution" in modern Western societies so vilified in the absolutist rhetoric—that may threaten to dampen interest in the services of the prostitute. This apparent increase in pre- and postmarital sex for affection and fun rather than profit may actually not only reduce the incentive to rush into, and perhaps even remain within, conventional types of marriage, but also spell the decline (though hardly the elimination) of the despised prostitute. As one streetwalker in London recently lamented: "This amateur competition is ruining our business." According to a study of organized crime in Illinois, even criminal syndicates are losing interest in prostitution as a profitable venture. The Chicago Crime Commission offers the explanation that prostitutes are experiencing difficulty these days because "sex is almost a free commodity in our modern society."[35] Like any efficient entrepreneur, even the mob apparently must keep up with the changing times and consumer tastes or risk going out of business!

Of course, the diverse functions and patterns of prostitution will vary in different societies reflecting different family structures, sexual norms and taboos, divisions of labor, and the kinds of prostitution that prevail. Yet while the available evidence is insufficient to document the extent of these alleged reductions in the rate of demand for the services of the prostitute as a consequence of greater sexual freedom, it seems quite paradoxical (if not always obvious) that the sacred and respectable values which have traditionally sanctioned female chastity and tabooed adultery may have inadvertently helped to support "the world's oldest occupation." In turn, prostitution has probably functioned in some respects—especially in the recent past—to buttress the conventional social order. It is clear that the absolutist emphasis on the "dysfunctional" and insidious consequences of prostitution and other kinds of "evil" hardly exhausts the study of the diverse functions of social deviance and their interrelationship with the culture, structure, and dynamics of a society.

Yet to sustain the absolutist perspective, the inclusion of such complexities is inadmissible. The acceptance of these multiple functions of "good and evil," of the paradoxes and dilemmas evident in many patterns of deviance, would considerably blunt the force of the absolutist moral dogma, eroding and, perhaps, puncturing its entire credibility. In the eyes of many absolutists, effective discreditation of deviance therefore requires total condemnation of deviance.

In many rapidly changing Western societies, however, challenges to the absolutist position are increasing. A small but growing number of social scientists and militant activists are beginning to contest the fundamental assumptions that support the absolutist perspective. Chapter 2 explores this growing conflict-ridden politicization of deviance and some of the strategies by which dominant groups attempt to deal with these moral and ideological challenges to the traditional social order.

FOOTNOTES

1   The use of the terms *relativist* and *absolutist* draws upon the discussion of these two perspectives in Jock Young, *The Drugtakers*, Paladin, London, 1971, Ch. 3; and Erich Goode, *The Drug Phenomenon: Social Aspects of Drug Taking*, Bobbs-Merrill, Indianapolis, 1973, pp. 26–37.

2   *The Chronicle of Higher Education*, Apr. 18, 1974, p. 8.

3   Jerry L. Simmons, *Deviants*, Glendessary Press, Berkeley, Calif., 1969, p. 4.

4   Thomas Szasz, *The Second Sin*, Doubleday, Garden City, N.Y., 1973, pp. 101, 112–113.

5   Szasz, *The Second Sin*, p. 25.

6   Kai Erikson, "Notes on the Sociology of Deviance," in Earl Rubington and Martin S. Weinberg (eds.), *Deviance*, Macmillan, New York, 1978, p. 26.

7   Simmons, *Deviants*, p. 73.

8   Simmons, *Deviants*, pp. 73–74.

9   Howard S. Becker, *Outsiders*, Free Press, New York, 1973, pp. 33–34.

10   Robert A. Scott, "A Proposed Framework for Analyzing Deviance as a Property of Social Order," in Robert A. Scott and Jack D. Douglas (eds.), *Theoretical Perspectives on Deviance*, Basic Books, New York, 1972, p. 14.

11   Albert K. Cohen, *Deviance and Control*, Prentice-Hall, Englewood Cliffs, N.J., 1966, p. 24.

12   Goode, *The Drug Phenomenon*, p. 35.

13   Thomas J. Scheff, *Being Mentally Ill*, Aldine, Chicago, 1966, p. 71.

14   This section on the view of deviance as pathology draws upon the discussions by Goode, *The Drug Phenomenon*, pp. 30–35; and by Young, *The Drugtakers*, pp. 51–68.

15   Scott, "A Proposed Framework for Analyzing Deviance as a Property of Social Order," p. 16.

16   Quoted in Goode, *The Drug Phenomenon*, p. 3.

17   Both quotations cited in Goode, *The Drug Phenomenon*, p. 34.

18   See Sidney Bloch and Peter Reddway, *Psychiatric Terror*, Basic Books, New York, 1977; Stephan L. Chorover, "Big Brother and Psychotechnology," *Psychology Today*, 6 (October 1973), pp. 43–54.

19   *The New York Times*, Nov. 24, 1973, p. 8.

20   Thomas Szasz, *Ceremonial Chemistry*, Anchor Books, Doubleday, Garden City, N.Y., 1975, p. 138.

21   Szasz, *Ceremonial Chemistry*, p. 138.

22   See Christina Milner and Richard Milner, *Black Players*, Bantam Books, New York, 1973; Alan G. Sutter, "Playing a Cold Game: Phases of a Ghetto Career," and Harvey Feldman, "Street Status and Drug Use," in Paul E. Rock (ed.), *Drugs and Politics*, Transaction Books, New Brunswick, N.J., 1977, pp. 191–205 and pp. 207–222.

23   See Dan Waldorf and Craig Reinarman, "Addicts—Everything But Human Beings," *Urban Life*, 4 (April 1975), pp. 30–53; Dan Waldorf, *Careers in Dope*, Prentice-Hall, New York, 1973.

24   See David M. Gordon, "Class and the Economics of Crime," and Andrew Hacker, "Getting Used to Mugging," in William Chambliss and Milton Mankoff (eds.), *Whose Law? What Order?* Wiley, New York, 1976, pp. 193–214 and pp. 215–224.

25   Philip Slater, *The Pursuit of Loneliness*, Beacon Press, Boston, 1970, p. 7.

26   Richard H. Blum and Associates, *Society and Drugs*, Jossey-Bass, San Francisco, 1969, p. 335.

27   Jock Young, "The Myth of the Drug Taker in the Mass Media," in Stanley Cohen and Jock Young (eds.), *The Manufacture of News*, Sage, Beverly Hills, Calif., 1973, pp. 314–322.

28   Quoted in Charles H. McCaghy, *Deviant Behavior*, Macmillan, New York, 1976, pp. 219–220.

29   Quoted in *The Progressive*, (January 1977), p. 17. For a discussion of white-collar crimes, see John E. Conklin, *"Illegal But Not Criminal,"* Prentice-Hall, Englewood Cliffs, N.J., 1977; Gilbert Geis and Robert F. Meier (eds.), *White-Collar Crime*, Free Press, New York, 1977; John M. Johnson and Jack D. Douglas (eds.), *Crime at the Top: Deviance in Business and the Professions,* Lippincott, Philadelphia, 1978.

30   Harrison Pope, Jr., *Voices From the Drug Culture*, Beacon Press, Boston, 1971, pp. 18–19.

31   Cohen, *Deviance and Control*, p. 7.

32   See "Pornography and Sex Crimes: The Danish Experience," *Psychology Today*, 6 (November 1973), pp. 13–14; Berl Kutchinsky, *Studies on Pornography and Sex Crimes in Denmark*, New Social Science Monographs, Copenhagen,

1970; *The Report of the Commission on Obscenity and Pornography*, Bantam Books, New York, 1970.

33 This analysis of prostitution draws upon the discussions by Cohen, *Deviance and Control*, pp. 7–8; Kingsley Davis, "Sexual Behavior," in Robert K. Merton and Robert Nisbet (eds.), *Contemporary Social Problems*, Harcourt Brace Jovanovich, New York, 1976, 245–252; and John Gagnon, *Human Sexualities*, Scott, Foresman, Glenview, Ill., 1977, pp. 277–285.

34 James H. Bryan, "Occupational Ideologies and Individual Attitudes of Call Girls," in Rubington and Weinberg (eds.), *Deviance*, p. 354.

35 *The New York Times*, Sept. 27, 1971, p. 39.

Chapter 2

The Politics of Social Deviance

To explain the shifting conceptions of deviance in modern societies, the relativist sociological perspective which emphasizes the crucial significance of differential power and conflict would seem most useful. Central to this perspective is the contention that much of what is considered deviance is actually a form of social conflict between relatively isolated, powerless individuals or groups and relatively large, powerful, well-organized groups.[1] Particularly in highly differentiated industrial societies, flux, diversity, and conflict seem more characteristic than a monolithic, static consensus and harmony of interests: a *plurality* of interests and subcultures, frequently in opposition ("countercultures"), rather than *one* commonly shared and consensually accepted culture. Complex modern societies increasingly have become arenas in which a great variety of moral and political struggles are staged.

DEVIANCE AND POWER

Some groups, however, are more successful than others in imposing their versions of conformity and deviance on the larger community or society, backed by a wide variety of resources and sanctions to use against persons seen as threatening the social rules promulgated or supported by these powerful dominant groups. In terms of its social *impact*, deviant behavior can be viewed simply as behavior that those who possess sufficient power label deviant. Such conflict-oriented relativists, of course, do not deny that a large consensus may prevail in terms of majority opinion regarding a particular type of behavior (for example, murder, heroin use, rape, burglary) in a particular society. However, even where a large majority of the citizenry concurs, such consensus of opinion may partly be a creation of the manipulation of the mass media by groups possessing sufficient power to propagate their own particular values and notions of proper and improper behavior.

For instance, is it "murder" or merely the exercise of legitimate police authority when a cop shoots an innocent fifteen-year-old black boy who flees from a grocery store in Harlem, failing to comply with the policeman's order to halt? Is it "rape" when a man has forcible sexual intercourse with his resisting wife, as many women's liberation groups would insist? Were the "long hot summers" of the 1960s in Watts, Detroit, and Newark "race riots" by "criminal hooligans" or spontaneous "rebellions" against intolerable and unjust conditions for black people in America? Is it a "criminal burglary" or protection of "national security" when men in the secret employment of the White House staff break into a locked office belonging to the psychiatrist of Daniel Ellsberg, the outspoken critic of the government's war policies in Indochina and alleged "thief" of the Pentagon Papers? The ambiguity evident to many readers in these questions—and the divergence of opinion that ripped across America in the wake of the national political scandals of the Nixon administration in the 1970s—suggests that the much-celebrated consensus of the absolutists may frequently be more fragile and precarious than popularly assumed. Recognition of this consensual instability is increasingly evident as deviant groups have become more self-consciously defiant, more militant and organized, more willing to boldly challenge dominant conventional views. As Howard Becker observes: "In addition to recognizing that deviance is created by the response of people to particular kinds of behavior, by the labeling of that behavior as deviant, we must also keep in mind that *the rules created and maintained by such labeling are not universally agreed to. Instead, they are the object of conflict and disagreement, part of the political process of society.*"[2]

The fact that most Americans currently define the use of heroin as "drug abuse" is also hardly evidence of a centuries-old "unanimity of values" or of a consensus in society regarding "drugs." Consider for a moment the shifting and divergent attitudes regarding alcohol and cigarettes, as well as the sizable groups who regularly use marijuana, barbiturates, and amphetamines. Attitudes toward narcotics use at the turn of the century were far different from today. In 1900, vast numbers of older, middle-class conventional Americans were addicted to various patent medicines saturated with opium—highly respectable citizens who were dependent on "their medicine" to deal with a variety of ailments ranging from menstrual pains and menopause to insomnia and headaches.

Indeed, the whole notion of a vast body of decent, rule-abiding, normal citizens within which lurks a tiny group of sinister, abnormal, or sick deviants—almost beyond the pale of humanity—becomes ludicrous. If one were to eliminate all marijuana users, persons who engage in homosexual acts or are involved in illegal abortion, embezzlers, income-tax evaders, alcoholics, radicals, hippies, perpetrators of assault, petty theft and fraud, white-collar occupational lawbreakers, prostitutes, the sexually promiscuous, and so on through the whole list of presumably deviant activity—there might be precious little left of society! As Jerry Simmons notes:

> We can't just say that deviance is the violation of institutionalized rules and expectations by a small minority of psychological freaks. The majority diverge to some extent from the laws and mores of every society and every organization. If you've never hedged a little on your income tax or done a bit of petty thieving or had a secret sexual adventure, you're either a rare and saintly person or you've lived an incredibly quiet life. Some divergence is often tolerated and sometimes even encouraged. Also, most organizations and societies have a number of sub-groups struggling with one another because their aims and standards and views conflict. The idea that deviants are a different species of men and women ranged against a vast majority of upright citizens falls apart under closer inspection.[3]

Despite the presence of numerous groups with *divergent* moral codes, it is in the interests of powerful groups in a society to foster the belief that "society's rules" are under attack and that official action, often of a repressive nature, is required. As one sociologist has put it: "[T]he 'myth' of a unified society with clear and firm rules is appropriated by powerful interest groups as a way of defining and stigmatizing relatively powerless opponents, people who, at least by implication, challenge the existing distribution of power."[4] This frequent use of power to stigmatize, harass, or punish persons who appear to threaten or publicly challenge the social rules and interests of the dominant groups was clearly evident in many communities in the persecution of persons considered "hippies" and "radicals" in the 1960s and early 1970s. The selective enforcement of drug laws was often the vehicle for such repression. For instance, in the Georgetown section of Washington, D.C., a narcotics squad of twenty officers raided (without a search warrant) a second-floor psychedelic shop and arrested thirty-seven persons. Of these, thirty were juveniles charged under the District's infrequently invoked antiloitering ordinance for persons under age eighteen. Three of the youths also were charged with marijuana possession, after a search which the police insist was legal since the offenders had been first arrested on the loitering violation. More than half of the juveniles, according to police reports, entered the psychedelic shop, which sells posters and other items, while the raid was still in progress. A narcotics-squad sergeant later admitted that "we had no evidence that they had anything to do with drugs." When asked to justify such raids, he offered this explanation: "Hippies are quite a problem for the city. People are screaming, ranting and raving to do something about it. We're doing it."[5]

Compare these two very different approaches to handling juveniles accused of violating marijuana laws, as reported in the press. In Naugatuck, Connecticut, teenagers arrested in a "good residential section" were handled gently by the circuit court judge and later released with dismissed charges: "I suspect that many of these youngsters should not have been arrested. . . . I'm not going to have these youngsters bouncing around with these charges hanging over them." In contrast, fifteen of twenty-five persons arrested in a "mass arrest" in Washington, D.C., were charged with mere presence in a place where they presumably had knowledge that marijuana was being smoked. The presiding judge was quoted as indicating his determination "to show these *long-haired ne'er-do-wells* that society will not tolerate their conduct."[6] It would seem, then, that in the decision to invoke criminal sanctions involving marijuana violations, the critical factor frequently is the imputed attributes of the suspected offender rather than his illegal behavior: *who he is*—and what he symbolizes—rather than *what he does* becomes paramount. The implied threat to the moral codes of dominant conventional groups in the offender's presumed life-style and values—commonly inferred by physical appearance, demeanor, and rhetoric as well as by the fact of illicit drug use—may become the decisive factor stimulating legal harassment or criminal prosecution.

Another revealing case is that of a Michigan man, Larry Belcher, who was sentenced to from twenty to thirty years in prison for selling five dollars' worth of marijuana to a police agent. Joel Fort's comments on this incident illustrate clearly the tendency for those values and interests treasured by dominant groups or important to the legal authorities to be protected not only through enactment of criminal laws but also through enforcement and judicial policies:

> This case is worth noting as an example of how the marijuana laws actually function in many instances. Belcher is the only individual in Grand Traverse County to receive this sentence in the past two years: 25 other marijuana arrestees were all placed on probation within that time. Belcher, it appears, was the author of a column called "Dope-O-Scope" in a local underground newspaper and had presented there some of the scientific facts incorporated into this article. People who publicly oppose the marijuana laws and marijuana mythology of our narcotics police have an unusually high arrest record.[7]

Occasionally, persons considered deviant are extremely useful to the interests of powerful groups precisely *because* of their deviant status, and therefore are not only tolerated but welcomed. Indeed it may become necessary to invent, to create, or at least to maintain and support their status as deviants. For example, many farmers in the Southwest welcome the influx of illegal Mexican immigrants—labeled "wetbacks"—desperate enough to risk arrest to escape their abject poverty (a per capita income in Mexico of less than $150 and severe unemployment).[8] However, *it is not a crime to employ wetbacks, only to be one.* Proposals to criminalize employers have been repeatedly deleted from legal codes. Yet exploitation of these illegal farm workers by both farmers and border immigration authorities is rampant. Smuggling wetbacks across the 1,800-mile border has become a lucrative business. Some swim or are rowed across the Rio Grande; others are smuggled in planes or car trunks, or are sealed in trucks for days without food or water:

> Patrol agents near Sullivan City, Texas, acting on a tip, stopped a 44-foot tank trailer which was supposed to be carrying oil. The driver, a United States citizen, opened a valve on the side of the truck and oil spilled out, but the driver appeared unusually nervous so the agents climbed to the top of the tanker, which had three 20-inch hatch openings. In the forward and rear compartments they found crude oil, but in the middle compartment—a crude tangle of 22 Mexicans; 22 illegal aliens in a space 6 feet long and 6 feet in diameter, crammed together on plastic sheets in four inches of inflammable oil. Each had paid $300 for standing room only all the way to Chicago.[9]

The farm entrepreneurs, however, have exerted various political pressures to ensure that border enforcement will not successfully seal off this valuable illegal human cargo. Several studies have noted the selective law enforcement in which the border patrol and local authorities conveniently overlook the wetbacks at harvesttime but stage "roundup" raids near the end of the work season in covert cooperation with these powerful farm interests. (In addition, effective political lobbying by these interests helps to keep down law-enforcement budgets, making inadequate both the size of patrol forces and the amount of surveillance equipment available.) The fact that the wetbacks are designated as illegal aliens—although those who employ them are not considered to be lawbreakers—assures the farmers of a cheap pool of labor. Since there need be no strict accounting of work records, many wetbacks are forced to work as much as 12 hours a day. The farmers need accept no responsibility for the provision of adequate health and medical services, sanitary facilities, or decent housing. No costly fringe benefits in case of injuries and accidents need be provided. Moreover, since the wetbacks are deviants—criminal felons—the employers can simply threaten to turn them in to the border patrol if they complain about the abominable working conditions or exploitative wages, which they are sometimes cheated out of completely. Preoccupied with survival and their statuses as criminal fugitives, they are hardly in a position to retaliate.

Thus the powerful farm interests have created a situation in which effective legislation to ensure enforcement of the immigration law is thwarted (ensuring an adequate labor supply which maximizes economic gains in low labor costs) while selective enforcement of the law is promoted when it suits them (disposing of a complaining or useless wetback—especially when the harvest is over). Such collusion between the farmers, the lawmakers, and law-enforcement agents also serves to undermine the bargaining power of the Mexican-American rural workers who lose out in job competition to the deviant wetback, depressing work-contract conditions to the lowest possible level. Through manipulation of the news media and effective political lobbying, these powerful farm interests thus help create an artificial labor shortage which functions advantageously to perpetuate the persistence of the illegal wetbacks.

MORAL ENTREPRENEURS AND THE LEGISLATION OF MORALITY

As society becomes more complex, secular, and heterogeneous, with opposing and frequently conflicting subcultures forming, consensus regarding the propriety of many different kinds of behavior tends to decline. Criminal law, therefore, becomes increasingly relied upon as a formal mechanism of social control, binding upon all those who live within its political jurisdiction.

Yet new products, ideas, and behavior patterns continually emerge in a dynamic society in areas where there may be no firm, settled community sentiment as to their social danger or immorality. Thus, interest groups that have a special stake in the outcome of the new situation interpret the events and exert influence to initiate, shape, or block legislation. Men and women arise—whom Howard Becker terms "moral entrepreneurs"—who by virtue of their initiative, political power, access to decision-makers, skillful use of publicity, and success in neutralizing any opposition are able to translate their interests into public policy. These highly committed individuals (and sometimes bureaucratic organizations) who insist that their particular version of good and evil become the law for everyone are frequently ideological imperialists. For the crusading reformer, the existing social rules are not satisfactory:

> . . . because there is some evil which profoundly disturbs him. He feels that nothing can be right in the world until rules are made to correct it. He operates with an *absolute ethic:* what he sees is truly and totally evil with no qualification. Any means is justified to do away with it. The crusader is fervent and righteous, often self-righteous.[10]

In addition, many of the thousands of criminal statutes are inconsistent and anachronistic—a casualty of changing social norms, new technology, scientific knowledge, and sometimes community hysteria. In the United States, many of these laws were hastily enacted as an emotional, morally indignant first reaction to troublesome and difficult situations—"moral panics" frequently triggered by the sudden and sensational treatment of some deviant activity in the mass media. In a somewhat cynical overstatement, Robert Park once said: "We are always passing laws in America. We might as well get up and dance. The laws are largely to relieve emotion, and the legislatures are quite aware of that fact."[11]

Under these varied legislative circumstances in a highly differentiated society, behavior that may be illegal in the light of new or old criminal laws may not be considered immoral or deviant relative to the social norms and values of the groups to which the lawbreaker belongs or identifies. The very legitimacy of the legal norms is thus open to challenge, resulting in either expedient compliance or widespread evasion of the laws. If such challenges widen and intensify among large dissenting segments of the citizenry—contesting the very legitimacy of the legal order itself by withdrawing their consent to be governed by official authorities—then the very nature of the problem becomes transformed from a simple case of criminality to that of a political power struggle.[12]

In considering the role of conflicting interest groups in the formulation of criminal law, it is important to note that such interests basically reflect particular desires, norms, and values. Indeed, moral values themselves may be considered worthy of legal protection when challenged and their basic rightness reaffirmed through the law in an attempt to control the threatening behavior of others. The long-standing American faith in the power of the law to *coerce men toward virtue* has led many European observers to comment on what appears to be a peculiarly American legal philosophy. As Lindesmith and Strauss note, *"This philosophy places special emphasis upon the idea that the law should express the highest ideals and make no compromise with evil."*[13]

The prohibitionist, police-suppression method of dealing with threatening behavior (particularly with "vice"), they suggest, is partly a manifestation of our traditional puritan "uplift" fervor—the attempt to educate the public through passing laws and to reaffirm thereby moral values cherished by certain powerful interest groups in the society. The European legal philosophy, in contrast, places a much greater emphasis on adapting laws to existing practices in order to avoid the adverse by-products of driving underground certain types of deviant behavior.

A consequence of this attempt to affirm one powerful group's version of morality through legal action is that it produces what Robin Williams refers to as large-scale "patterned evasion" of our laws.[14] Even where a certain kind of behavior is widely condemned, many members of the society may nevertheless desire to indulge in the forbidden conduct; yet consensus is often insufficient to prevent this demand or deter others from serving it. But there is still enough community agreement—or sufficiently powerful interest groups—to preserve the norm itself from public repudiation and to prevent a repeal of the law. Since many of those persons who violate these criminal prohibitions are otherwise quite respectable and hold functionally important positions in the society, there is strong resistance to massive, wholesale punishment. Consequently, the situation is typically handled by a symbolic public affirmation of the values embodied in the law and only periodic, token ("ritualistic") sanctions or mild punishment if the violation becomes too flagrant. Public policies toward illegal gambling, drinking, marijuana use, abortion, prostitution, and sexual deviation among consenting adults ("victimless crimes") in many communities are common manifestations of such systematic, widespread evasion of criminal laws.

THE SYMBOLIC FUNCTIONS OF THE LAW

To explain the persistence of such widely violated and often unenforceable laws, it is important to emphasize the symbolic functions, in contrast to the more instrumental, social-control functions, of these criminal statutes. In an excellent study of the American temperance movement culminating in the Prohibition laws, Joseph Gusfield argues that such symbolic functions do not depend necessarily on the successful enforcement of the law for their effect; *rather the mere existence of the laws symbolizes the public affirmation and dominance of certain social ideals and norms at the expense of others.*[15] This symbolic function of the law serves to enhance and glorify the social status and prestige of groups holding the affirmed values and to demean and degrade groups whose moral patterns and life-styles reject these values.

The American Temperance movement became a conflict between abstinent, small-town and rural evangelical Protestant middle classes and drinking, urban Catholic and Lutheran lower-class immigrant groups. Victory or defeat became symbolic of the status and power of the subcultures in opposition. As Gusfield notes: "Even if the law was broken, it was clear whose law it was."[16] When the legitimacy of the norms of the dominant group is under threat, the need for symbolic restatement in legal terms intensifies. In such instances as illegal drinking, drug use, gambling, and other "moralistic crimes," the criminal law is not a reflection of any consensus within the community. Rather it is when widespread agreement is least attainable that the pressure to legislate the private moral conduct of others becomes greatest:

> When Temperance forces were culturally dominant, the confrontation was that of the social superior. He sought to convert the weaker member of the

society through persuasion backed by his dominance of the major institutions. Where dominance of the society is in doubt, then the need for positive governmental and institutional action is greater. The need for symbolic vindication and deference is channeled into political action. *What is at stake is not so much the action of men, whether or not they drink, but their ideals, the moralities to which they owe their public allegiance.*[17]

In many ways, marijuana has become the "new Prohibition" in contemporary American society, with upwards of 40 million persons having used this illicit drug, perhaps one-third of them using it on a more or less regular basis. Effective enforcement of the law has become impossible. The use and sale of marijuana remain illegal, however, primarily because most of the older adult public are *ideologically* opposed to total decriminalization. Use of the drug is symbolically associated in much of the public mind with many kinds of activities, life-styles, and moral and political beliefs that these dominant groups find repugnant (for example, hedonism, sexual promiscuity, altered states of consciousness, radicalism, irreverence toward authority, and so on). The various medical and psychiatric arguments warning of possible dangers to personal health and welfare are primarily used as rhetorical devices—portraying antimarijuana opposition as reasonable, rational, and humane—to mask these more fundamental moral and ideological sentiments which largely block repeal. Although some legal reforms are occurring, the complete legalization of marijuana would dramatically *symbolize* the already significant loss in the prestige and societal dominance of the moral codes of these older and conventional but still powerful segments of the population.[18]

DEVIANT BEHAVIOR AND MORAL PASSAGE

Public attitudes toward deviance, of course, do not necessarily remain constant, but over a period of time may change in response to changing social conditions, hierarchies of power, group norms, and scientific knowledge. Behavior that is defined as criminal at one period in time may be reevaluated as "sick," viewed as legitimate, or even positively valued. Demonstrating suffragettes early in this century were arrested as criminals for their deviant behavior in trying to gain women the right to vote. Until the 1930s, labor unions attempting to engage in collective bargaining were often harassed as "criminal conspiracies" in many states. The alcoholic in nineteenth-century America was mostly viewed as an immoral degenerate but today is labeled by most as sick, impelled by an uncontrollable compulsion, a person to be pitied and cured rather than harshly condemned. In this sense, as Joseph Gusfield has emphasized, the designation of behavior as deviant or criminal may have a history, as public definitions change with modifications in the relative power of various interest groups and with the emergence of social movements and moral crusades. The deviant behavior undergoes a "moral passage," as its designated moral status is transformed.[19]

The considerable variability in public reactions to different forms of deviance is mostly a reflection of the different "norm-sustaining implications" imputed to the deviant acts. Gusfield, for example, describes four basic kinds of deviants in terms of their implied support or threat to the social norms and values of the dominant groups in the society: the repentant, the sick, the cynical, and the enemy deviant. The *repentant deviant* openly admits the wrongness of his or her behavior, thereby confirming the legitimacy of the dominant moral code (for instance, the shamed shoplifting housewife and the remorseful drunken driver who admit the rightness of the laws they have violated; the ex-drug addict who goes on the lecture circuit to high schools and colleges preaching on the evils of dope). The actions of the *sick deviant* are, in one sense, largely irrelevant to the legitimacy of the dominant social norms, neither challenging nor affirming them. Behavior which is seen as the product of sick persons (for example, the kleptomaniac or sexual exhibitionist) is not likely to be defined as a great threat to the dominant morality; rather, the behavior is viewed as the result of a temporary, uncontrollable condition, excusing the person from official criminal liability for the consequences of his or her behavior. The offender who is assigned the status of "sick person" thus supposedly becomes a target for help, therapy, and welfare; hostile attitudes are viewed as improper and inappropriate. Law-enforcement agencies are mobilized not to punish the offender but to allow other agencies to "treat" that person (although, from the perspective of the offender, the coercion frequently involved in "treatment" may result in deprivations even more severe than those in official punishment).[20]

The attempt to define certain deviant acts as illnesses, however, can become the controversial focus of a conflict and power struggle; various official agencies may vie with each other over their vested interests in maintaining or expanding their care and control of different kinds of deviants:

> As the movement for redefinition of the addict as sick has grown, the movement to strengthen the definition of addiction as criminal has responded with increased legal severity. To classify drug users as sick and the victims or clients as suffering from "disease" would mean a change in the agencies responsible for reaction from police enforcement to medical authorities. Further, it might diminish the moral disapproval with which drug use, and the reputed euphoric effects connected with it, are viewed by supporters of present legislation.[21]

Moreover, law-enforcement agencies are not always unaware that deviant groups, whose political power is weak, may attempt to manipulate the public labeling process by conveying the impression that their behavior is involuntary—encouraging a status designation of sick in order to avoid the criminal sanctions administered for willful, deliberate deviance. Clearly, rule breakers do not always play a passive role but may, in a tactical ploy, try to manage the impressions held by those who have the power to assign public labels, and may thereby help shape the legal reactions to their deviant behavior.[22]

The widely condemned, reprehensible, and basically self-seeking acts of the *cynical deviant* (for example, the professional safecracker, the hired killer, the embezzler, the corrupt narcotics agent who extorts money from drug dealers) also represent no significant threat to the legitimacy of the dominant social norms. Although such deviants must be effectively dealt with or at least contained, the designation of their actions as wicked, immoral, or wrong generally receives widespread support throughout the society. Such deviants may, of course, cynically feign illness ("temporary insanity"), pretend repentance (become a temporary "born-again Christian" to gain early parole), or fabricate a higher loyalty ("national security") to reduce the severity of the penalties for their deviant behavior.

It is the acts of what Gusfield refers to as the *enemy deviant*, however, that most endanger the official dominant morality. These activists are neither repentant nor ill, and they defend their behavior as morally legitimate, openly contesting the moral codes embodied in the criminal law or in the official political and economic policies of the society. The behavior of these *moral provocateurs* is dramatically evident in the actions of such militant groups as the Symbionese Liberation Army and the Black Panthers, the Chicago Seven war protesters, the environmentalists who disrupted the construction of nuclear reactor plants, members of the American Indian Movement who raided the treaty files in the Bureau of Indian Affairs, and the ideologically inspired skyjackers and urban terrorists. Enemy deviants are personified in vocal critics such as Aleksandr Solzhenitsyn, the exiled Russian writer, who has accused Soviet officials of mass extermination and detention of innocent citizens in Siberian penal camps; such as the South African novelist whose depiction of the tabooed black-white racial love affairs has provoked an official ban of his books; such as Allen Ginsberg and Timothy Leary, who have championed the right to indulge in the mind-expanding pleasures and discoveries of hallucinogenic drugs; such as Larry Flynt, publisher of the raunchy *Hustler* magazine, who has been convicted of pandering to obscenity—all are thus cast in the role of enemy deviants—if not that of Satan himself—threatening the legitimacy of the dominant social norms, values, and legal policies.

Whether it be an attempt by hippies to smoke marijuana openly by staging a "puff-in" at the Hall of Justice in San Francisco and demanding legalization of the drug, a raid on a Maryland draft board by militant priests and nuns who spill blood on selective service files, a parade of homosexuals down Fifth Avenue chanting "gay is good," a takeover of parts of beaches by nude bathers, or an open defiance of local "committees for decency" by theater owners showing films such as *Deep Throat*, a direct clash in moralities is precipitated. Thus any increasing power of enemy deviants, flouting and challenging the rightness of the social or legal norms, threatens the social and political dominance of the cultural group in power. Such threats tend to stimulate renewed efforts to shore up symbolically the dominant morality. New repressive laws are passed, and already existing criminal sanctions are strengthened and enforced (such as the recent federal conviction of publisher Al Goldstein by a Wichita jury on eleven counts of mailing "an obscene, lewd, lascivious, indecent, filthy, and vile tabloid entitled 'SCREW'" from New York City to Kansas).[23] The clash becomes not just a legal struggle but a confrontation over which group has social power over the others and the right to legitimate its own social values.

If successful, the moral passage of deviant acts may result in narrowing the reach of the criminal sanction or in its elimination altogether (for example, the decriminalization of private homosexual acts among consenting adults in many states, the legality of abortion for any reason within the first three months of pregnancy, the legalization of casino gambling in selected resort areas and the proliferation of state lotteries). Changing modes of social control may occur (the substitution of "treatment" and civil commitment for imprisonment of drug addicts, civil detoxification centers and "after-care" treatment instead of jailing alcoholics, the removal of official arrest from the records of first-offender marijuana users who demonstrate subsequent "good behavior," the establishment of segregated districts for sex-oriented "adult entertainment" as in Boston's "combat zone"). The dean of a Catholic university, commenting on the revival of witchery on college campuses, illustrates the changing social reactions to deviant behavior:

> We've really become progressive around here. A couple of hundred years ago we would have burned them. Twenty-five years ago I would have expelled them. Now we simply send them all to psychiatrists.[24]

Gradually, widespread public acceptance of the new moral status of the behavior in question may crystallize, with a possible symbolic loss in social dominance of the moral codes held by certain segments of the population. For example, the chronic problem drinker has undergone in much of the nation a moral passage from the status of habitual drunken "sinner" to the "diseased" alcoholic who should be medically treated. So too, the illicit drug user appears to be partially experiencing a moral passage from "dope fiend" and "acid head" to the pitied "sick addict" or "emotionally disturbed drug user"—and even to the eventual possibility of the legitimate moral status of "social user," especially among marijuana, cocaine, and hallucinogenic drug devotees. The outcome of this moral transition is by no means clear, as various contesting interest groups use their power, status, and organizational resources in struggles to control the public designation of these and other deviant acts:

> The "lifting" of a deviant activity to the level of a political, public issue is thus a sign that its moral status is at stake, that legitimacy is a possibility. Today the moral acceptance of drinking, marijuana and LSD use, homosexuality, abortion, and other "vices" is being publicly discussed, and movements championing them have emerged. Such movements draw into them far more than the deviants themselves. Because they become symbols of general cultural attitudes, they call out partisans for both repression and permission.[25]

Over the last 15 years, hippie countercultures, gay rights and feminist liberation movements, and other activist groups have emerged to challenge the traditional and absolutist order, offering alternative ways to be human and liberated. The participants in these movements have become central actors in helping to change conceptions of what constitutes deviant behavior. A recent example of such efforts to reconstruct social reality is evident in the National Hookers Convention held in the chic Hyatt Regency hotel in San Francisco, sponsored by COYOTE ("Call Off Your Old Tired Ethics"). The prostitutes angrily charged the police and courts in America with an unconstitutional invasion of their privacy and the right to control their own bodies. They protested the sexist harassment and jailing of prostitutes while police ignore the "johns" and men who openly solicit women. These militant prostitutes called for the decriminalization of prostitution, rousing support for a view of prostitution as an economic activity rather than a moral offense. One streetwalker, dramatizing the depriving economic and social conditions that frequently propel some women into prostitution, reported: "It looked good to me; I didn't have any money, I was on welfare, trying to raise a baby, getting high, running the streets."[26]

Some prostitutes are also attempting to erode the stigma of their activity —and speed the process of moral passage—by relabeling themselves as "paraprofessional sex therapists." According to COYOTE, persons opposed to prostitution are "stuffy old Puritans in advanced stages of sexual repression." Margo St. James, a vocal leader in COYOTE, sums up this feminist challenge to traditional views and male dominance which oppress not only prostitutes but all women:

> Women are an oppressed class living in a patriarchy. The casualties fill the mental institutions and jails. Incarceration of the prostitute is an object lesson for ALL women. Keeping her behavior illegal is absolutely necessary for the subjugation of women. Myths are perpetrated about the "fallen woman"; she's unclean, she's sick, she's hostile to men, she's criminal, an unfit mother and

wife . . . no vestige of respectability is allowed the whore. Her mate will be called a pimp and ostracized along with her. He's the object lesson for men who will let a woman be the breadwinner. (There are no laws which protect men from having women live off them.) . . . A woman is put in jail if she capitalizes on the Sexsystem . . . [is] directly excommunicated if she attempts to take control of her own body . . . but her image is used to sell almost everything for man's profit.[27]

THE PROTECTIVE COCOON

From the perspective of the dominant groups many deviants are dangerous, for example, murderers, rapists, and muggers. Many such persons, of course, do represent a threat to life, limb, or property, lashing out in sporadic violence or causing financial loss. Most persons considered deviants, however, are relatively harmless in the sense that they are unlikely to do direct physical or property injury to others. Yet in another more basic sense, various kinds of persons labeled as deviants are indeed dangerous. Their very existence implicitly challenges the prevailing conceptions of order, normality, and reality. Anomalies and incongruities like lepers, transvestites, homosexuals, transsexuals, or schizophrenics may threaten in a deeply fundamental way our most basic beliefs about the nature of man and social reality—beliefs that provide a basic sense of anchorage and certainty in our lives. As Robert Scott observes, "Anything that threatens to strip us of this protective cocoon will inevitably be seen as evil. . . . The madman whose rantings challenge our system of meanings is in a sense just as dangerous as the madman who is a threat to our physical being. The practice early in our history of beating and killing heretics is strong testimony to this fact."[28] Berger and Luckmann describe the threat that deviance poses to our basic world view, our very conception of social reality. Deviant phenomena, they note,

> . . . constitute the most acute threat to taken-for-granted, routinized existence in society. If one conceives of the latter as the "daylight side" of human life, then [deviance] constitutes a "night side" that keeps lurking ominously on the periphery of everyday consciousness. Just because the "night side" has its own reality, often enough of a sinister kind, it is a constant threat to the taken-for-granted, matter-of-fact, "sane" reality of life in society. The thought keeps suggesting itself . . . that, perhaps, the bright reality of everyday life is but an illusion, to be swallowed up at any moment by the howling nightmare of the other, the night-side reality.[29]

Persons who do not fit into these dominant conceptions of normality and reality—who threaten our security—thus must be dealt with: annihilated, exiled, confined, or corrected—thereby reaffirming the validity and potency of the established, institutionalized world view.

However, it is the enemy deviants who perhaps pose the most effective challenge to the "protective cocoon" of dominant group notions of what is right, good, and proper. Such persons expose the precarious nature of this absolutist conception of social reality, threatening the assumption of a widely shared, well-integrated consensus in which conventional behavior patterns and beliefs are the only viable, authentic, healthy ways of acting, feeling, and thinking. Anita Bryant, campaigning against a homosexual rights ordinance in the Miami area and leader of the "Save Our Children" crusade, clearly perceives this danger:

> What these people really want, hidden behind obscure legal phrases, is the legal right to propose to our children that there is an acceptable alternative way of life—that being a homosexual or lesbian is not really wrong or illegal.[30]

Consequently, various strategies come in to play to discredit these competing views. These strategies typically take on an aura of *mystification*: by obscuring the fact that both deviant and normal activities are basically arbitrary, the dominant group masks the underlying conflict of interests and the mainsprings of power.

THE COOPTATION OF SCIENTISTS

Increasingly in modern Western societies, scientists are contributing— sometimes unwittingly—to these ideological struggles. Interest groups use scientific research data as moral armaments to bolster their contention that there is only *one* possible view of the world—the *real* world, and to assign an almost semisacred or natural status to certain institutionalized patterns of behavior that are humanly produced. In so doing they mystify human behavior by imputing an *inexorability* and *inevitability* to those man-made social creations. In effect, scientists and their ostensibly impartial research are used to make both establishment rules and their enforcement appear rational, humane, and just. All other views must be seen to be in error. Persons who challenge the conventional rules must be discredited as *individual* wrongdoers (as sick, pathological, or criminal), not accepted as willful, normal participants involved in legitimate *political conflict* and viable social movements.

As Erich Goode reminds us, during an earlier period this "mystification process was religious in character: views in competition with the dominant one were heretical and displeasing to the gods—hence, Galileo's 'crime.'" Today, however, "nothing has greater discrediting power . . . than the demonstration that a given assertion has been 'scientifically disproven.'"[31] Scientists, Goode notes, have become our contemporary "pawnbrokers of reality" (and, I would add, psychiatrists our arbiters of normality), operating under a value-free cloak of objectivity that Western civilization assigns to this prestigious enterprise. Dominant interest groups thus mobilize psychologists, physicians, pharmacologists, criminologists, psychiatrists, and other highly regarded "experts" operating under the scientific banner to render unconventional behavior meaningless, harmful, or unnatural. If such impeccable authorities certify behavior as pathological or dangerous, the labels become potent rhetorical weapons of social control. These controls, designed to keep others from doing things dominant groups dislike, are effectively cloaked in reasonable, humanitarian garb—restriction of certain kinds of behavior is *morally* desirable and *scientifically* correct, good for both the individual and the society. The clearly political uses of psychiatry, for example, occur not only in such totalitarian societies as the Soviet Union, but occasionally even in the United States. Social psychiatrist Robert Coles describes his shock on discovering the ease with which a civil-rights worker in the early 1960s was committed to a Southern state hospital:

> But I was not so prepared . . . to see how convenient it would be for that judge, and many others like him, to have people around who could summon all the authority of medicine and science to the task of defending the status quo—which meant putting firmly in their place (a hospital or a clinic) those who choose to wage a struggle against that status quo.[32]

In every complex society there are "hierarchies of credibility," by which some prestigious and respectable persons have greater power than others to define what is true and false, what is proper and improper, what is normal and abnormal, what is safe and dangerous. It is partly through such control over definitions of social reality that dominant groups enforce their conceptions of deviance. As Howard Becker argues:

> Elites, ruling classes, bosses, adults, men, Caucasians—superordinate groups generally—maintain their power as much by controlling how people define the world, its components, and its possibilities, as by the use of more primitive forms of control.[33]

Whether it be statements from the American Medical Association, the Federal Bureau of Narcotics, or "drug experts"; the American Psychiatric Association or the FBI; the director of the National Institute of Mental Health, the U.S. Attorney General, or the president of the American Bar Association—all may be enlisted to uphold dominant ideological views and to stigmatize and condemn persons who display unpopular or threatening modes of belief and behavior—in short, to sanctify existing social, economic, and political arrangements and privileges. Such prestigious organizations and their bureaucratic functionaries help filter out scientific findings that do not conform to official prevailing views—attacking, debunking, or ignoring them—and publicize in the mass media research findings that support the conventional wisdom. For example, in the early 1970s Dr. Wesley Hall, newly elected president of the American Medical Association, was quoted in a widely publicized news story as saying that an AMA study left "very little doubt" that marijuana would cause a significant reduction in a person's sex drive (observing that a thirty-five-year-old man might have his sex drive reduced to one more typical of a seventy-year-old man). He also implied that certain scientific evidence demonstrated that this illicit drug caused birth defects. In an interview several weeks later, Dr. Hall said he had been misquoted but added that he didn't mind:

> I don't mind . . . if this can do some good in waking people up to the fact that, by jingo, whether we like to face it or not, our campuses are going to pot, both literally and figuratively. . . . If we don't wake up in this country to the fact that every college campus and high school has a problem with drug addiction, we're going down the drain not only with respect to morality, but . . . the type of system we're going to have.[34]

When confronted by the comment that such misleading statements might damage the credibility of the AMA, Dr. Hall answered: "I'm tired of these phrases about the credibility gap. *We're talking about the morality of the country . . . and respect for authority and decency.*[35] Dr. Hall not only disapproves of marijuana but also exploits such drug use as a vehicle for expression of his own ideological views toward other kinds of activities and attitudes that he deplores. But in view of the AMA's prestige and power, such selective and distorted use of empirical evidence is not likely to significantly impair the credibility of future pronouncements on the dangers of illicit drug use.

Research and writing on deviance are replete with such value-laden language as "social maladjustment," "sexual promiscuity," "inadequate personality," "hedonism," "perversion," "escape from reality," "artificial euphoria," "social irresponsibility" and "underachievement"—terms and expressions which, used under the pretext of unbiased, scientific objectivity, serve to further mystify the nature of deviance.

EXISTENTIAL PARADOXES

The mystification of deviance, however, is not without its powerful effects on the deviant himself. The responses of others to persons stigmatized as deviant may affect the deviant's world in such *self-fulfilling* ways that they would seem to substantiate the validity of popular and scientific views. Thus some deviants also may come unwittingly to embrace, internalize, and act out the stereotypical conceptions. Heroin addicts or persons diagnosed as mentally ill and incarcerated for therapeutic reasons in prison hospitals and asylums may come to see themselves in the absolutist's terms—as dependent, inadequate, psychotic, asocial, or demoralized. Some homosexuals echo the imagery pervading their community and come to hate themselves as unworthy, dirty "queers." Some heavy drinkers may come to embrace the stigmatizing label of alcoholic, thereby excusing their own and others' failures in marriage, family, or career.

The self-fulfilling effects of criminal stigmatization are particularly harsh and may inadvertently entrench the offender in a persistent criminal life-style. The conferral of criminal status may not only transform the identity of the offender in the eyes of others and reshape to some degree his self-image, but may also impel the offender into various behavior patterns that will further confirm his negative public identity, increasing the probability of further criminal processing and stiffer penalties. The imprisoned drug addict released on parole, for example, may find jobs difficult to secure and may be denied access to the very kinds of legitimate conventional opportunities that he needs to demonstrate his "fitness" to re-enter society and effectively remove the label of "dope fiend." Skepticism, suspicion, and withdrawal of trust are likely to prevail long after the offender has "paid his debt to society." ("Once a junkie, always a junkie.") Unlike some primitive societies, American society has a legal process that lacks any special ceremonial rites of passage that clearly mark the termination of a criminal status, the resumption of a noncriminal identity, and the readmission of the offender to a legitimate position in the social order.

Unable to slough off the stigmatizing label of criminal, the convicted assailant, petty thief, or drug addict may experience a variety of disabilities—employment and housing restrictions, loss of voting rights and access to military service, increased police surveillance and harassment, and disrupted family and personal relations. Denied the opportunities to engage in conventional routines of everyday life, such offenders' experiences of rejection and suspicion are likely to intensify their feelings of alienation and despair, impelling them toward further criminal behavior.

Without legal access to heroin, the ex-convict who becomes addicted may be forced to commit income-producing crimes (robbery, burglary, larceny), to break into pharmacies or doctors' offices, to peddle drugs, or to turn to prostitution to pay for the exorbitant black-market prices. Since the sale of stolen goods to underworld "fences" provides only about 20 percent of their value, an addict with a $60-a-day drug need, unless wealthy, must steal merchandise each day worth $300. "The male addict becomes a continuing one-man crime wave and is unlike other criminals in that he *must* 'score' every day."[36] In New York City alone, it is estimated that drug addicts are involved in about one-quarter of all known crimes involving property.

The beleaguered addict must also often confront the dangers of diseases such as hepatitis and tetanus from dirty, unsterilized needles used communally. Inexperienced heroin users may inadvertently inject the drug into an artery rather than a vein, resulting in gangrene. Improper handling of the needle may produce air bubbles, which can be fatal. With no standardized potency or quality control in black-market drugs, the threat of death from overdose or impurities in the adulterated opiate is a constant hazard. Pneumonia and nutritional deficiencies may occur from the scrounging, hand-to-mouth life-style of the junkie who must raise from $20 to $150 daily for a drug that costs but pennies to produce legally. Thus, most of the crime, disease, and death commonly associated with heroin use are not particularly a result of the pharmacological properties of heroin but the social conditions —the *illegality*—under which the addict must secure the drug. In such ways do repressive legal policies help artificially *create* some of the very features of drug use that dominant groups in society find most repugnant.[37]

Cast apart from legitimate society, stigmatized criminal offenders may gravitate toward others similarly branded. Here they may discover deviant subcultures and groups whose social norms and participants provide them with the emotional support and rationalizations to neutralize guilt feelings from any lingering adherence to the norms of conventional morality. With continued participation in such a milieu, incipient criminal self-images may crystallize as the offenders withdraw their commitment to conventional norms; new standards and ideologies are adopted which justify their deviance and provide a positive self-evaluation. Forced to operate in an atmosphere of secrecy, deviousness, and illegality, the offenders may come to depend on criminal sources for protection and aid. (The prostitute, for example, may depend on other prostitutes to train her and to help her to build a clientele, and on a pimp to protect her from incursions by police, customers, or other criminals. The heroin addict requires a dependable drug supplier, a grapevine information system to protect him from informers and police, and fences to dispose of stolen goods.)

In these subcultures and groups the stigmatized deviants may obtain a number of rewards: status and positive evaluation from peers, enhancing the offender's self-image; access to illegitimate means to obtain material and monetary gain with a minimum of trouble; access to opportunities and techniques to gratify illicit desires; and escape from conventional role demands and pressures. Often embittered, cynical, hostile—perhaps even brutalized from their prison or jail experiences—many offenders may drift further toward a persistent criminal life pattern. Still others may vacillate ambivalently in a twilight zone of conventionality and criminality, often zigzagging in episodic movements into and out of criminal activities as employment opportunities and other circumstances vary.

The adverse consequences of obscuring the humanly created quality of many disturbing features of social deviance, however, are not simply the result of the viewpoints and social policies of dominant conventional groups in the society. *Deviant subcultures, with their belief systems and social pressures, also may mystify,* creating stereotypes and alienative mechanisms of their own. These dissident groups may have their own "hierarchies of credibility," affirming the desirability or legitimacy of only certain values, ideologies, and life-styles, while discrediting other normative orientations and options as square, unreal, or undesirable (e.g., only "gay is good," bisexuality is a lesbian cop-out, prostitutes are the only women free of hypocrisy, the Jesus movement is the only way).

Indeed, some subcultures are so constricted that many of their participants may come to take on the character of "one-dimensional" men or women. For example, some "cool" drug users—using mood and mind-altering substances experientially to push beyond the narrow confines of the conventional socially constructed reality—may become transmuted into the frantic street junkie, whose life-style becomes narrowly tailored to the incessant demands of feeding his increasingly expensive drug habit. The chemically induced "rush"—the exhilarating sense of euphoria—diminishes in power and pleasure as the long-term addict only rarely "cops" a dose potent enough to "take off." Instead, he must shoot up several times a day merely to feel "normal," to stave off the misery of withdrawal sickness. Ironically, the hip drug user who attempts to explore the boundaries of human freedom and experience with narcotics may come to act out a more stereotypical role, a more confining and alienating round of life than prior to such drug use. Contrast the accounts given below of the experiences of two heroin users. First a twenty-two-year-old college senior describes her attraction to the excitement of the drug world and the boredom and banality of her parent's straight world:

> I tend to think that the primary target of my striving for deviance is possibly the sterility and blandness of the life I had always been exposed to. . . . My parents . . . gave me a life devoid of real, deep feeling. I wanted to feel! I wanted to play in the dirt. I wanted to transgress those lily-white norms, break those rules designed to make me a good little Doris Day. And when the first transgression was followed not by the wrath of God . . . but by a feeling of being alive, and free, and different, that I had never known before, then I guess after that, all rules and norms lost their meaning and power over me. . . . I knew that there was a way for me to declare my independence from the straight, conventional and BORING! life my mother wanted me to lead. . . . When I shot up, I felt so superior, so wicked, so unique. . . . I thought I had found the ultimate rebellion, the most deviant act possible. I was drawn to it because it set us apart from, and above, everyone—even the other drug users, the "soft" drug users. . . . I was irresistibly attracted to and proud of the deviance and anti-sociability of the act. . . . The "badness" of shooting heroin was precisely why I did not hesitate to do it.[38]

An interviewer relates the decision of a black ex-convict to give up heroin after having reached "rock bottom" in his life—an existence so repugnant that even other addicts ostracized him:

> After leaving prison at Hart Island he became addicted once more and started to steal from home, pawning his mother's new radio and shoplifting. His mother forced him out of the house, and he started to sleep in cellars, which he had always hated, and developed pustular fungus sores all over his body. Although he had formerly been very careful and neat about his appearance and bathing, he now no longer cared, went downhill, and did all the things he had previously loathed. He slept in a rat-infested cellar that frequently drained human waste from overflowing toilets down on him. He lived this way for nearly three years, going home on and off, until he became an outcast among junkies, no mean feat. They could not understand how he could live the way he did and described him as disgusting.[39]

Seeking authenticity, some participants in deviant subcultures may inadvertently get locked into their deviant identities and roles. Instead of an emphasis on the human process of *becoming*, such persons may confuse their behavior or *doing* with their *being*. The individual who acts out his occasional erotic desires for persons of the same sex, for example, may insist that he *is* gay, the essence of his character—his inescapable destiny—thereby closing other sexual options, relationships, and identities that being human permits. As Edward Sagarin notes:

> [P]eople become entrapped . . . [into] identifying themselves as *being* homosexuals. They believe that they discover what they are (and by implication, since this is a discovery, they must have been this all along). Learning their "identity," they become involved in it, boxed into their own biographies, and they adjust to the reified images of a language-reinforced belief. There is no road back because they believe there is none, and they see the search for escape as a renunciation of identity.[40]

These mystifications, by either the conventional or the deviant world, may function to amputate a significant portion of a person's human potentiality. Such moral and ideological straitjackets severely limit people's capacity to conceive of radically alternative social arrangements and forms of human consciousness—the ability to create, to *choose* their action rather than be propelled and imprisoned by current social structures, labels, and circumstances.

The fact is, however, that most persons engage in some deviance and break some law or moral code during their lives. But most such deviance is experimental, irregular, or seldom harmful to others. Many kinds of unconventional behavior are simply options that may be tried, but do not necessarily lock a person into a rigid or chronic deviant life-style. Most people experience deviant impulses; they flirt with deviance, fantasize, sound out others, explore, backtrack, zigzag, and only occasionally persist. People may find their deviant impulses and actions frightening, disgusting, or unsatisfying; or, conversely, they may find such experiences gratifying and rewarding. Choices can be made at various points to change or continue. Sometimes, however, the social reactions from the conventional or deviant world may combine with one's own beliefs to imprison one in a role or identity that is not desired. Herein lies the real tragedy of the mystification of deviance.

FOOTNOTES

1   For example, see John Lofland, *Deviance and Identity*, Prentice-Hall, Englewood Cliffs, N.J., 1969, pp. 13–23; Alex Thio, "Class Bias in the Sociology of Deviance," *American Sociologist*, 8 (February 1973), pp. 1–12; Nanette J. Davis, *Sociological Constructions of Deviance*, William C. Brown, Dubuque, Iowa, 1975, Ch. 8; Ian Taylor and Laurie Taylor (eds.), *Politics and Deviance*, Penguin Books, Baltimore, 1973; Richard Quinney, *Criminology*, Little, Brown, Boston, 1979; Ian Taylor, Paul Walton, and Jock Young, *The New Criminology: For a Social Theory of Deviance*, Harper Torchbooks, New York, 1974.

2   Howard S. Becker, *Outsiders*, Free Press, New York, 1973, p. 18. Italics added.

3   Jerry L. Simmons, *Deviants*, Glendessary Press, Berkeley, Calif., 1969, p. 42.

4   *Society Today*, CRM Books, Del Mar, Calif., 1971, p. 347.

5   Carl Bernstein, "Hippie Busting by the Narcotics Squad," *The New Republic*, Feb. 24, 1968, p. 20.

6   Both quotations cited in Michael E. Brown, "The Condemnation and Persecution of Hippies," *Transaction*, 6 (September 1969), p. 46.

7   Joel Fort, "Pot: A Rational Approach," *Playboy*, (October 1969), p. 218. See also, Paul Rock (ed.), *Drugs and Politics*, Transaction Books, New Brunswick, N.J., 1977; John Helmer, *Drugs and Minority Oppression*, Seabury Press, New York, 1975.

8   See Jorge A. Bustamante, "The 'Wetback' as Deviant: An Application of Labeling Theory," *American Journal of Sociology*, 77 (January 1972), pp. 706–718; Julian Samora, *Los Mojados, the Wetback Story*, University of Notre Dame Press, Notre Dame, Ind., 1971; Alejandro Portes, "Return of the Wetback," *Society*, 11 (March/April 1974), pp. 40–46; Alejandro Portes, "Labor Functions of Illegal Aliens," *Society*, 14 (September/October 1977), pp. 31–37.

9   Leslie Aldridge Westoff, "Should We Pull Up the Gangplank?" *The New York Times Magazine*, Sept. 16, 1973, p. 82.

10 Becker, *Outsiders*, pp. 147–148. Italics added.

11 Quoted in Edwin H. Sutherland and Donald R. Cressey, *Principles of Criminology*, Lippincott, Philadelphia, 1978, pp. 10–11.

12 See Jerome H. Skolnick, *The Politics of Protest*, Simon and Schuster, New York, 1969, pp. 323–324; Paul G. Schervish, "The Labeling Perspective: Its Bias and Potential in the Study of Political Deviance," *American Sociologist*, 8 (May 1973), pp. 47–57; Ian Taylor et al. (eds.), *Critical Criminology*, Rout-

ledge and Kegan, Boston, 1975; Irving L. Horowitz and Martin Liebowitz, "Social Deviance and Political Marginality: Toward a Redefinition of the Relation Between Sociology and Politics," *Social Problems*, 15 (Winter 1968), pp. 280–296; Davis, *Sociological Constructions of Deviance*, Ch. 8.

13 Alfred R. Lindesmith and Anselm L. Strauss, *Social Psychology*, Holt, Rinehart and Winston, New York, 1968, p. 420. Italics added.

14 Robin M. Williams, Jr., *American Society*, Knopf, New York, 1970, p. 421.

15 Joseph R. Gusfield, *Symbolic Crusade*, University of Illinois Press, Urbana, Ill., 1963.

16 Joseph R. Gusfield, "Moral Passage: The Symbolic Process in the Public Designation of Deviance," *Social Problems*, 15 (Fall 1967), p. 178.

17 Gusfield, *Symbolic Crusade*, p. 177. Italics added.

18 See John Kaplan, *Marijuana—The New Prohibition*, World, New York, 1970; Erich Goode, *Drugs in American Society*, Knopf, New York, 1972, Ch. 7; National Commission on Marijuana and Drug Abuse, *Drug Use in America*, U.S. Government Printing Office, Washington, D.C., 1973.

19 Gusfield, "Moral Passage," pp. 175–188.

20 See Nicholas N. Kittrie, *The Right to be Different: Deviance and Enforced Therapy*, Penguin Books, Baltimore, 1973; Peter Schrag, *Mind Control*, Pantheon Books, New York, 1978; Thomas Szasz, *Psychiatric Slavery*, Free Press, New York, 1977; Stephan L. Chorover, "Big Brother and Psychotechnology," *Psychology Today*, 6 (October 1973), pp. 43–54.

21 Gusfield, "Moral Passage," p. 188.

22 See Judith Lorber, "Deviance as Performance: The Case of Illness," *Social Problems*, 14 (Winter 1967), pp. 302–310.

23 See Robert Yoakum, "An obscene, lewd, lascivious, indecent, filthy, and vile tabloid entitled 'SCREW,'" *Columbia Journalism Review*, 15 (March/April 1977), pp. 38–49.

24 Quoted in Irving K. Zola, "In the Name of Health and Illness: On Some Socio-Political Consequences of Medical Influence," *Social Science and Medicine*, 9 (February 1975), p. 86.

25 Gusfield, "Moral Passage," p. 188. See also Charles Winick, "From Deviant to Normative: Changes in the Social Acceptability of Sexually Explicit Material," in Edward Sagarin (ed.), *Deviance and Social Change*, Sage, Beverly Hills, Calif., 1977, pp. 219–246.

26 Quoted in Nanette J. Davis, "Feminism, Deviance and Social Change," in Sagarin (ed.), *Deviance and Social Change*, p. 267.

27 Margo St. James, "The War on Women," *Coyote Growls*, (June/July 1975), p. 1.

28 Robert A. Scott, "A Proposed Framework for Analyzing Deviance as a Property of Social Order," in Robert A. Scott and Jack D. Douglas (eds.), *Theoretical Perspectives on Deviance*, Basic Books, New York, 1972, pp. 30–31.

29 Peter L. Berger and Thomas Luckmann, *The Social Construction of Reality*, Anchor Books, Doubleday, Garden City, N.Y., 1967, p. 98.

30 *The New York Times*, Mar. 28, 1977, p. 52.

31 Erich Goode, *The Marijuana Smokers*, Basic Books, New York, 1970, pp. 52–53. For a discussion of various strategies of mystification, see also Scott, "A

Proposed Framework for Analyzing Deviance as a Property of Social Order," pp. 24–32; Thomas Szasz, *The Second Sin*, Anchor Press, Doubleday, Garden City, N.Y., 1973; Jock Young, *The Drugtakers*, Paladin, London, 1971, Ch. 3.

32   Cited in Fitzhugh Mullan's review of Charles Steir (ed.), *Blue Jolts: True Stories From the Cuckoo's Nest*, New Republic Books, Washington, D.C., 1978, in *The New York Times Book Review*, Feb. 5, 1978, pp. 13, 30.

33   Becker, *Outsiders*, p. 204.

34   Quoted in Goode, *Drugs in American Society*, p. 15.

35   Quoted in Goode, *Drugs in American Society*, p. 16.

36   Charles Winick, "Drug Addiction and Crime," *Current History*, 52 (June 1967), p. 349.

37   See Goode, *Drugs in American Society*, Chs. 6–7; Dan Waldorf, *Careers in Dope*, Prentice-Hall, Englewood Cliffs, N.J., 1973. For a history of American legal policies and narcotics, see David F. Musto, *The American Disease*, Yale University Press, New Haven, 1973; Charles Reasons, "The Politics of Drugs: An Inquiry in the Sociology of Social Problems," *Sociological Quarterly*, 15 (Summer 1974), pp. 381–404; Troy Duster, *The Legislation of Morality*, Free Press, New York, 1970.

38   Erich Goode, "The Criminology of Drugs and Drug Use," in Abraham S. Blumberg (ed.), *Current Perspectives on Criminal Behavior*, Knopf, New York, 1974, pp. 171–172.

39   Waldorf, *Careers in Dope*, p. 148. For a discussion of the street addict's perspective toward his life-style, see also Leory Gould et al., *Connections: Notes From the Heroin World*, Yale University Press, New Haven, 1974; Dan Waldorf and Craig Reinarman, "Addicts—Everything But Human Beings," *Urban Life*, 4 (April 1975), pp. 30–53; Edward Preble and John H. Casey, "Taking Care of Business—The Heroin User's Life on the Street," *International Journal of the Addictions*, 4 (March 1969), pp. 1–24; Seymour Fiddle, *Portraits From a Shooting Gallery*, Harper & Row, New York, 1967.

40   Edward R. Sagarin, "The Good Guys, and Bad Guys, and the Gay Guys," *Contemporary Sociology*, 2 (January 1973), p. 10. See also Edward R. Sagarin, *Deviants and Deviance*, Praeger, New York, 1975, pp. 144–154.

Part Two

Studies in Deviance and Conformity

Chapter 3

Rape and the Masculine Mystique

"Lock your car doors . . . Look into the back seat before entering your car . . . If you must walk alone at night, walk along the curb side of the sidewalk . . . Don't open your door to a stranger." These warnings to reduce the possibility of becoming a rape victim are now commonplace. Although the taboo subject of rape has come out of the closet to become a popular feature of magazine articles stressing methods of crime prevention, this well-intentioned advice may inadvertently reinforce widespread stereotypes of the pathology of the typical rapist. Such emphasis on the alien danger "out there" may divert attention from the relationship of rape and other forms of sexual assault to normal and *culturally approved* patterns of behavior, particularly the deeply entrenched sexism in American life.

MEDIA IMAGES AND SOCIAL REALITIES

The lower-class sex-crazed *stranger* lurking in the alleys. The crazy, sadistic *psychopath*—the lone mad stalker—masquerading as a delivery man or hiding concealed in the backseat of the parked car. The *freaks* of society. Such is the powerful stereotypical imagery of the typical rapist in the news media. These are the kinds of people we occasionally read about in the big-city newspaper or hear about on the 10 o'clock television news out of New York City. Thus the myth is perpetuated that rape is a rarity—except in certain dangerous urban areas—and is predominantly the result of a small number of psychopaths and weirdos, deviants who are distant strangers to their victims. Rape is not likely to be seen, therefore, as having any further implications for the dominant culture and established social arrangements.

In reality, there are many different kinds of rapists. They vary in their needs, motivations, and approaches to rape. As social scientists devise research methods that go beyond the limited and biased official police statistics, they discover that rape is much more commonplace than most people realize and that it certainly is not the exclusive product of a small number of demented psychopaths or alienated lower-class blacks. In fact, it is quite likely that the majority of rapists are the kinds of men that women from all social classes and communities are likely to *know:* a friend, acquaintance, relative, coworker, employer, date, lover, former-lover, husband—quite *normal* people.

The discussion that follows will particularly explore the "rape date" and some of the cultural patterns that help provoke, justify, and culminate in rape. We shall especially probe some of the idealized attributes of the masculine mystique—the cult of male virility and machismo—the mythical beliefs, values, and expectations that justify treating some women as legitimate targets of violence and contempt.

SOCIAL STIGMA AND THE REPORTING OF RAPE

Rape typically refers to the oral, anal, or vaginal penetration of a woman by force and without her consent and willingness. It is one of the least studied and most underreported kinds of violent crime in America. For example, a victimization study in the late 1960s by the President's Crime Commission found that women were almost *four times* as likely to report in an interview that they had been raped (in the previous year) than they were to report it to the police.[1] A 1972 study of the five largest American cities, in which respondents were asked if they had ever been victimized by certain crimes, found that of women who were willing to admit that they had been sexually assaulted, only 46 percent (Los Angeles) to 61 percent (NYC) reported it to legal authorities.[2]

Moreover, recent studies reveal that rape is not only more widespread than official records indicate, but also that rapists quite frequently, probably typically, choose women who are *known* to them. (Therefore, it should not be surprising that the vast majority of rapes also involve persons of the same race. Overwhelmingly white rapists victimize white females and, contrary to the fears of white racists, black rapists predominantly prey upon black females.) A District of Columbia Crime Commission study, for example, found that only 39 percent of the rapists were total strangers to their victims.[3] In a seventeen-city survey done by the National Commission on the Causes of Violence, about one-half of the assailants were strangers.[4] These and other kinds of official and unofficial studies, however, grossly overstate the proportion of rapes involving strangers and vastly understate the actual incidence of rape in America. Certainly stranger-victim rape is much more likely to be reported and admitted—officially or unofficially in interviews—than rape occurring among friends, acquaintances, and relatives. For example, in one study of ninety rape victims, with three exceptions, only women who were raped by strangers reported it to legal authorities.[5]

Furthermore, when the assailant is the woman's own husband, the law in most states does not even define such forcible intercourse as rape, even in late pregnancy and when she is physically harmed. (In common law tradition, the husband is only exercising his "conjugal rights.") According to an estimate by the Federal Bureau of Investigation, probably no more than 10 percent of all rape is reported. As the Kinsey Institute for Sex Research points out:

> These percentages of strangers, acquaintances present . . . a false picture of rape. . . . It is known that many rape cases go unreported, especially if the two people concerned have been dating. No girl likes to advertise her misfortune through court action, and she is especially loath to do so if the defendant is someone with whom she has been friendly, lest there be some question about the validity of her charge.[6]

To be raped by a stranger may possibly make one a martyr; to be raped by a friend, business colleague, blind date, or your husband's fishing buddy clearly makes a complaining woman an object of suspicion. The female must convince legal officials that she was coerced, not seduced; that it was a degrading, not a joyful experience. If the woman chooses not to risk serious injury by resisting—or is paralyzed by fear or shock—she becomes even further suspect and often humiliated in a criminal courtroom where the victim's virtue "goes on trial." Even when brutally raped by a stranger, a woman may be compelled to undergo a degradation ceremony and demeaning experiences in a male-dominated "criminal-justice" system:

> "If I had it to do again, I would never have gone through with the prosecution. I wouldn't even have reported it," said one twenty-seven-year-old woman who suffered through months of legal proceedings and publicity only to see her rapist found innocent because she was unable to prove that she did not consent to the act. Despite extensive body bruises and a wound in her forehead

that took six stitches to close, the defense attorney argued that "vigorous love play" did not necessarily indicate nonconsent and, in fact, could even indicate enthusiastic approval and passionate involvement in the act.

"From the beginning I had this feeling I was the one who was on trial rather than the guy they picked up and charged," said the woman, raped by an intruder who entered her apartment through a window, from an adjacent rooftop. She was at the time sleeping in the nude . . . a fact that is frequently alleged in rape cases to prove "willingness to have intercourse."

"Right after it happened . . . I mean here I was lying on the floor, my face was streaming with blood, I was damned near hysterical when I called the police. They arrived and the very first question this one guy asked me was, 'Did you enjoy it? Did you really try to resist the guy?'

"Then the questions really started. I couldn't believe what they asked me. About five officers were crowded into my bedroom. They said things to me like 'Lay on the bed exactly as you were when the guy came in. Why did you spread your legs if you didn't want to be raped? Did you see his penis? Describe it. Did you touch his penis? Did you put it in your mouth? Did you have an orgasm?'

"Then there was the hospital they took me to. There were maybe three dozen people sitting around in this large ward. This one guy in a white coat takes my name and he yells down the ward, at the top of his lungs, 'Hey Pete, I got a rape case here. Check her out, will you?' It was just incredible. The guy checking me out left me sitting on this table for like an hour. One of his questions was, 'Did you give the guy a blow job or what?'

"Later at the police station. They caught the guy from my description. He was sitting there and one of the cops went out to get him a cup of coffee and gave him a cigarette. They told me, 'Sit over there, lady, we'll get to you in a minute.'

"Over and over again, the police, the district attorney, the defense attorneys, even my own goddamned private lawyer asked me the same thing: 'Are you sure you really resisted? Did you really want to get raped subconsciously?'

"In the end the guy who did it got off. They even brought in this one boy—a man now—that I knew in high school. That was ten years ago. He testified he had intercourse with me, after a prom. The defense attorney said, 'She was pretty easy, wasn't she?' The guy grinned and shook his head.

"I learned. I still live alone, but now I have a gun. I have a permit and everything like that for it. I keep it right on the night table, loaded. If someone ever comes in my apartment again, I'll kill them. If I don't kill them with the first shot, I'll keep shooting until they are dead. I also keep a knife right below the headboard of my bed. No one is ever going to put me through that again."[7]

There are many kinds of motives in the reluctance of women to report that they have been raped: a sense of futility, a fear of reprisal by the rapist, ambivalent feelings of shame, guilt and self-blame, or even a protective, affectionate feeling for the man, not wanting to get him into trouble. The woman may wish to avoid the indignities she may suffer, not only from the police and courts but also from her friends, neighbors, relatives—even her husband. One woman, who had been attacked and raped by an apparent good samaritan who walked a mile to obtain gas when her car ran out of gas on a highway, returned home after being hospitalized several days for shock. Her husband greeted her with the angry query: "If that's what you wanted, why didn't you come to *me?*" Although she was totally devoid of any feelings for sex immediately following her traumatic experience, her husband proceeded to give her what he assumed she desired—he raped her.[8]

Clearly, there is a strong social *stigma* to being raped. It is one of the few forms of crime in which the victim experiences as much moral devaluation and loss of status as the offender—and sometimes more. The fact that a most intimate but illicit sexual experience becomes a public and open topic for conversation may foster a social identity in the community—and sometimes self-identity—as "the kind of woman who gets raped." Her tainted identity may make her less desirable ("damaged goods") for serious courtship but ripe for further sexual exploitation.[9] A twenty-eight-year-old insurance underwriter describes some of the postrape trauma and damaged self-esteem that many rape victims experience:

> I always thought my attitudes were so sophisticated. . . . But I found myself feeling terrified, embarrassed, ashamed. Over and over I kept blaming myself, thinking how I should have prevented it. . . . I really wanted to tell my boyfriend, but I was afraid he'd reject me. I needed someone to talk to.[10]

Her assailant had knocked her to the ground, kicked her in the groin, repeatedly bashed her head against a concrete floor, and then raped her. Months after getting help from a rape crisis center, she was able to purge herself of guilt feelings, reorganize her life, and move to another community, angrily observing:

> I'm not a freak, I'm not a novelty. It's just that the stigma is so brutal. . . . The stupid myths even got to me for a while. It's society's attitudes that can destroy you.[11]

SEXUAL ASSAULTS ON COLLEGE CAMPUSES

Understandably, with such severe stigma inflicted on rape victims, very few women are willing to report that they were raped, especially when living on a college campus. Yet such assaults, successful or attempted, are not uncommon. In a study of college females in the 1950s at Indiana University, one-fifth of the respondents reported that they had recently been offended by forceful attempts at sexual intercourse while on *dates.*[12] Within the previous year of the study, 6 percent of the students studied indicated that they had experienced physical pain or menacing threats to gain their submission. Interestingly, seven out of the ten most violent incidents reported involved college girls in regular dating, "pinned," or engaged relationships. A study of social science undergraduates at two universities in 1968 revealed that almost 25 percent of the nonvirgin females had their initial experience of intercourse because they were forced or because they felt an obligation to the male.[13] Although some of these episodes would not be considered rape, they clearly indicate that many women submit to male pressures contrary to their personal desires.

In a mid-1960s study of *males* at a large Midwestern university, one-fourth of the respondents admitted that they had engaged in coercive physical attempts at intercourse to the extent that the girl cried, fought, screamed, or pleaded.[14] Doubtlessly, few of these young men would conceive of themselves as having attempted rape.

It would appear that only a fraction of rapes or attempted rapes on college campuses across America are ever reported to the police and collected and published by the FBI in the official Uniform Crime Reports. In 1973, for example, the FBI report told of about 100 known cases of rape involving thirty-one different college campuses. Yet in that same year, a representative at one Big Ten university reported that during the last three years on his campus alone there were over 200 known cases of rape.[15]

Although it is difficult to document accurately offender characteristics in the absence of more detailed and reliable data, confidential surveys of sexual aggression on college campuses clearly suggest that assailants cut across social class boundaries in America. Contrary to the impression given by official police statistics, rape is not a near monopoly of lower-class offenders but also involves middle- and upper-class males—both young and old. The greater access to their own private cars and single-dwelling sound-proof homes, however, helps reduce the visibility of the sexual depredations committed by these high-status males and minimizes the prospect of legal intervention. If rape takes place in an automobile, the probability that legal action will occur depends mostly on a complaint by the victim, with the feeling of shame or futility often deterring such an official complaint. If rape occurs in an alley or in a crowded tenement apartment where the shouts are heard by neighbors, the likelihood of a report to the police increases. In this instance the offended women herself may initiate the legal complaint, if for no other reason than to protect her reputation against neighbors who might otherwise suspect her complicity in the act. When the event occurs in private, there is less incentive to file a formal complaint. Unlike the female in a lower-class slum neighborhood who may call a police officer, the upper-middle-class rape victim is more apt to turn instead to a family physician, counselor, or psychiatrist for aid. In addition, the cooperation of public relations–conscious university officials and all the other protective shields that money, power, and respectability provide help contribute to the relative immunity from arrest or prosecution for these more advantaged males.[16]

By the late 1970s, a tremendous increase in female sensitivity to the threat of sexual assault on campuses had occurred at numerous colleges.

This heightened awareness was largely triggered by the women's movement, although the focus of anxiety still appeared to be overwhelmingly on the kinds of rapes committed by marauding strangers who invade large urban-based campuses or pick up hitchhikers in university towns. On hundreds of campuses across the nation new rape awareness programs proliferated—films, discussion panels, crisis centers, escort services, 24-hour "hotlines," newly installed security systems, and burgeoning courses in karate and judo.[17] While hard data on the actual frequency of rape and attempted rape and on offender characteristics still remain elusive, the end of the decade has witnessed increased feminist challenges to the conventional wisdom and traditional perspectives on rape in American society.

THE IMAGE OF MASCULINITY

Feminist sociologist Diana Russell contends that much rape is not so much a *deviant* act as it is an *overconforming* act, an exaggerated form of "normal" relations which often exist between the sexes. Sexual aggression, even violent assault, represents qualities regarded by many men as *super masculine*: strength, power, independence, forcefulness, domination, toughness. To conquer, to be successful, to win, to induce respect through force—all of these attributes are commonly associated with masculinity in our culture (and also in many other societies). Sexual activity particularly is an occasion on which these qualities of masculinity are often most intensely acted out. Especially for men who feel powerless or inadequate in other areas of their lives, the conquest of a woman may become an important instrument for the achievement and maintenance of a man's sense of masculinity, status, and self-esteem.[18]

Growing numbers of feminists and sociologists thus would insist that rape can be adequately understood only by an examination of dominant notions of masculinity and feminity: that in a deeply ingrained sexist culture, rape and other forms of aggression are an integral part of a larger sexist ideology that serves to perpetuate the power of men over women.

In the tradition of *machismo*, an extreme version of the masculine image which is widespread, women are to be cynically manipulated and exploited if possible. The opposite sex is viewed as weak, passive, dependent, inferior, and submissive. Such contempt and one-dimensional conceptions of women encourage the use of females as a mere vehicle for a man's pleasure or for an expression of his hostility and feelings of aggression. Although the estimated 200,000 women raped by enemy soldiers in Bangladesh received some publicity, the thousands of Vietnamese women raped by American soldiers have barely received any mention. In Vietnam, one of the few GIs in Charlie Company who was willing to talk candidly about rape said: "That's an everday affair. You can nail just about everyone on that—at least once. The guys are human, man."[19] For some men who subscribe to the macho perspective, "seduction is for sissies"; as Ogden Nash put it, "a he-man wants his rape." According to Susan Brownmiller, American soldiers who refused to participate in group rapes and subsequent murder of Vietnamese women were regarded as "queers" by their buddies, lacking in sufficient masculinity.[20] For men socialized into the dominant cultural tenets of machismo, "to be dependent on a woman and especially to show her tenderness and consideration because she deserved it as a human being rather than because it is a useful device for overcoming her resistance, is thought to be foolish."[21]

Central to this image of maleness is the belief in a powerful masculine *sexual force* which once unleashed is almost beyond rational control. To be confronted by a "cock teaser" who titillates or suggests but does not deliver is unforgivable. Such perceived female provocation is considered unfair, offensive to male sensibilities, and deserving of retaliation. By *blaming the victim* and by evoking the self-serving belief that the woman's provocation puts the man temporarily "out of control," the rapist shifts the responsibility for the rape to the female. The message communicated is clear: women who walk or talk or dress in a manner that is sexually provocative to men do so at their own risk. Nor do such woman have any right to change their mind about sex if they seemingly hint or contemplate such desires. This masculine perspective, of course, puts women in a double bind. Although American society normally *rewards* women for looking sexually attractive—indeed they are *expected* to be enticing and a little "sexy"—if they become a rape victim they are immediately held blameworthy. As one convicted California rapist put it:

> I believe that women who want to be fashionable in some of the styles that are sexually stimulating to men should try to realize some of the consequences of wearing some of these styles before they wear them. . . .
>   Once again, I would say again, by body language—or unconsciously they flirt—sometimes the way they dress—their minds say one thing—their bodies say another—or some come on with their seduction-type overall tone—that says one thing but could possibly mean something else. Or they put themselves in the position of being alone.[22]

Sexist views which hold the victim responsible are not a monopoly of rapists but are widely held in American society. Such sentiments are reinforced in the value-laden language of social scientists who emphasize "victim-precipitated" rape.[23] Or consider the frank remarks of Wisconsin Judge Archie Simonson. In 1977, he ruled that a boy who raped a schoolgirl in a stairwell was reacting "normally" to the provocative clothing that women now wear and sentenced the boy to the protective custody of his parents:

> I'm trying to say to women stop teasing. There should be a restoration of modesty in dress. . . . Whether women like it or not they are sex objects. Are we

supposed to take an impressionable person 15 or 16 years of age and punish that person severely because they react to it [scanty female attire] normally?[24]

The widespread view that girls who exercise their personal freedom by hitch-hiking are really "asking for it" is also the apparent sexist reasoning applied by a California Court of Appeals recently in reversing the conviction of an accused rapist. The presiding judge wrote for a unanimous court:

> The lone female hitchhiker in the absence of an emergency situation, as a prac-tical matter, advises all who pass by that she is willing to enter the vehicle with anyone who stops and in so doing advertises that she has less concern for the con-sequences than the average female. Under such circumstances it would not be unreasonable for a man in the position of the defendant here to believe that the female would consent to sexual relations.[25]

The force of this sexist mythology in America also contributes to the common notion that it is mostly "bad girls" that get raped. Yet a District of Columbia study, for example, reported that 82 percent of the rape victims had a "good reputation."[26] A common observation accompanying such statistics is for some writers to note that even "nice girls" get raped too. (No one, of course, ever inquires whether a robbed service station operator "asked for it" or observes that "nice guys get mugged too.") The chauvinistic implication is that nice girls follow prescribed and passive sex roles, never actively seek sexual relationships, and confine their sexual intimacies to only a husband, a fiancé, or, at best, a single, exclusive, long-term lover. It is precisely such sexist assumptions that the women's movement is attempting to combat in instigating legal reforms that make prior sexual conduct of the rape victim inadmissible evidence in court. As Baril and Couchman note, "Liberation precludes having to convince anyone of one's niceness."[27]

THE DATING GAME AND JUSTIFICATIONS FOR RAPE

Dating is a widespread social practice in American society that sometimes leads to a serious, committed relationship or marriage—and sometimes to rape. The expectations that each partner brings to the encounter may be ambiguous and unfilled. Misunderstandings, confused signals, and mis-perceptions are a common part of many dating relationships, especially in casual pickups in singles' bars. As Charles McCaghy notes, on many dates,

> the expectations of the male stem from the attention, time, and money he ex-pends. But it is more than pleasant and witty conversation that is to be his reward. He anticipates a progression of sexual intimacies with each date with the ultimate goal of "going all the way." But somewhere in this progression a point of contention can arise over how much he is "buying" and how much she is "selling." This is particularly likely to occur when there is no emotional commitment to the relationship by either party. For many such couples con-

frontations over rewards end dramatically, one way or another, with the demand: "Put out or get out!"[28]

Traditionally, males take the initiative and press for increasing sexual intimacies until stopped by the female. However, in an ambiguously defined social situation where the male may assume that a show of resistance is merely a coquettish ploy or female game of feigning reluctance, many males will pay no heed and continue to persist and cajole. The woman's "no" is not to be taken seriously, especially in a sexually permissive era. Indeed some resistance is *expected* but so is eventual submission. Some men may even assume that the girl may feel less guilty about enjoying sex if she is overwhelmed in caveman style. But regardless, many males are so convinced that women desire sexual intimacies with them that they are unable to hear their protestations to the contrary—even their desperate struggles and cries.

The fact that otherwise respectable and relatively normal males can sexually assault women is facilitated by a vocabulary of socially shared motives or rationalizations that consistently tend to blame the victim. These male justifications for rape typically reflect heavily stereotypical views of women, which enable sexual aggressors to maintain a favorable self-image and to treat some women as *legitimate* targets of violence. McCaghy pinpoints three common kinds of male justifications for forcibly abusing women.[29]

1. "Some women *need* to be raped." These accounts given for sexual aggression concern the importance of keeping females in their place—beneath men.

> These dumb broads don't know what they want. They get you worked up and then they chicken out. You let 'em get away with stuff like that and the next thing you know they'll be walking all over you.

> Women like a strong man who will knock them around once in a while—that way they know the man is in charge.[30]

Or consider the motives offered by this middle-class salesman with two years of college who feels he must prove his superiority and punish an "uppity" woman for being "snobbish and phony":

> I met a girl at a party, and I considered her snobbish and phony. She latched onto me at the party, and we laughed and had a good time and went somewhere else. She was an attractive woman in her thirties, but she irritated me. When I took her home to her apartment she was telling me goodnight and I raped her. I didn't really feel the urge. As a matter of fact, I had a hell of a time getting an erection. . . . I'd had quite a bit of booze. But I forced myself to do it to prove a point to her, to prove that she wasn't as big as she thought she was.[31]

These sentiments perhaps illustrate what many feminist writers contend: that there is frequently very little sexual desire in such violent assaults. At best, militant feminists insist, lustful motives play a minor role in the assault. Rape is more accurately seen as a *power* play, a violent expression of male dominance, a way of subjugating and humiliating women against their will. As Susan Brownmiller succinctly puts it: "Rape is the quintessential act by which a male demonstrates to a female that she is conquered— vanquished—by his superior strength and power."[32]

2. "Some women *deserve* to be raped." These verbalized motives relate to the social reputation of the victim. A female stigmatized as sexually experienced, as promiscuous or "a slut," may become a legitimate target for all forms of sexual aggression. "Her prior experience qualifies her as public property for all interested males and cancels her prerogative to accept or reject sexual partners."[33] Once the label of "an easy lay" has been affixed, the refusal of a girl to accommodate all comers may threaten fragile male egos and precipitate assault:

> OK. There was this chick, see. I took her out. It was my first date with her, but I knew from some other dudes that she liked sex, you know what I mean? So I'm driving back to my pad and she says she wants to go home. Well that's a put down. *That's saying to me that I'm not a man.* Well no broad in the world is gonna give me that shit! So I messed her around a little bit.[34]

When asked to justify his use of force to obtain sex, a college student replied:

> When a male doesn't respect a girl and knows she is nothing but a whore anyway, I feel he is entitled to use force because he knows it isn't her first time.[35]

Such tarnished female reputations also may aid males in participating in group rapes—a not uncommon form of sexual assault. The pervasive use of such slang terms as "gang-bangs" or "trains" appears to mitigate the horror of such violence for many young men. Even for assailants who feel some qualms, the fear of losing status in the eyes of their male peers may become a more pressing concern. In one study of group rape, the author describes the dynamics of such peer-group expectations and fears:

> The leader of the male group . . . apparently precipitated and maintained the activity, despite misgivings, because of a need to fulfill the role that the other two men had assigned to him. "I was scared when it began to happen," he says. "I wanted to leave but I didn't want to say it to the other guys—you know—that I was scared."[36]

3. "Some women *want* to be raped." The myth that only willing women get raped, that no female can be actually raped who doesn't wish to be is a

fallacious but widely shared chauvinistic contention. This "victim in search of a rapist" perspective is evident in the remarks of this convicted rapist:

> *Interviewer:* I'd like to know how you can tell if women are susceptible to rape and how they respond.
>
> *Fred:* All right, I'd say most of the women that are susceptible to rape are pretty broadminded and pretty sexy. Sometimes a woman who tries to hide sexuality is very susceptible to rape. What she's really saying is, "I'm a woman but I'm not gonna let anybody know about it, but I dare you to find out." So you find that she is a woman and most of the time she's the best lay.[37]

Some scientific studies may also reinforce the common belief that many women subconsciously desire to be raped. The writer may insist that a woman who claims rape is suffering from self-deceit or selective recall, camouflaging her ambivalent—but real—sexual desires:

> Even the woman who is quite sane but who is possessed of strong guilt feelings, may convince herself in retrospect that her own conduct was really blameless and she was forced. This conviction is the more easily arrived at because it is quite likely that her conscious response at the time could not accurately be labeled either as consent or non-consent. There may have been an ambivalent and confused mixture of desire and fear, neither of which was clearly dominant. Most women want their lovers to be at least somewhat aggressive and dominating. *Some consciously or unconsciously want to be forced.* Their erotic pleasure is stimulated by preliminary love-play involving physical struggle, slapping, scratching, pinching and biting. The struggle also saves face for the girl who fears she would be considered "loose" if she yielded without due maidenly resistance; it also relieves that guilt feeling that might exist if she could not tell herself that "he made me do it." Many of the wrestling matches in parked cars come within this category.[38]

It is perhaps not surprising in a male-dominated society that some women also belittle and scorn raped women by denying the credibility of their claims. Steeped in the notion that only willing women and those who "ask for it" get raped, these women insist that such abused females precipitated their own victimization or that they were not really raped. Indeed, the mystifying power of the male mystique may psychologically so oppress some women that, even when they are assaulted themselves, they may find it difficult to define what occurred as rape.

Yet as Russell points out, it is men who benefit from this myopic "wishing away of rape." For if females cannot be raped ("you can't thread a moving needle"), the implication is clear that all women desire sexual intercourse with men whenever men feel the itch, despite whatever rigorous resistance and emphatic denials they offer. This male fantasy that the "penis is irresistible" is a standard theme not only in pornography but also frequently in popular films.[39] In the movie *Straw Dogs*, for example, a macho local handy-man attacks the bored and frustrated sexy wife of Dustin Hoffman, who portrays an effeminate college professor oblivious to his wife's needs. In the rape scene, the camera zooms in on the struggling, screaming wife as her cries gradually fade into a whimper and soft moans of ecstasy; her arms encircle the assailant, drawing him into her.

The belief that women enjoy being victims, that they secretly like to be "manhandled" and ravished is also reinforced in other areas by the popular culture. For example, record album covers and advertisements have shown women being "bound, gagged, collared, beaten, bruised, chained, stamped like a piece of meat—sometimes smiling in pleasure." An advertising billboard for the Rolling Stones musical rock group featured a bound female saying, "I'm 'Black and Blue' from the Rolling Stones—and I love it!"[40] Such portrayal of female images in the media may thus help sustain the deeply held belief that women's resistance—physical or verbal—is merely a female gambit of pretending reluctance and an indication of a desire to be forcibly overcome—to liberate basic animal passions.

The myth that there is no such thing as rape may also partly explain why some men who rape women maintain a self-concept of lovers rather than rapists. Several days after a young woman had been raped by her friend's husband, the man returned to her home, banged at the door and yelled: "Jane, Jane. You loved it. You know you loved it."[41] Another woman reported that

> . . . her date finally succeeded in raping her after a two-hour struggle but he could not understand why she was so upset, and he was unable to comprehend why she accused him of raping her. He considered himself a lover in the tradition of forceful males and expected to have a continuing relationship with her.[42]

In one study of rape victims, two women even received marriage proposals from their assailants, who were total strangers. In another instance, after being raped by two men, the victim was asked which of the two rapists she enjoyed the most. Still another victim reported that her rapist was "furious because I wasn't getting turned on."[43]

SEXUAL SOCIALIZATION OF MALES

Many men in American society, perhaps most, have the ability to compartmentalize their purely sexual desires from sentiments of caring, affection, and love. Traditional socialization since preadolescence permits them to separate easily their sexual responsiveness from any feelings of emotional warmth, friendship, commitment, or respect. Men can become "turned on," for example, in the presence of a sexually attractive female. Some males can become sexually aroused to the point of erection from mere pictures of "sexy" scantily clad female bodies (supporting a multimillion-dollar industry of "girlie" magazines such as *Playboy, Hustler, Penthouse*, and *Oui*).[44]

Especially for males who have internalized the importance of appearing virile, and who are unsure of their masculinity, "scoring" with a sexually attractive woman—the more frequently the better—may become a kind of ritualistic test of their manhood. In the lockerroom tradition, the virgin and inexperienced male becomes an object of ridicule, taunted to show that he is a "real man" by "making it" with a woman. An upper-middle-class man who had attacked a nurse in a doctor's office when he was a seventeen-year-old virgin, recalls his attempted rape:

> I was seventeen, and I was trying to prove that I was a man. . . . It was difficult for me at that time to admit that I was dealing with a human being when I was talking to a woman, because, if you read men's magazines, you hear about your stereo, your car, your chick.[45]

Over six feet tall and weighing 240 pounds, this would-be rapist slammed the nurse against the wall and hit her several times in the face. Finally she stopped struggling and said, "all right, just don't hurt me. . . . All of a sudden it came into my head," the man exclaimed, "My God, this is a human being!"[46] He indicated that he wished he could have subsequently told the nurse that his assault on her was "nothing personal." Indeed, many rape victims have reported that their rapists have viewed them as if they were nonpersons—as simply convenient "cunts," "pieces of ass"—rather than as people.

In a rather chauvinistic remark, one psychologist was recently quoted as saying: "I don't think there's a man worth his salt who hasn't seen some chick walking by and wanted to screw her."[47] Obviously, not all men forcibly attempt to act out such desires. However, it should not be surprising that some men socialized into these feelings and attitudes toward women succumb to the temptation of rape. Such acts of human degradation are to be expected—regardless of what psychodynamic or situational factors are involved—as long as our culture continues to equate sexual aggression and dominance with masculinity, and as long as women are perceived as sex objects rather than as full human beings.

Yet there *are* cultures in which men are reared to be gentle, tender, nurturing, and sensitive. In these societies, men find rape an incomprehensible act. Anthropologist Margaret Mead, for example, points out that the Arapesh, a "primitive" people of New Guinea, "know nothing of rape beyond the fact that it is the unpleasant custom of the Nugum people to the southeast of them."[48] As advocates of women's and men's liberation have argued, radical changes in deeply ingrained values and in the socialization of males and females must occur if rape is to diminish significantly:

> If our culture considered it masculine to be gentle and sensitive, to be responsive to the needs of others, to abhor violence, domination, and exploitation, to want sex only within a meaningful relationship, to be attracted by personality and character rather than by physical appearance, to value lasting rather than casual relationships, then rape would indeed be a deviant act, and . . . much less frequent.[49]

Greater sex-role liberation in America would also reduce the prevalence of what some feminist writers call "petty rapes" or "the little rapes."[50] This kind of pervasive female degradation includes sexual exploitation by men who control promotions and the hiring and firing process in highly desirable jobs. Or the form of sexual blackmail in which men threaten to discredit a female's reputation by openly talking about her intimate sexual behavior unless she "comes across." Or the deceit practiced to gain momentary sexual conquest by phony gestures of tenderness and personal interest. Such petty rapes, as Germaine Greer notes, are a persistent hazard in the dating game, as are those situations when the man who picks up the tab for the evening's entertainment and owns the car threatens to throw his date out on a deserted road if she doesn't respond with the swiftness and degree of sexual intimacy he desires.

A particularly crass instance of this kind of sexual rip-off is that of a thirty-six-year-old man who succeeded in "seducing" into bed a twenty-year-old woman in her own apartment after informing her that he was a psychologist doing research. A New York judge hearing the case stated that a man may use any nonviolent or nonthreatening means, "even deceit," to gain female compliance. The judge added, "Bachelors and other men on the make, fear not. It is still not illegal to feed a girl a line."[51]

Perhaps the most destructive aspect of these insidious "little rapes" is that they may gradually, almost imperceptibly erode a female's self-esteem and dignity, and make her more callous and suspect in her dealings with men. Such self-alienation and "hardening of the heart" may invite still further exploitation in a self-perpetuating manner, deepening her malaise and oppression.[52]

THE FUTURE OF RAPE

Rape is a social creation. It involves human judgment, social values, and differential power. As previously noted, forcible intercourse by a husband against his wife's wishes is not traditionally or legally defined as rape in most states. An ambiguous gray area also frequently exists in judging the degree of physical force in dating situations or among lovers. Rape depends on the social meanings we *impute* to behavior. Clearly, the same objective behavior may be subject to different evaluations and classifications. Perhaps what is most critical in terms of social consequences is who does the classifying and who holds the power to make his—or her—definition stick.

Therefore, it is difficult to assess accurately or in what sense it can be said that the frequency of rape is or is not increasing. There may well be a real rise in sexual assaults by American males along with other forms of violence. With the growth of women's liberation, however, greater numbers of women are perhaps *defining* forcible sexual aggression as rape and officially *reporting* it to legal officials more frequently than in the past. Such willingness to report may reflect an increase in female pride, an awareness of more sensitive handling of rape complaints by some legal authorities (especially with use of female police officers in "rape squads"), a decrease in the stigma of rape, or an altered conception of rape. Whatever the actual increase in sexual assault may be, if any, more women appear unwilling to remain passive victims of male aggression. As Goode and Troiden observe:

> It is likely that women's conceptions as to what constitutes rape have changed, making rape more common *because more male sexual behavior is seen—and experienced*—as rape. In other words, the greater the pride and self-confidence that exists among women, the more likely it is that male sexual aggression against them will be reported and recorded officially.[53]

It is also possible that the women's movement and the increasing atmosphere of sexual permissiveness in American society may both contribute indirectly to an actual increase in sexual assaults in the population. The new assertiveness of many women may threaten insecure male egos, triggering a violent backlash to keep such women in their "place," and thereby affirm male dominance and a precarious sense of superiority. Moreover, women's assertion of their independence and quest for equal rights may increase their vulnerability to rape because they may discard male escorts, walk alone, hitchhike, explore singles' bars and places of entertainment by themselves—in short, act as if they were free human beings.

In addition, the "sexual revolution," much discussed in the mass media, may deepen many men's feelings of *relative deprivation*. In a sexually permissive era, when "free and easy" sex is seemingly more available for the asking, a spurned male may find such rejection more threatening to his sense of male adequacy. His feelings of anger and frustration may intensify if he lacks legitimate opportunities to fulfill his rising sexual expectations. At the same time, he is also perhaps denied the kinds of rationalization that were once available in a more repressive culture to protect his "beleaguered self-image."[54] In a sexually prohibitionist era, as Gilbert Geis notes, the rejected male could blame his lack of success in sexual conquest on the nonpermissive sexual environment of the time (for example, greater female inhibitions, stricter religious and parental norms or other moral constraints). Without the availability of such facile defenses to account for sexual failure— or unable to affirm his virility or power in this manner—sexual aggression may increase in response to such subjective experiences of deprivation.

Thus during this abrasive transitional period in American society, feelings of hostility, frustration, misunderstanding, and resentment between men and women may increase, at least in the short run, and so possibly will the occurrence of rape.

Without a fundamental restructuring of our society, no significant reduction in rape is likely. Since rape behavior thrives in a sexist cultural atmosphere, the essential nature of male-female relationships must change. Such a transformation will require not only a veritable revolution in childhood training of both sexes, but also a more equitable sharing of political, legal, and economic power in America. Whether the ruling male patriarchy will willingly submit to such profound changes remains to be seen.

Relatively little is still known about rape in our society. Although changes are occurring, only a handful of carefully researched studies exist of rapists, rape victims, and the dynamics of this social behavior. This fact itself is perhaps indicative of traditional male dominance in the behavioral sciences and the lowly status of women. As feminists have argued, since rape victims are overwhelmingly women, men have historically viewed the "rape problem" more as a threat to their "property" and masculine pride than as a violation of the right of women to control their own bodies and to determine their own lives. As Kate Millett writes, "Traditionally rape has been viewed as an offense one male commits against another—a matter of abusing his woman."[55] Interest in the forcibly violated woman reflected a husband's concern with his status, family lineage, inheritance rights, and loss of male honor by a decline in the "value" of his sexual property. (The Old Testament, for example, instructs the rapist to pay fifty shekels of silver to the father as compensation for the violation of an unbetrothed virgin daughter.)[56]

Whatever the origins of our attitudes toward rape and the laws about it, until very recently rape was the most ignored violent kind of behavior in society. But as a by-product of the feminist movement, a highly politicized antirape movement has in recent years gained growing support for the definition of rape as a serious social problem.[57] Feminists have been successful in achieving significant legislative reexamination and revision of rape laws in numerous states, which may make it easier to convict offenders. And in many cities, a more sensitive handling of rape victims by law-enforcement officials and medical staff is evident (epitomized in the comment of one Chicago doctor who noted that because of improved procedures, the police officers he meets no longer barge crudely through the emergency room yelling, "I got a rape for ya, Charlie!")[58] Women's groups have also organized task forces for research on rape, lobbied for federal funding, offered rape-prevention instruction, and established centers to assist rape victims and ease the trauma of their experience.

Attempting to change traditional attitudes and beliefs about rape—often reflected in and reinforced by existing legislation and judicial procedures—feminist activists have adopted various strategies to raise the public consciousness: debunking rape myths through educational campaigns, protesting sexual exploitation and brutalization of women in the mass media, demonstrating during courtroom trials, even marching with placards ("You're marrying a rapist") outside the church wedding of a notorious accused rapist who had escaped conviction. Women have also raised funds for the nationally publicized defense of thirty-year-old Inez Garcia, a Chicano woman convicted in 1974 of the murder of a 300-pound man, who, she testified, held her down while another man raped her:

> [T]he Garcia case became a rallying point for feminists. Feminine support was demonstrated by packing the courtroom and demonstrating outside the courthouse during the trial, and calling for a nationwide women's strike following her conviction. Inez Garcia became a "national symbol" for the antirape movement . . . as well as . . . a potential role model for all women because she fought back.[59]

This deeply felt sense of moral outrage that energizes a large segment of the antirape movement is also evident in buttons proclaiming "Castrate Rapists," conspicuously worn by militants, and in the encouragement given to rape victims by feminist counselors to express anger rather than guilt.

While the antirape movement has made great progress—particularly in the legislative and judicial arena—the movement is not without its critics, especially some civil libertarians who fear vigilante action and express concern that far-reaching changes in rape laws might run roughshod over the defendant's rights and erode due process.[60] But whatever the final shape of this reform legislation, the view of women as sex objects is still widespread in America. And this deeply ingrained sexism, combined with the increasing liberalization of female attitudes toward sexual intercourse, will continue to spark debate and legal confusion in the 1980s regarding the meaning of rape and its prevalence, prevention, and control.

FOOTNOTES

1 President's Commission on Law Enforcement and Administration of Justice, *The Challenge of Crime in a Free Society*, U.S. Government Printing Office, Washington, D.C., 1967, p. 21.

2 U.S. Department of Justice, *Crime in the Nation's Five Largest Cities: National Crime Panel Surveys of Chicago, Detroit, Los Angeles, New York and Philadelphia*, Advance Report, April 1974, U.S. Department of Justice, Washington, D.C., 1974, p. 28.

3 Cited in President's Commission, *The Challenge of Crime in a Free Society*, p. 40. For a discussion of race and rape, see Lynn A. Curtis, *Violence, Race, and Culture*, Lexington Books, Lexington, Mass., 1975, Ch. 7.

4 Donald J. Mulvihill and Melvin M. Tumin, *Crimes of Violence*, Staff Report Submitted to the National Commission on the Causes and Prevention of Violence, vol. 11, U.S. Government Printing Office, Washington, D.C., 1969, p. 217.

5 Diana E. H. Russell, *The Politics of Rape*, Stein and Day, New York, 1975, p. 260.

6 Quoted in Erich Goode and Richard R. Troiden (eds.), *Sexual Deviance and Sexual Deviants*, William Morrow, New York, 1974, p. 301.

7 Freda Adler, *Sisters in Crime*, McGraw-Hill, New York, 1976, pp. 214–215. See also Gerald D. Robin, "Forcible Rape: Institutionalized Sexism in the Criminal Justice System," *Crime & Delinquency*, 23 (April 1977), pp. 136–153; Lynda Lytle Holmstrom and Ann Wolbert Burgess, *The Victim of Rape: Institutional Reactions*, Wiley-Interscience, New York, 1978; Pamela Lakes Woods, "The Victim in a Forcible Rape Case: A Feminist View," in Leroy G. Schultz (ed.), *Rape Victimology*, Charles C Thomas, Springfield, Ill., 1975, pp. 194–217.

8 Russell, *The Politics of Rape*, p. 226.

9 Kurt Weis and Sandra S. Borges, "Victimology and Rape: The Case of the Legitimate Victim," *Issues in Criminology*, 8 (Fall 1973), pp. 103–104.

10 Quoted in Laurie Lucas, "Against Their Will," *Syracuse Herald-American Empire Magazine*, Nov. 6, 1977, p. 4. Victim's reactions to their experiences are discussed in Russell, *The Politics of Rape*; Ann W. Burgess and Lynda L. Holmstrom, *Rape: Victims of Crisis*, Robert J. Brady, Bowie, Md., 1974; Marcia J. Walker and Stanley L. Brodsky (eds.), *Sexual Assault: The Victim and the Rapist*, Lexington Books, Lexington, Mass., 1976; Nancy Gager and Cathleen Schurr, *Sexual Assault: Confronting Rape in America*, Grosset and Dunlap, New York, 1976.

11 Lucas, "Against Their Will," p. 12.

12 Clifford Kirkpatrick and Eugene Kanin, "Male Sex Aggression on a University Campus," *American Sociological Review*, 22 (February 1957), p. 53.

13 Harold T. Christensen and Christina F. Gregg, "Changing Sex Norms in America and Scandinavia," *Journal of Marriage and the Family*, 32 (November 1970), pp. 625–626.

14 Eugene J. Kanin, "Reference Groups and Sex Conduct Norm Violations," *Sociological Quarterly*, 8 (Autumn 1967), pp. 495–504.

15 Leslie Maitland, "Colleges Acting to Protect Students Against Rape," *The New York Times*, Jan. 11, 1975, p. 18. See also Leroy G. Schultz and Jan DeSavage, "Rape and Rape Attitudes on a College Campus," in Schultz (ed.), *Rape Victimology*, pp. 77–90.

16 William J. Chambliss, *Crime and the Legal Process*, McGraw-Hill, New York, 1969, pp. 87–88, 102.

17 Maitland, "Colleges Acting to Protect Students Against Rape," p. 18.
18 Russell, *The Politics of Rape*, p. 260. See also, Weiss and Borges, "Victimology and Rape," pp. 85–87.
19 Seymour M. Hersh, *My Lai 4: A Report on the Massacre and Its Aftermath*, Vintage Books, New York, 1970, p. 185.
20 Susan Brownmiller, *Against Our Will*, Simon and Schuster, New York, 1975, Ch. 3.
21 William Goode, "Violence Among Intimates," in Donald J. Mulvihill and Melvin M. Tumin, *Crimes of Violence*, Staff Report Submitted to the National Commission on the Causes and Prevention of Violence, vol. 13, U.S. Government Printing Office, Washington, D.C., 1969, p. 971.
22 Quoted in Gilbert Geis, "Forcible Rape: An Introduction," in Duncan Chappell, Robley Geis, and Gilbert Geis (eds.), *Forcible Rape*, Columbia University Press, New York, 1977, p. 28.
23 See Menachem Amir, *Patterns in Forcible Rape*, University of Chicago Press, Chicago, 1971, Ch. 15.
24 *Time*, Sept. 12, 1977, p. 41.
25 *The New York Times*, July 24, 1977, p. 16E.
26 Cited in Susan Griffin, "Rape: The All-American Crime," in Goode and Troiden (eds.), *Sexual Deviance and Sexual Deviants*, p. 315.
27 Cecile Baril and Iain S. B. Couchman, "Legal Rights," *Society*, 14 (July/August 1976), p. 15.
28 Charles McCaghy, *Deviant Behavior*, Macmillan, New York, 1976, p. 135. See also Weiss and Borges, "Victimology and Rape," pp. 87–89.
29 McCaghy, *Deviant Behavior*, pp. 135–136.
30 Paul H. Gebhard et al., *Sex Offenders: An Analysis of Types*, Harper & Row, New York, 1965, pp. 177–178, 205.
31 Russell, *The Politics of Rape*, p. 253.
32 Brownmiller, *Against Our Will*, p. 49.
33 Kanin, "Reference Groups and Sex Conduct Norm Violations," p. 502.
34 Quoted in John Perry and Erna Perry, *Face to Face*, Little, Brown, Boston, 1976, p. 481. Italics added.
35 Eugene J. Kanin, "Selected Dyadic Aspects of Male Sex Aggression," in Schultz (ed.), *Rape Victimology*, p. 71.
36 Gilbert Geis and Duncan Chappell, "Forcible Rape by Multiple Offenders," *Abstracts on Criminology and Penology*, 11 (July/August 1971), pp. 435–436.
37 Robert W. Winslow and Virginia Winslow, *Deviant Reality*, Allyn and Bacon, Boston, 1974, p. 305.
38 Quoted in Nanette J. Davis, *Sociological Constructions of Deviance*, William C. Brown, Dubuque, Iowa, 1975, p. 155. Italics added.
39 Russell, *The Politics of Rape*, p. 257. See also Aljean Harmetz, "Rape—An Ugly Movie Trend," *The New York Times*, Oct. 1, 1973, p. 1D.
40 Holly Hyans, "Media Mistreatment of Women," *McCalls*, January, 1978, p. 43. See also, Judith Coburn, "S & M," *New Times*, Feb. 4, 1978, pp. 42–50.
41 Griffin, "Rape: The All-American Crime," p. 308.
42 Russell, *The Politics of Rape*, p. 258.
43 Russell, *The Politics of Rape*, p. 258.

44 Russell, *The Politics of Rape*, pp. 263–264.
45 Russell, *The Politics of Rape*, pp. 249–250.
46 Russell, *The Politics of Rape*, p. 249.
47 *Newsweek*, Aug. 20, 1973, pp. 67–68.
48 Margaret Mead, *Sex and Temperament in Three Primitive Societies*, Dell, New York, 1935, p. 110.
49 Russell, *The Politics of Rape*, pp. 264–265.
50 See Germaine Greer, "Seduction Is a Four-Letter Word," in Goode and Troiden (eds.), *Sexual Deviance and Sexual Deviants*, pp. 333–342; Andra Medea and Kathleen Thompson, *Against Rape*, Farrar, Straus, & Giroux, New York, 1974, pp. 49–55.
51 *Time*, May 12, 1975, p. 55.
52 Greer, "Seduction Is a Four-Letter Word," p. 333.
53 Goode and Troiden (eds.), *Sexual Deviance and Sexual Deviants*, p. 300.
54 Duncan Chappell et al., "A Comparative Study of Forcible Rape Offenses Known to the Police in Boston and Los Angeles," in Chappell, Geis, and Geis (eds.), *Forcible Rape*, pp. 230–231.
55 Quoted in Griffin, "Rape: The All-American Crime," p. 319.
56 Deuteronomy, 22: 28–29, *The Holy Bible*, Revised Standard Version, Thomas Nelson, New York, 1952, p. 208.
57 See Vicki McNickle Rose, "Rape as a Social Problem: A Byproduct of the Feminist Movement," *Social Problems*, 25 (October 1977), pp. 75–89.
58 "'Code R' for Rape," *Newsweek*, Nov. 13, 1972, p. 75.
59 Rose, "Rape as a Social Problem," p. 84. See also Nan Blitman and Robin Green, "Inez Garcia on Trial," *Ms.*, May 1975, pp. 49–54; "Revolt Against Rape," *Time*, Oct. 13, 1975, pp. 48, 53–54.
60 Edward Sagarin, "Forcible Rape and the Problem of the Rights of the Accused," *Intellect*, 103 (May/June 1975), pp. 515–520.

Chapter 4

Beyond the Godfather: Organized Crime and the American Way of Life

In popular discussions on crime, relatively little attention has been directed to the recognition that organized crime is an integral and vital part of the American way of life. The reasons for the existence and vitality of this pattern of criminal activity cannot be fully comprehended—much less adequately coped with—if we persist in viewing it as an essentially separate and detached social phenomenon, alien to our country's values, social institutions, and legal policies. Perhaps in no other area of deviance are the dysfunctional consequences more apparent of legislating morality and mystifying the causes of troubling behavior by blaming it solely on an internal alien conspiracy.

STEREOTYPES IN THE MASS MEDIA

Since the 1890s, it has been commonplace to depict organized crime—variously known as the Mafia, the Syndicate, the Mob, La Cosa Nostra—as a foreign cancer that has invaded an otherwise essentially healthy society. To root out this pathology, therefore, it is argued that the nation must declare war on this elusive and sinister internal evil. The criminal-justice system must lengthen prison sentences for criminal conspirators, centralize the fragmented and overlapping police agencies that touch on aspects of organized crime, permit greater investigative freedom for grand juries, expand "no-knock" laws, wiretapping, electronic "bugging," and so forth. Although such an arsenal of legal and judicial weapons may be useful, such strategies will not suffice in themselves, and the dangers of abuse and erosion of civil liberties may outweigh the benefits.

Most sociologically oriented criminologists tend to see the scope and vitality of organized crime as interrelated with basic cultural values, private-profit markets, legal policies, political corruption, restricted opportunity structures, and the complicity of respectable groups in American society. Yet the utility of this perspective is obscured in popular treatments of the topic that attempt to explain it by reciting a long list of unsavory gangsters—with Italian-sounding names—sworn to codes of silence in their secret monolithic Mafia organization, which threatens to overwhelm the innocent citizenry of our large metropolitan cities. As Dwight Smith observes, the Mafia is the prototypical alien conspiracy theory, so popular in American history as an explanation of disturbing social trends,

> . . . a recurring apprehension that somewhere "out there" is an organized, secret, alien group that is poised to infiltrate our society and to undermine our fundamental democratic beliefs. "It" is more foreboding . . . because conspiracies can set to work in our midst without a public declaration of intent or an overtly hostile act; even before we know it, "they" can be overrunning our internal defenses and overwhelming any instinct to resist.[1]

Information on organized crime generally has been presented to the public in a lurid, sensational manner that prevents an understanding of the true nature and ramifications of the problem. In this stereotypical imagery, there has been a tendency to portray the participants as either romantic folk heroes or villains in a "ghetto western," minimizing the involvement of organized crime with the rest of society. As Donald Cressey points out, newspapermen typically depict the participants as nothing but "gangsters," "muscle men," and "gorillas" who mainly prey on each other in their "gangland slayings" or victimize shady characters in such illicit activities as "the juice racket," "the scam racket," or "the fix."

> For example, there are few newspaper accounts in which Mr. Lucchese is called "Mr. Lucchese" or Mr. Ricca is called "Mr. Ricca." The writer always displays his "inside knowledge" about how things *really* are by using the first name, parenthesis, corny "alias," parenthesis, last name. "Mr. Lucchese," when he was alive, could possibly have been someone who was corrupting my labor union, but "Three Finger Brown" could only have been a somewhat fictitious

character in a "cops and robbers" story. Similarly, usury is almost always
called the "juice racket," and this terminology lets the reader believe that the
activity has nothing to do with him or the safety of his community. The criminals' terminology is similarly used when the word "scam" is used to describe
bankruptcy fraud. Most of us can understand the seriousness of usury, bankruptcy fraud, and bribery, but we have a hard time realizing that our friends
and neighbors are, in the long run, the victims of "the juice racket," "the scam
racket," or "the fix."[2]

Moreover, the news media penchant for using colorful nicknames in
crime stories such as Joe Bananas, Sam the Plumber, Frankie the Bug, and
Matty the Horse sometimes inadvertently lends a Damon Runyonesque
quality to the participants that further undermines the credibility of the
real threat and nature of organized crime in America. Nathan Detroit and
Nicely-Nicely Johnson were fictitious characters in *Guys and Dolls*. But
Mr. Lucchese and Mr. Ricca are hardly harmless, fun-loving, laughable
characters.

The treatment of organized crime in the mass media tends to be not
only unrealistic and superficial but also sporadic in coverage. In between
periodic exposés and crusades which generate much fanfare, organized
crime continues unabated, its *inherent*—rather than alien—relationship
with the core of American life largely ignored by television and Hollywood.
Perhaps such vivid images in blockbuster films like *The Godfather* and in
best-sellers like *The Valachi Papers* and *My Life in the Mafia* function to
reassure Americans who envision organized crime as essentially a foreign
transplant—brought to this country by persons who remain incompletely
assimilated minority-group members—and, therefore, help to absolve us
from any responsibility for the persistence and strength of these illicit enterprises. As Gus Tyler has noted, through this scapegoating process the
"culture is not only relieved of sin but can indulge itself in an orgy of righteous indignation."[3] A popular bumper sticker perhaps sums up best the
myopic conception of organized crime and its Italian coloration in much
of the popular consciousness: Mafia Staff Car—Keepa You Hands Off!!

The discussion that follows will attempt to articulate some of the diverse kinds of close relationship between organized crime and the American
way of life—together with some of the injurious consequences. An awareness of the nature and strength of these linkages must be a starting point
for any successful comprehension of the difficulties of effectively limiting
the operations of these large-scale criminal enterprises.

LEGISLATION OF MORALITY AND THE CRIMINAL TARIFF

Organized crime can be viewed essentially as an adjunct to our private-
profit economy. It is a large-scale business that has provided goods and ser-

vices demanded by sizable segments of the American public but not permitted under our legal codes: gambling, drugs, alcohol, high-interest cash
loans, prostitution, and so on. Many quite respectable citizens support the
legal prohibition of such activities, yet may have little interest in seeing the
laws enforced at their expense. Al Capone, the Chicago gangster, clearly
perceived this hypocrisy:

> I call myself a business man. I make my money by supplying popular demand.
> If I break a law, my customers are as guilty as I am. When I sell liquor, it's
> bootlegging. When my patrons serve it on a silver tray on Lake Shore Drive,
> it's hospitality.[4]

The attempt to curb the human appetite by passing laws reflects, in
part, our puritanical tradition which allows no compromise with "evil" but
insists that the laws must express the highest ideals of dominant interest
groups—even if they are unenforceable. Daniel Bell incisively pinpoints
this feature of the American way of life:

> Americans have had an extraordinary talent for compromise in politics and
> extremism in morality. The most shameless political deals (and "steals") have
> been rationalized as expedient and realistically necessary. Yet in no other
> country have there been such spectacular attempts to curb human appetites
> and brand them as illicit, and nowhere else such glaring failures. . . . Crime as
> a growing business was fed by the revenues from prostitution, liquor, and gam-
> bling that a wide-open urban society encouraged and that a middle-class Prot-
> estant ethos tried to suppress with a ferocity unmatched in any other civilized
> country.[5]

In such a situation, as Herbert Packer notes, a kind of protective "crime
tariff" goes into operation:

> Regardless of what we think we are trying to do, when we make it illegal to traf-
> fic in commodities for which there is an inelastic demand, the effect is to se-
> cure a kind of monopoly to the entrepreneur who is willing to break the law.[6]

Although the degree of monopoly and organization in different types of
illicit traffic varies (for example, less in abortion and more in gambling and
narcotics), Thomas Schelling points out that

> . . . any successful black marketeer enjoys a "protected" market in the same
> way that a domestic industry is protected by a tariff, or butter by a law against
> margarine. The black marketeer gets automatic protection, through the law
> itself, from all competitors unwilling to pursue a criminal career. The law gives
> a kind of franchise to those who are willing to break the law.[7]

In few instances are American citizens forced to patronize the criminal syndicate. It is the public's desire for entertainment after regular clos-

ing hours that supports the syndicate's illegal after-hours establishments. It is not the syndicate which provokes violations of the blue-laws, but the demand of the American public. Similarly, no one initially coerces the customers of the multibillion-dollar loansharking business (the lending of money at illegal, usurious interest rates, with payment insured by force) who come from all segments of society—professionals, industrialists, contractors, bookmakers, stockbrokers, bar and restaurant owners, drug addicts, gamblers, and factory workers:

> In an era when the nation's economy has been rapidly expanding, punctuated by periods of tight money in which even the most legitimate businessman can be desperate for cash, everything is fair game. A Wall Street securities house caught short by a sudden market reversal. A builder trapped in a credit squeeze. A garment manufacturer who guessed wrong on this year's line.[8]

All such customers have in common an urgent need for ready cash and no recourse to regular channels of credit. In highly profitable, though risky, businesses like the garment industry, loan sharks are almost a necessity. As one garment manufacturer explained: "If it wasn't for loan sharks, I'd be out of business. The sharks and Chapter Eleven [a bankruptcy statute]—they're my only partners."[9]

> There are times when the economy restricts banks from making the kinds of speculative loans needed to begin a new line, open a small non-union factory in the South or, for that matter, cash in on a truckload of dubiously acquired cloth at a 70 percent discount. Mob bankers are always available for such deals.[10]

Once deeply in debt, borrowers may sometimes be pressured into criminal activities to pay off, such as embezzlement, stealing negotiable securities from brokerage houses, or acting as illicit lottery ticket sellers; still others may be pressured into giving up a piece of their business to the loan shark or becoming a fence for the syndicate's stolen goods. Vincent Teresa, a government informer, describes an arrangement whereby a Boston warehouseman deeply in debt to a loan shark paid his bills by setting up hijackers to steal shipments of Polaroid film from a factory loading dock:

> One skid [a portable loading platform used by a forklift] . . . contained sixteen thousand . . . small packages of film, and each one of those sold for three bucks in the stores. We could sell skid loads for twenty-five to thirty grand all day to fences. The film was the hottest product the mob could lay its hands on. . . . There's no way to trace film, and there were businessmen standing in the line waiting to buy our loads at half price or less.[11]

The ultimate collateral for the loan shark is the borrower's body. Although the loansharking racket *encourages* the victim to remain in constant debt, thereby providing a lucrative weekly return, borrowers who miss too many payments due on the interest may face intimidating threats and, occasionally, terrifying physical beatings. A District Attorney from Nassau County in New York relates the ordeal of a taxi driver who refused to pay the 100 percent interest due on a $10,000 loan:

> [He was] beaten with brass knuckles, taken for a wild ride, forced at gunpoint to watch while a grave was dug for his body and then was driven home with the threat that his house would be bombed if he failed to pay his debt.[12]

The profits from loansharking are tremendous, reportedly topping even gambling as the most lucrative source of syndicate profits.[13] The typical "6 for 5" loan, where $1 of interest is charged weekly for each $5 borrowed, can bring an enormous return, especially when compounded *weekly* on the unpaid balance. For example, $1,000 lent out at this 20 percent interest rate would return $1,200 after the first week, $2,073.60 the first month, and $10,699.30 within three months. Yet even at interest rates that range as high as 150 percent (depending on the size of the loan, the relationship with the loan shark, the probability of repayment, and the purpose of the loan), there is no shortage of customers. As former loan shark and government informer, Joseph Valachi noted: "Jesus, if you gave to everybody who wanted money, you'd have to be the Bank of Rome."[14]

The President's Crime Commission estimates that the income derived from loansharking, gambling, and other illicit goods and services is nearly *twice* that generated by all other kinds of conventional criminal activities combined.[15] Illicit gambling alone grosses an estimated $50 billion a year and nets organized crime perhaps $15 billion in profit. Drug trafficking, which is increasing at a rapid rate, represents a $75 billion industry. Loansharking, hijacking, and the sale of stolen merchandise bring an estimated $100 billion annually.[16]

KEEPING UP WITH CHANGING TIMES

As with any efficient entrepreneur, criminal businessmen must keep up with changing consumer habits and tastes or go out of business. For example, with the increasing permissiveness of sexual norms resulting in a reduced demand for commercial prostitution and the increasing legalization of alcohol, organized crime is moving into other areas to keep up with changing times, reportedly even supplying black-market gasoline and oil during the energy crisis of the mid-1970s. Clearly, whether it be the theft of credit cards and securities, the hijacking of cargo at Kennedy Airport, the pirating of stereo recordings, the sale of black-market amphetamine pills and hard-core pornographic films, or the use of coercion and fear to peddle "labor harmony," organized crime is not restricted to a particular kind of illegal activity but will participate in any criminal enterprise that promises high profits and relatively low risks.

The willingness of organized crime to exploit profitable opportunities, especially where there is a strong public demand, is evident in the increasing involvement of syndicates in bootleg cigarettes. Because of the vast differences in state tobacco taxes, more than 1 billion packs of cigarettes are smuggled annually into nine states in the Northeast, creating illicit profits of more than $105 million and losses of more than $500 million to legitimate wholesalers and state tax bureaus.[17] The smuggling chain begins in Virginia, Kentucky, and North Carolina where the state tax is only 2 or 3 cents a pack and a carton sells for $2.60. In New York or New Jersey, the same carton from a legitimate dealer sells at $6.50 to $7.50. The combined state-city-county tax structure in New York City adds an additional 26 cents to the cost of a pack, forcing legitimate wholesalers to sell to the customer at 63 cents—in contrast to the syndicate price of 35 cents. At such bargain prices there is no shortage of willing buyers.

According to one recent study, more than 128,000 cartons of contraband cigarettes arrive every day in New York State, with the smugglers using sophisticated communication equipment and traffic monitors as they transport the cigarettes northward. Shortly after arrival by trailer truck, rented van, or airplane, the cigarettes disappear into warehouses or suburban homes rented by the syndicate.

> Within hours, they are redistributed by an army of mob peddlers who take orders in advance of the arrival of incoming loads, delivering and selling the bootlegged cigarettes to construction sites, apartment houses, factory complexes, beauty salons, bars and discount stores. What is left over quickly disappears into special mob outlets that include gas stations, vending machines, bookmakers and dealers in stolen property.[18]

Although the customers for these cigarettes are satisfied, others are deeply hurt by these illicit transactions. Because of the growing mob involvement in smuggling, more than 2,500 drivers, packers, and salesmen in New York State alone have lost their jobs and almost half of the state's legitimate wholesalers have gone out of business. Those wholesalers still struggling for survival face higher overheads due to soaring insurance premiums and fees for additional guards to protect against further hijacking and theft.

Adapting to the urbanization and industrialization of society and the increasing scale and scope of their operations, some of the large, successful criminal syndicates tend to become more formal in structure. They possess many of the characteristics of any sizable business: a hierarchy of authority, a complex division of labor (complete with secretaries and college-trained accountants, financial advisors, and lawyers), departmental specialization, impersonality, the profit motive, and a desire for continuity and survival. Such criminal businesses attempt to effect some control over their markets and engage in "mergers" and "consolidations" to eliminate "cut-throat" competition, though without the normal restraints imposed by the courts, governmental agencies, and laws. Historically this process was rather crude, as in the famous St. Valentine's Day Massacre of February 14, 1929, when several of Al Capone's thugs lined up seven mobsters working for George Moran and machine-gunned them down in a dispute over the control of bootlegging operations. As one observer wryly notes, some of Mr. Moran's business associates "were victims of the free enterprise system in its extreme form."[19] Although violence is still sometimes involved in the destruction of business competition, contemporary business takeovers typically involve more varied, sophisticated, and complex procedures.

ORGANIZED CRIME AND LEGITIMATE BUSINESS

Today organized crime is increasingly moving into such *legitimate* enterprises as the coin-operated machine industry, night clubs, hotels, food products, garment manufacturing, banking and finance, oil, steel, trucking, meat-packing, and dozens of other business areas. One criminal syndicate has real estate holdings with a value estimated at $300 million.[20] This infiltration of legitimate enterprises may result partly from force and intimidation, from acceptance of business interests in payment of gambling debts, or from foreclosure of usurious loans. But increasingly, control of such businesses has been acquired by inconspicuous investments funded from the multibillion-dollar profits in gambling, narcotics, loansharking, and other illegal operations. It is the tremendous profits from illicit trafficking that primarily undergird and enrich these criminal syndicates. And today, legitimate businesses provide the only major investment source available that can absorb rapidly enough such vast illicit wealth (and thus the ability of the professional "money mover" or financial expert to arrange to "launder" the investment funds becomes indispensable).

After obtaining control, the syndicate may operate the newly acquired business in a variety of ways: as a front to conceal other illegal activities, using fear and strong-arm tactics to gain a monopoly on the product or service provided by the business, or liquidating the business through bankruptcy fraud or arson to collect the insurance. The President's Crime Commission describes some of these syndicate modes of operation in action:

> Control of certain brokerage houses was secured through foreclosures of usurious loans, and the businesses then used to promote the sale of fraudulent stock, involving losses of more than $2 million to the public. . . .
> In one city, organized crime gained a monopoly in garbage collection by preserving the business's nonunion status and by using cash reserves to off-

set temporary losses incurred when the criminal group lowered prices to drive competitors out of business.[21]

Another report describes the actual looting of a captive company through bankruptcy fraud:

> The management of a large meat wholesaler in New York made the mistake of borrowing money from the Cosa Nostra. Under the guise of safeguarding the loan, the company was required to accept [a syndicate member] as its new president. Once he was installed, his colleagues went to work. In ten days they made $1,300,000. They did it by buying huge quantities of meat and poultry on credit and selling it immediately for cash at below-market prices. Then, when they were through, they blithely ordered the thoroughly cowed firm to declare bankruptcy.[22]

The thin line that often exists between the operations of criminal syndicates and legitimate businesses is further breached by some presumably respectable owners of businesses who purchase stolen goods or hire labor-boss racketeers to strike competitors to gain a more favorable trade advantage. Or companies may turn to syndicate-supplied workers to break the back of a labor strike. Mobile Oil, for example, recently "got caught paying Mafia strikebreakers $14,000 a day."[23] Businesses may also seek the services of a syndicate-connected "fixer" who can smooth the path through the maze of zoning, licensing, and other governmental regulatory requirements. And the lure of big savings deposits may provide the inducement for legitimate banks to launder the illicit mob profits. In 1977, New York's Chemical Bank was fined $225,000 for failing to report $8.5 million in hundreds of all-cash transactions from suspected organized criminal figures.[24] Even when the company is the victim of organized crime itself, legitimate businesses may cooperate with the ring of thieves to recoup some of their losses. In 1974, Pan American World Airways secretly paid "ransom" money to a criminal syndicate to purchase nearly 2,000 blank flight tickets stolen from the airline. Although the transaction drew some industry criticism, Pan Am defended its business with organized crime as "strictly a commercial decision."[25]

The systematic way in which legitimate businesses *encourage* and *sustain* organized crime is revealed in a recent study of crime in the construction industry in California. Here cooperative relations exist among syndicate-supplied burglars, illicit sales personnel, legitimate warehouse owners, and construction companies—all mutually involved in the theft and purchase of large heavy equipment such as big-wheeled earth movers, bulldozers, and even cranes and shovels. After serial numbers are altered and fake invoices provided, the stolen equipment is sold back to other contractors who are aware they are purchasing "hot goods" but cannot resist bargain "discounts" of nearly 75 percent off the normal price. Ralph Thomas describes this interdependent network of supportive relationships:

> There are indications that the Mafia or other organized racketeering groups sometimes supply the burglars for an operation. . . . The burglars could not profit if the contractors did not buy the goods; yet the contractors would not be able to purchase the goods at cut-rate prices if the burglars did not steal them. Each makes a handsome profit. Warehouses provide burglars with a legitimate avenue for disposing of their goods. They sell the stolen equipment to construction equipment supply centers where, after appropriate alteration, it is sold back to the contractors at discount rates. Thus both the warehouses and the contractors make a substantial profit from the outwardly legitimate purchase and sale of stolen goods.[26]

In addition, the infiltration of some labor unions by criminal elements has resulted in "sweetheart contracts" (which cheat workers out of wages and benefits) in collusion with management, while in others it has prevented the legitimate unionization of some industries. Such syndicate control has led to the theft of union funds, extortion through threat of economic pressure, and manipulation of welfare and pension funds to finance dubious construction projects and mob-controlled business ventures. Waterfront, trucking, and construction businessmen have been persuaded for the sake of labor tranquility to tolerate gambling, pilfering, loansharking, and kickbacks.

A conservative estimate puts the annual total take of the operations of organized crime at about one-tenth of our gross national product.[27] The consequences of this expansion of organized crime into the legitimate business area are clear: reduction of product quality, increase in prices, loss of revenue to the state, creation of fear and anxiety, defrauding of workers, businessmen and the public, and the malfunctioning of the economy.

SOCIAL MOBILITY AND MINORITY GROUPS: THE ETHNIC SUCCESSION

Organized crime viewed from another perspective is a vehicle for upward social mobility for various disadvantaged minority groups in the United States. Historically, organized crime, along with the political machine, has represented an important means to obtain wealth, power, and fame. Each major immigrant group has taken its turn successively in the upper echelons of syndicated crime. With the rags-to-riches paths preempted by earlier arrivals, opportunities in organized crime have provided shortcuts to the great American dream of individual success. When the members of each group found increasing opportunities in more conventional forms of enterprise as discriminatory barriers declined, the group itself became less prominent in the world of gangs and rackets.

As Gus Tyler has pointed out, the roots of organized crime run deep in American history. The colonial period had its pirates and smugglers. The early nineteenth century produced the urban mobs of New York and San Francisco, reflecting the poverty, ethnic strife, and ruthless politics of the times. The Old West had its highwaymen, gamblers, and slave snatchers. New Orleans had its river and port pirates. The frontier lawlessness and social unrest of the last half of the nineteenth century produced the James, Dalton, and Younger gangs. By the end of the century, numerous frontier gangs, often consisting of mercenaries, struggled for control over land, cattle, grazing fields, mining and timber properties. The early part of the twentieth century gave way to great citywide gangs, often in alliance with the new wealth and political talent of the growing urban centers, as seen in the Irish gangs of New York. To the chagrin of the Jewish community in the mid-1920s, the "Jewish racketeer" emerged, only to be replaced by the Italian-Sicilians who gained dominance by the 1930s. This great immigrant group consolidated and expanded the structure and scope of criminal operations and cooperated in loose alliances to delimit geographical and trade jurisdictions to minimize gang warfare.[28]

The Italian-Sicilians were the last of the large-scale waves of European immigrant groups to arrive in America. And like their predecessors, some of these newcomers turned to illicit activities to attain their fame and fortune. Beginning late in the nineteenth century, they brought with them a peasant distrust of corrupt local government officials and a familiarity with the exploitation and terror of predatory groups such as the kinship-based Mafia of Sicily and the Camorra of Naples that had victimized them in their towns and villages of southern Italy. Although patterns of small-scale organized crime *preceded* the arrival of the Italian-Sicilians in this country, undoubtedly some members active in criminal gangs in the old country transferred their criminal habits to the United States; particularly during the 1920s when the Italian government was under the dictatorial grip of Mussolini, some members of local Mafia groups were forced to seek refuge in America.

Thus it is possible that a diffusion of these old-world criminal patterns and traditional perspectives was one important factor in the success of Italian-Sicilians in assuming the leadership of organized crime in America, along with the special strength of kinship bonds and group loyalties facilitating cooperative criminal ventures. In a recent study of the Horatio Alger-like rise of one Sicilian-American family from its early immigrant poverty and involvement in organized crime in New York City's "Little Italy," Francis Ianni emphasizes particularly the importance of these traditional familial ties and sense of group allegiance in the social mobility of this now affluent upper-middle-class family clan (most of whose fourth-generation members are college graduates and uninvolved in organized criminal activities). The

American-born son in the family recalls the advice given by his immigrant father, Giuseppe:

> If he told us once, he told us a thousand times, you couldn't trust the judges and politicians to do anything for you because they were crooks who hid behind the law. The only protection was to take care of yourself and to make sure that you had people around you that you could count on when the time came. Pop always said he trusted his family first, relatives second, Sicilians third, and after that, forget it![29]

Probably the most significant factor in the rise of this immigrant group to the highest levels of organized crime, however, was its adaptation to the indigenous experiences of life in America: the relative recentness of arrival, the prejudice and discrimination by established groups restricting legitimate paths to prosperity, the acculturation to American values and symbols of success, and the criminal opportunities provided by the economic, political, and social conditions of American society during the first few decades of this century.

It was national Prohibition, in particular, that provided the catalyst for the *expansion* of organized crime and the rise of Italian-Americans. The earlier-arriving Irish and the Eastern European Jews were already deeply entrenched in politics, prostitution, and gambling, and the Eighteenth Amendment in 1919, which outlawed the manufacture and sale of alcohol, provided a new opportunity for some Italian-American immigrants to escape the poverty of their urban slums. An entire new illegal trade with a national market was now available, one not already monopolized by other ethnic groups. Prohibition, however, resulted in two important changes for the illicit entrepreneurs: (1) large-scale *organization* and (2) *respectability*. The illicit alcohol had to be manufactured, transported, and distributed to thousands of retail outlets. Successful bootlegging required complex operations involving huge breweries and distilleries, giant warehouses, fleets of tank cars and trucks, and protection from hijackers. It required the bribery and cooperation of the Coast Guard, customs officials, politicians, and police. Since the liquor came from Europe or Canada, it required international as well as interstate connections. Thus bootleg alcohol necessitated a level of organization and coordination unknown to earlier gangs.

But above all, Prohibition provided gangsters with wide-spread legitimacy and respectability in American life:

> In the Roaring Twenties America was a nation of outlaws enjoying bathtub gin, speakeasies, and hipflasks. The Prohibitionists had grossly miscalculated; America had a thirst that was not eliminated by the passage of a law. The bootleggers who satisfied the thirst were accepted as part of the public scene. There

were few raised eyebrows as politicians, businessmen, and any manner of good citizens openly rubbed elbows with gangsters. The funerals of major bootleggers brought mourners from the highest echelons of government and finance.[30]

The creation of this new mass market gave the Italian-Sicilians an unusually lucrative source of illicit wealth and power as they warred among themselves and with the earlier Irish, German, Polish, and Jewish bootlegging gangs to exploit this futile experiment in the legislation of morality. In the aftermath of a series of bloody intergang battles in the early 1930s, some authorities believe a loose confederation of these victorious Italian-Sicilian gangs was formed under the leadership of Charles Luciano—the great consolidator—who helped hammer out "peace treaties" and jurisdictional boundary agreements among the various competing gang factions.[31] With the repeal of Prohibition in 1933 and the expansion of a nationwide communications system, the Italian-Sicilian gangs successfully adapted to the changing society, switching from prostitution and bootlegging to gambling, drug trafficking, loansharking, labor racketeering, and control of legitimate businesses. Through bribery, violence, and intimidation they further consolidated their power to reach their present influential position in organized crime today.

Perhaps the American cultural tendency to emphasize the symbols of success and their display, rather than the means of obtainment, helps to account for the begrudging admiration and celebration of some of these notorious leaders of organized crime and the ease with which some gain entrée to the more polite circles of society. (It is reported that Al Capone received over 1,000 fan letters a day and served on a welcoming committee in Chicago during a goodwill visit of an emissary from the Italian government.)[32] As their success increases with movement into legitimate business areas, such leaders may polish up their manners, change their taste in clothes, move into exclusive suburbs, contribute to popular charities, and send their children to our finest private schools and colleges. Consider the style of life of Frank Costello, one of the major figures in organized crime and a man who once sponsored a charity dinner for the Salvation Army attended by more than twenty judges and scores of other civic and political dignitaries:

> He lived in an expensive apartment on the corner of 72nd Street and Central Park West in New York. He was often seen dining in well-known restaurants in the company of judges, public officials, and prominent businessmen. Every morning he was shaved in the barbershop of the Waldorf Astoria Hotel. On many weekends he played golf at a country club on the fashionable North Shore of Long Island. In short, though his reputation was common knowledge, he moved around New York conspicuously and unashamedly, perhaps ostracized by some people but more often accepted, greeted by journalists, recognized by children, accorded all the freedoms of a prosperous and successful man.[33]

High-ranking members of organized crime usually attempt to blend into the local community as good neighbors—often rather successfully. A resident of the Long Island suburb of the late Thomas Lucchese is quoted as saying: "If he's a gangster, I wish all of them were."[34] In Buffalo, New York, a prominent businessman and member of various local civic, fraternal, and political organizations (including the Elks, Buffalo Athletic Club, Erie Downs golf course, Chamber of Commerce, and city council) was voted Man of the Year for his civic contributions one year before his exposure as a member of organized crime, when he was apprehended at a conclave of more than 100 syndicate chieftains and associates at a private estate in Apalachin, New York.[35]

In the early 1970s Joseph Colombo, a real estate man convicted of perjury and facing probable jail after an indictment for grand larceny, conspiracy to commit extortion, and income tax evasion, was honored at a posh Long Island restaurant before some 1,450 guests. Each had contributed $125 at this testimonial dinner to hear him extoled for "restoring dignity, pride and recognition to every Italian."[36] Instrumental in the formation of the Italian-American Civil Rights League, Mr. Colombo, reputed head of one of New York City's most powerful criminal syndicates, drew nearly 100,000 demonstrators to the League's first major rally in New York's Columbus Circle to protest FBI and media defamation of Italian-Americans as Mafia criminals. Singer Frank Sinatra, together with a Hollywood cast of entertainers, raised nearly $500,000 at a Madison Square Garden benefit for the League, whose membershp reportedly had grown to 45,000 in thirty-three chapters throughout the country. A short time later Joe Colombo lay in a coma, paralyzed by bullet wounds fired by a black assailant (subsequently murdered) apparently hired by rival syndicate leaders suspicious of Mr. Colombo's motives and disdainful of his public activities.

One can almost sympathize with the chagrin felt by the wife and children of Italian-American syndicate members residing in the prestigious suburb of Grosse Point, Detroit, when their neighborhood was invaded by television camera operators intent on a documentary exposé. But as the taint of new money gained by questionable means subsides—along with some of the déclassé traits of occupation and background—the great-grandchildren of these syndicate leaders may come to revere them, much as the inheritors of the great financial dynasties of this country honor the founders ("robber barons") who were not always above using illicit and ruthless methods to obtain their wealth.[37]

The present preoccupation in the news media and entertainment industry with Italian-dominated criminal syndicates ("families"), however, encourages the belief that as soon as the assimilation process has been completed in another generation or two, the entire problem of organized crime will disappear. This is a dubious assumption, and it blinds us to the considerable involvement of those of other ethnic backgrounds in organized crime.

With the opportunity structure only gradually widening for our racial minorities, it is likely that we shall see a continuation of this route to upward mobility, with blacks, Puerto Ricans, Mexican-Americans, Cubans, and other Latin Americans moving into the higher ranks of organized crime. Currently, however, these minority groups comprise mostly the very lowest—or at best middle—levels of this kind of criminal activity. Shortly before his death, Martin Luther King denounced the "organized crime that flourishes in the ghetto—designed, directed, and cultivated by white national crime syndicates operating numbers, narcotics, and prostitution rackets freely in the protected sanctuaries of the ghettos. Because no one, including the police, cares particularly about ghetto crime, it pervades every area of life."[38]

But as the racial minorities gain increasing political control in many of our large central cities, their rise to the higher levels in organized crime should accelerate. Ralph Salerno, a former New York City police intelligence expert on organized crime, and John Tompkins describe these changes:

> Today, the Italian-Jewish Syndicate is in control of the important organized criminal activities, but it is fighting a carefully planned rearguard action as newer racial groups—Negroes, Puerto Ricans, Japanese, Mexicans, Chinese— move up in the power structure. In the near future, the old guard will largely abandon the big cities to such groups as it follows the middle class to the suburbs and out to megalopolis. Some kinds of crime, particularly those that flourish in the ghetto, will also be surrendered.[39]

> Negroes have long been employees of organized crime, but mostly in the menial jobs of narcotics pusher and policy runner. In recent years, though, a few Negroes have risen to what might be called the "junior partner" level of the Confederation in such cities as Detroit, Buffalo, and Chicago. It is these rising executives of organized crime who are pushing hardest for ghetto crime to become black, so they can control it and be equal in status to their present white bosses.[40]

Growing signs of more intensive participation in organized crime are apparent in the increasing numbers of blacks and Spanish-speaking persons who are being arrested with wholesale amounts of heroin and cocaine as they move up to the smuggler and dealer levels.

> According to federal sources, some black dealers are purchasing large quantities of heroin in individual deals involving hundreds of thousands of dollars in Asia and Mexico. Some black drug organizations supervise the entire distribution process, from smuggling to "milling" or the packaging of heroin, and the final street sales. . . .[41]

Police estimate that in New York City, Newark, and Jersey City, forty black and Hispanic dope dealers were gunned down within a 2-month period in

1977, apparent victims of "gangland-type" slayings. Blacks and Puerto Rican gangs are also joining in alliances, increasingly "banking" their own gambling operations as they challenge the dominant Italian and allied Jewish criminal power structures.

As the movement toward "community control" in ghetto neighborhoods grows, it is unlikely that the white dominance of illicit trafficking will be able to withstand completely these pressures. At a meeting of the First National Black Economic Conference in Detroit, Professor Robert Browne of Fairleigh Dickinson University summed up this growing mood when he told a group of 350 black militants: "Racketeering, prostitution, and the numbers, if they are to continue, must be put into the hands of the Black community."[42] The stakes are high. The numbers racket is said to be one of the major income-producing industries in Harlem, employing thousands of persons; its control would become a significant source of black political power:

> Harlem experts estimate that more than 100,000 players dreaming of a big hit—600 to 1 if they get three numbers right in a row, or 8 to 1 on a single-number play—put down $2,000,000 to $4,000,000 a month in Harlem and the Bedford-Stuyvesant section of Brooklyn. More than 10,000 persons reportedly make a living from the game.[43]

> From the gross play, a banker, nowadays generally an outsider [i.e., a white rather than a black], takes perhaps 65 percent, out of which he pays the wins—perhaps 20 to 25 percent of the play. From this he pays runners, lawyers, bondsmen—and also rumors say, the police for as much as 15 percent at low echelons of the department. Thus [the] argument is that 50 percent of the play—derived from wages, pensions, relief checks—flows out of the [black] community in a monthly total of at least $1,000,000.[44]

Thus it appears that these most recent challengers for the dominant position in large-scale criminal enterprises are only repeating an old American tradition. How successful they will become remains to be seen. Francis Ianni sums up this historical process of ethnic succession in organized crime:

> The Irish came first, and early in this century they dominated crime as well as big-city political machinations. As they came to control the political machinery of large cities they won wealth, power and respectability through subsequent control of construction, trucking, public utilities and the waterfront. By the 1920's and the period of prohibition and speculation in the money markets and real estate, the Irish were succeeded in organized crime by the Jews, and Arnold Rothstein, Lepke Buchalter and Gurrah Shapiro dominated gambling and labor racketeering for over a decade. The Jews quickly moved into the world of business and the professions as more legitimate avenues to economic and social mobility. The Italians came next, and . . . what is now becoming increasingly obvious [is] that as the Italians are leaving or are being pushed out of

organized crime they are being replaced by the next wave of migrants to the city: blacks and Puerto Ricans. Ethnic groups move in and out of organized crime and their time in control comes and goes. Even the specific crimes may change, as bootlegging is replaced by drug pushing and prostitution gives way to pornography. But organized crime as an American way of life persists and transcends the involvement of any particular group and the changing social definitions of what is illegal and what is not.[45]

POLITICS, CORRUPTION, AND LAW ENFORCEMENT: SYMBIOTIC RELATIONS

It is doubtful that organized crime could thrive so successfully in America without the cooperation and outright connivance of a portion of our political and law-enforcement machinery. From the Prohibition era to the present, most of the various municipal, state, and federal committees investigating political corruption have consistently revealed an unholy alliance of syndicate members, politicians, public officials, and law-enforcement agents. Well-intentioned political reforms, however, have been typically short-lived. As Henry Ruth points out:

> When the influence and effect of organized crime bursts above the surface, local governments are forced to act. But after a few gambling raids, perhaps a public corruption case or two, and the defeat of some public officials at the next election, the public becomes satisfied that the situation has been cured. Law enforcement returns to policing unorganized crime, and public officials proudly proclaim that there is no cleaner, finer place to live than their community.[46]

A case in point is Westchester County in New York. In the 1960s a State Criminal Investigations Committee discovered widespread gambling in many parts of the county and considerable corruption in a number of the thirty-nine police departments. But only a few years later, *The New York Times* reported:

> Some of the suspected police officers have since been promoted, some repudiated politicians have since been returned to office, gambling is as wide open as before, and inroads have been made [by organized crime] in other areas of criminal activity.[47]

As Ruth pessimistically observes, undoubtedly there will be cries of public anguish at this publicized revelation of events. Unless the climate is changing, he notes, heated denials by public officials will occur; abortive grand juries will convene; a flurry of law enforcement is predictable—perhaps even a few persons will lose their positions—and then things will return to the next phase of this cycle of "hit-and-run" law enforcement as the community's attention is diverted to other concerns.

The trouble with the "new broom" philosophy designed to sweep out the rascals is that it does not basically alter the structural and cultural conditions that facilitate and encourage political corruption. The local cycles of corruption, reform, and more corruption do little to modify the insistent demands from those large segments of the public who still want to place a bet on a horse with their favorite bookie or match their luck against a football-card point spread; from builders who seek special consideration to secure a contract to do business with the city and bypass competitive bidding; from speculators who want to "bend" the zoning ordinance to permit a windfall in their real estate purchases; from businessmen who want to snare a lucrative liquor license; or from politicians who must finance a party campaign war chest. Running for political office in America, for instance, tends to be costly, and most large financial contributors to political campaigns expect some favors in return—including simply being "left alone." In Mount Vernon, New York, a local political party turned to organized gamblers for campaign funds because, in the words of the city committee, "we were poor and couldn't get the money from anywhere else."[48] A conservative estimate puts the level of all local and state political contributions stemming from criminal sources at 15 percent.[49]

The sordid story of bribes, delivery of votes, fixes, payoffs, and public officials beholden to the syndicate continues ad nauseam, allowing organized crime in many large and small cities to operate in comparative immunity. At various times, organized crime has been the dominant political force in such small cities as Cicero, Illinois; Long Branch, New Jersey, and Reading, Pennsylvania—as well as in Chicago, New York, Miami, and New Orleans; in fact, few sizable metropolitan centers have been immune to such corrupting influences. The impact of syndicate control on such communities is vividly revealed in this report of corruption in the city of Reading, in the middle of the bucolic Pennsylvania Dutch region:

> Operating in conjunction with a local underworld figure, most of the municipal administration from the mayor on down was corrupted. As a result, the biggest illegal still since Prohibition was tied into the city water supply, the biggest red-light district on the East Coast was set up, and the biggest dice game east of the Mississippi, within an easy drive of either Philadelphia or New York, was launched. Nothing was done for the city. Industry started leaving; downtown Reading became an eyesore. When murmurs of public discontent grew too loud, mob-controlled "reformers" were promptly whisked on the scene. As the city steadily began to wither, a Justice Department task force noticed that the only sign of civic improvement was new parking meters. The company involved in the installation of these meters had a history of kicking back to municipal governments to get the business. It was this thread that eventually unraveled the whole mess, but until outside aid arrived, the local citizenry was truly helpless.[50]

The manner in which organized crime may effectively sink its claws into public officials can be seen in the case of James L. Marcus, former Commissioner of Water Supply, Gas, and Electricity in New York City and a close advisor and member of Mayor Lindsay's inner circle. Deeply in debt from business investments and Wall Street plunges, Marcus was referred by a business associate to Anthony Corallo, reputedly a high-ranking member of the Thomas Lucchese syndicate "family" with a reputation as a labor racketeer and loan shark. Paying interest to Corallo on cash loans said to be at an annual rate of 104 percent, Marcus sank further in debt, and was finally pressured into doing business "favors" to the mob shylock and his associates. The result was a tangled web of rigged municipal contracts, bribes, and illegal real estate deals. Marcus pleaded guilty to taking a $16,000 kickback in return for awarding a $835,000 city contract to clean a Bronx reservoir and received a 15-month sentence for his part in this and several other conspiracies.[51]

The close interdependence of organized crime and the law-enforcement process operates at various levels. For instance, when a bookie "talked" in New York City a number of years ago, 450 policemen of all ranks either resigned, retired, or were dismissed.[52] In Chicago, Captain William Duffy of the Police Intelligence Division, along with federal authorities, raided a multimillion-dollar North Side lottery operation, confiscating so-called "ice lists"—compilations of payoffs to various police officials for protection:

> [T]his one lottery was paying off police in 10 of Chicago's 21 police districts, officers in three of the department's six roving Task Forces, and others in the Robbery Detail and the Intelligence Division. Also, there were payoffs to the Vice Control Division, the outfit specifically charged with suppressing gambling.[53]

(A short time after the gambling raid, an enraged syndicate gambling chief boasted publicly: "We got a promise that Duffy will go." He was apparently right. Only six weeks after the raid, Captain Duffy was relieved of his position as intelligence chief.)[54]

Numerous mayors and district attorneys have also been found to have friendly relations with criminal elements. Even judges have been indebted to the syndicate for their positions. One of the best authenticated of many such cases is the famous wiretapped telephone conversation in which a newly appointed judge thanked gangster Frank Costello for arranging his nomination as justice of the State Supreme Court of New York and pledged his undying loyalty.[55]

Even in those rare instances in which high-ranking syndicate members have been jailed or imprisoned, special favorable treatment by correctional authorities has often occurred. Sam Giancana, reputed Chicago syndicate boss, was the recipient of steaks and cigars personally delivered to the most comfortable cell in a Chicago county jail while a federal prisoner. In Jersey City, another notorious criminal had private accommodations in the warden's quarters and access to female companions. Vito Genovese, former New York City syndicate chieftain, reportedly continued to transmit major policy decisions to his "family" members during his eight years of federal imprisonment and to arrange cell assignments for friends.[56]

The wide scope of political corruption is also visible in the city of Newark, New Jersey, which in 1970 was rocked by a major scandal involving public officials, law-enforcement agents, and organized crime. In the first of two mass indictments resulting in subsequent convictions, a federal grand jury charged the mayor, Hugh Addonizio, with income tax evasion and sixty-six counts of extortion involving a share in payoffs totaling $253,000 from a business firm that had contracts with the city. Also included in the indictments were eleven current or former city officials and a reputed prominent member of a New Jersey crime syndicate. Barely a day before this grand jury action, a series of gambling raids by some 100 FBI agents (apparently sparked by information derived from wiretaps) in Newark and surrounding suburbs resulted in scores of arrests and led to another mass indictment of fifty-five persons. Almost a dozen of those indicted were reported to be syndicate members, including Simone Rizzo Decavalcante, alleged boss of one of the six major Italian-dominated syndicate "families" in the New York metropolitan area. (This huge interstate operation, extending as far as Troy, New York, reportedly brought the syndicate $20 million a year.) The indictments of these gambling figures also charged that some of them had "solicited and obtained" tip-offs from Newark City Police on any impending gambling raids.[57]

Publicly released transcripts of FBI eavesdropping on alleged syndicate *capo* Angelo DeCarlo revealed that he had raised money for Addonizio's Newark mayoralty campaign. "I'll guarantee, we'll own him," boasted DeCarlo. Tapes from these electronic bugs also showed the syndicate's participation in the appointments of New Jersey county prosecutors, judges, state and local police chiefs, and an assortment of police officers of all ranks.[58]

It is not necessary, of course, to attempt to bribe most local law-enforcement agents and public officials. That would be much too expensive and is quite unnecessary. The syndicate need only corrupt certain strategically placed key officials—perhaps a supervisory lieutenant or captain in a vice-control squad, a police chief, an assistant district attorney, a judge, a mayor, or especially the non-office-holding political leaders to whom elected officials are responsive. When a zealous rookie police officer investigates a suspicious-looking gathering in the neighborhood he patrols that turns out to be a gambling enterprise and finds that his reports are repeatedly ignored, that the persons he arrests are later dismissed, or that he is reassigned to a new beat—he and the rest of the police force are likely to "get the message." Especially when high-ranking officials are involved, a policy of nonenforcement becomes quickly established, breeding police demoralization, cynicism, and suspicion (even envy) that large numbers of fellow officers are "on the take." As Ruth comments:

> When a mayor orders the transfer to an outlying district of a police officer who has raided one of organized crime's gambling establishments, the climate of nonenforcement is created. . . . When a police officer senses that the political figures do not desire a program against organized crime (despite their public statements to the contrary), police officials realize correctly that they cannot accomplish the task alone; and they are not going to risk their careers in an attempt to prove otherwise. Law-enforcement officers and others concerned about organized crime, when left standing alone, are soon branded as hysterical fictionalists, flailing away at a mythical enemy, whose existence public officials and other parts of the community deny. Indeed it is difficult for the public to believe what their elected officials will not permit them to see.[59]

Cooperation between law-enforcement agencies and organized crime operates in a variety of ways. The police, for example, may in effect sell "crime-committing licenses" to certain criminal groups. By selectively enforcing the law against other criminal gangs that might offer potential competition, the police assist one criminal group to obtain a local monopoly— an exclusive franchise—on some illicit activity such as a gambling lottery operation. A number of years ago in New York City, Adam Clayton Powell, a former black Congressman from Harlem, accused the police of systematic discrimination by raiding gambling operations and arresting primarily black bankers and harassing black numbers runners to prevent successful black-controlled operations independent of the Italian and allied Jewish groups in control.

> At this time, no arrests have been made in East Harlem, the center of Italian and syndicate activity. Until action begins in that area and higher up, it is apparent that . . . arrests are an attempt to embarrass the Negro community while continuing the policy of allowing the higherups to go scot-free.[60]

From the police perspective, by permitting one criminal group a monopoly, the kind of violence and organizational strain for the police that might result from ruthless, open competition—compounding their problems—is minimized. Moreover, any such "tolerance policy"—restricting illicit bet-taking operations to certain sections of the city—enables the police to accommodate those persons in the community who wish to gamble and those who seek its suppression, or at least its diminished visibility. All these considerations, together with the wide-spread conviction that gambling isn't *real* crime, offer a seductive logic for many police officers that helps sustain these symbiotic relationships between law enforcement and organized crime. Thus, given the diverse and conflicting pressures operating in the community, the loud and insistent complaints by some influential persons about illicit gambling are likely to be viewed by the police as both naive and unwelcome.

Frequently, however, the tolerance policy of the police evolves into a shakedown racket whereby law-enforcement and government officials align themselves with organized crime. Consider the case of Seattle, where the mayor had closed down all card parlors in the city. Within two years the police began to permit selected syndicate-run card parlors to stay in business in return for monthly cash payoffs:

> Within six years an extensive network of police payoffs was discovered. A grand jury later alleged that some patrolmen were collecting $10 to $1,000 each month from operators of gambling establishments on their bets. Some portion of the payoffs . . . was passed up the chain of command as far . . . as the chief of police. Several police officials were reported to have earned as much as $12,000 annually. . . . Moreover, several prominent city officials, including the past county prosecutor, the president of the city council, and the county license director, were indicted for receiving bribes in the form of campaign contributions to cover up the corruption.[61]

In New York City, the Knapp Commission estimated that gambling shakedowns provided police with $7 to $12 million annually, with even higher profits in payoffs from narcotics dealers. Moreover, the Commission discovered that some policemen were dealing in confiscated drugs themselves. Of 97 pounds of heroin seized from one ring of narcotics smugglers, which became the basis for the film *The French Connection*, 80 pounds were later stolen from the police department's own vaults and security installations. The Commission estimated that over half of the New York City police force took some form of graft.[62]

During spasms of political reform, a flurry of gambling and "vice" raids may occur, but these usually only temporarily upset the negotiated relationships with the criminal groups which provide the illicit but widely patronized services. Many such raids, are, of course, merely staged "tip-over" raids, generating much publicity but few convictions. It is not uncommon for a member of the raiding party who is on the syndicate payroll deliberately to engage in illegal search and seizure and commit other violations of constitutional due-process procedures, thus making difficult successful prosecution by honest prosecutors and judges.

These police "favors" to appreciative criminal groups may, in addition to cash payoffs, be reciprocated in other ways. Cressey tells of a city official who had entertained a prostitute in his home while his wife was out of town and later discovered that the prostitute had stolen a fur coat belonging to his wife:

> He called a trusted police official, explained the situation, and that it would be embarrassing if the coat were still missing when his wife returned. The police official called on a dozen prostitutes, with no success. He then revealed his plight to a Cosa Nostra lieutenant, keeping the name of the city official confidential. The lieutenant returned the coat two days later but the police kept it for another two days, then "explained" to the city official that diligent and delicate detective work was necessary for its retrieval.[63]

Crime-committing licenses are also issued by corrupt district attorneys and judges, providing a virtual immunity against prosecution, conviction, or severe sentences. As the Kefauver Committee concluded, in referring to William O'Dwyer, former District Attorney of Kings County, New York:

> [Mr. O'Dwyer failed to take] effective action against the top echelons of the gambling, waterfront, murder, or bookmaking rackets. His defense of public officials who were derelict in their duties, and his actions in investigation of corruption, and his failure to follow up concrete evidence of organized crime, particularly in the case of Murder, Inc., and the waterfront, have contributed to the growth of organized crime, racketeering, and gangsterism in New York City.[64]

Occasionally, corrupt judges may blatantly attempt to intervene in behalf of a syndicate member. For example, a New York judge was convicted for accepting a $35,000 bribe from gangster Anthony Corallo to "fix" a sentence for a defendant in a $100,000 bankruptcy fraud. Similarly, the New Jersey Supreme Court suspended a trial judge charged with offering a prosecutor a $10,000 bribe to squelch a gambling case involving two syndicate members. More typically, however, a mob-linked judge might serve syndicate members by warning in advance that a search warrant for a raid had been issued, by assigning cases to certain trial judges, by suppressing incriminating evidence in court, by instructing the jury in ways likely to produce a not-guilty verdict, and by imposing only nominal fines or short jail terms rather than a lengthy prison sentence.

It is clear that organized crime requires the passive—and at times the active and conscious—cooperation of diverse elements of *respectable* society to flourish and effectively neutralize any opposition. Indicative perhaps of either the naiveté, political expediency, or outright corruption of the presumably respectable sectors of the society is an episode that occurred in Philadelphia. In federal court a man who had been convicted of operating a huge interstate gambling operation and who had been arrested fourteen times—seven for violent crimes—petitioned for reduction of his sentence. (Before this gambling conviction, he had served but 30 days in jail on five different convictions in the past 40 years.) Although a federal attorney had informed the court that the man was a notorious figure in organized crime,

> . . . officials from both political parties, including a United States congressman, publicly testified as to the convicted person's good character. A lawyer who testified for the felon subsequently became the nominee for district attorney in his county. Another United States congressman defended the nominee's character testimony.[65]

In countless cities throughout America, these various patterns of cooperation and corruption continue. In this sense then it can be said that organized crime represents an *alliance with government*—a point often glossed over in such films as *The Godfather* and in other popular accounts of this allegedly "alien" criminal conspiracy and its "foreign" mafia characteristics.

Indeed, respectable government officials and legitimate businessmen may actually *initiate* and *control* the criminal activity to the point where "organized crime" and "white-collar crime" become almost indistinguishable. In 1977, for example, thirty-three persons in Boston were indicted as members of an arson ring charged with thirty-five fires that killed at least three persons and cost insurance companies $6 million. According to the Massachusetts attorney general, however, "this is just the tip of the iceberg." Included in this lucrative criminal conspiracy were lawyers, insurance adjusters, businessmen, police and fire officials, and professional arsonists. An investigative report describes the arson setup:

> Businessmen buy rundown buildings planning to burn them, usually hiring professional "torches." After minor renovations, these buildings are insured for far more than their worth and sometimes traded back and forth between partners and dummy corporations to artificially inflate their value. The insurance settlements can be enormous, and they are tax-free because they are not considered income.[66]

The discovery of this high-profit illicit enterprise in Boston came as a result of probes initiated by the victims themselves who grew impatient and frustrated with investigation by local authorities—and with good reason: "[S]ome of the officials they complained to are among those indicted."[67] Arson is now one of the fastest growing major crimes in America. And the consequences can be devastating. Across the nation arson has resulted in the deaths of hundreds of innocent people, the loss of an estimated $2 billion in property losses, and the destruction of entire inner-city neighborhoods.

Even the White House may not be immune to the advantages of doing business with persons connected with organized crime. During the revelations of the scandals involving the Nixon Administration in the 1970s, evidence mounted that the President of the United States may have had close relationships with syndicate figures. Los Angeles mobster Mickey Cohen claims he contributed to Nixon's political campaigns as far back as 1945.[68] One of the most damaging allegations surrounded the strange circumstances under which Nixon pardoned Jimmy Hoffa after a federal parole board had twice denied parole to the former Teamster boss. Frank Fitzsimmons, Hoffa's replacement as Teamster president, was subsequently invited to the White House after his mob-connected union supported Nixon in the 1972 election, reportedly contributing as much as $250,000 to the Committee to Reelect the President. According to the press, shortly after the union's support of President Nixon, the politically sensitive Department of Justice abruptly ordered the FBI to terminate its court-authorized wiretapping of Teamster officials and their contacts with crime syndicates.[69]

Further, there is convincing evidence from a U.S. Senate committee investigation that the CIA even hired two notorious syndicate mobsters, Sam Giancanna and John Roselli, to arrange the assassination of Cuba's Fidel Castro. Although plans were apparently drawn up, the Bay of Pigs invasion aborted the plan to poison the Cuban leader and the murder contract was canceled. In 1976, shortly after Roselli testified before the Senate Select Committee of Intelligence investigating the CIA involvement, he was strangled and stabbed, his partly decomposed body found floating in a 55-gallon drum in Biscayne Bay. Giancanna also was mysteriously killed days before he was to appear as a Senate witness. To deepen the intrigue, it seems that both Roselli and Giancanna were close friends of Las Vegas show girl Judith Campbell Exner. Allegedly, Exner spent some of her evenings with John F. Kennedy, to whom she had been introduced by singer Frank Sinatra at a Nevada resort. The exact reasons for the death of the two syndicate mobsters—and who ordered it—still remain a mystery.[70]

The involvement of this secret U.S. intelligence agency in covert activities in Cuba also ironically may have supported organized crime in America in other ways. In his recent study of the ascendency of new ethnic groups into prominent positions in organized crime, Francis Ianni found that the Cubans appear to show the most structural development and cohesion in their criminal gangs. In addition to the importance of strong kinship bonds among Cuban-Americans, several of Ianni's informants attributed this structure not only to contacts with Italian-American and Jewish syndicates operating in Havana during the pre-Castro days, but also to experiences with the CIA. These informants claimed that the more disciplined organizational structures of Cuban syndicates emerged partly from their military and paramilitary training by the CIA in connection with the Bay of Pigs invasion and other military ventures. They then utilized this organizational network to move into drug smuggling—especially the cocaine connection—from South America.[71]

Yet there is another kind of governmental response that supports organized crime—the "corruption of indifference."[72] For example, when elected officials sense that important segments of the public want to gamble, they are unlikely to attempt zealously to disrupt the organizational apparatus that provides this illicit service. Only when gambling becomes "flagrant or notorious" or a major flap is instigated by influential persons are many public officials likely to take action. Referring to a former Superintendent of the Louisiana State Police, Governor John McKeithen of Louisiana is quoted as saying:

> Look at Grevemberg. He cracked down on gambling. He was tough. He went around with a flashlight and an ax, busting up little honkey-tonk places. Do you know where he placed when he ran for governor? *Fifth!*[73]

There is also the corruption of indifference that occurs when citizens are unwilling to pay sufficient salaries to attract efficient, skilled prosecuting attorneys. It is quite unnecessary for syndicate operators to bribe mediocre law-enforcement officials if they are already lazy or inept in the performance of their jobs or if their departments are understaffed and starved for operating funds. Communities may be unwilling to provide such alleged "frills" as police intelligence units (something most police departments do not have) that would permit the unheralded—and therefore, to the taxpayer, invisible—continuous surveillance and investigative work so necessary for any successful attempt to combat organized crime. Consequently, police agencies may concentrate on securing a high number of arrests—a superficial and misleading index of the "success" of a law-enforcement agency—to impress fund-allocating city councils and legislatures, diverting police resources away from potentially more fruitful long-term intelligence work. The result is likely to be a flurry of periodic low-level arrests among gambling and "vice" offenders with little real impact on the functioning of the criminal organization that operates or controls these illicit operations.

Today, corruption of all kinds is more threatening than ever. Such corruption is becoming less visible, more subtle, and thus more difficult to detect and evaluate than during the Prohibition era. The need to corrupt public officials at every level of government has grown as the scale of organized-crime activities and the scope of government regulatory controls have broadened: "As government regulation expands into more and more areas of private and business activity, the power to corrupt affords the corrupter more control over matters affecting the ordinary life of each citizen."[74]

INDIVIDUALISTIC BIAS IN LAW ENFORCEMENT

A major difficulty in combating organized crime in America reflects our cultural tendency to view criminality in terms of *individual* maladjustment, rather than as a consequence of an individual's participation in a structure of group relationships. The failure to perceive and cope with the organizational nature of our crime problem is, in fact, generally inherent in our criminal codes. Our law-enforcement process is largely designed for the control of individuals—not for the control of organizations.[75] Police and investigative agencies, consequently, are more concerned with collecting evidence that will lead to case-by-case prosecution of individuals than with securing evidence of the relationships between criminals or the structure and operation of illicit business organizations. This selective view also affects the way we compile and publish data on crime, thereby allowing the public—and the police, too, if they so desire—to ignore organized crime because it does not show up in the statistics. Neither the much-publicized FBI Index of Serious Crimes nor its list of the ten most wanted men alerts the public to the immense economic costs and political dangers of organized crime.

This individualistic bias creates various legal loopholes through which most of the high-ranking participants in these criminal organizations escape arrest, prosecution, and imprisonment. As Cressey notes:

> "[O]rganized crime" is not against the law. What is against the law is smuggling and selling narcotics, bookmaking, usury, murder, extortion, conspiracy and the like. Except when conspiracy statutes are violated, it is not against the law for an individual or group of individuals rationally to plan, establish, and develop a division of labor for the perpetration of crime, whether it be bookmaking or murder. Neither is it against the law for an individual to participate in such a division of labor. . . . The legal lacunae permit directors of illicit businesses to remain immune from arrest, prosecution, and imprisonment unless they themselves violate specific criminal laws such as those prohibiting individuals from selling narcotics.[76]

In general, this cultural astigmatism makes it difficult for most of the citizenry—as well as many social scientists—to view organized crime as a serious social problem. Many of the customers who place a friendly bet with that nice old man in the corner bar do not perceive, in fact, that this criminal bookmaker is a *businessman*—not an unorganized individual gambler. He is typically linked to a far-reaching organizational network that channels and pools thousands of $5 bets, that can finance a professional murder of a government informer, corrupt a judge or a district attorney, manipulate the price of shares on the stock market, or fund the takeover of a legitimate business. The successful operation of any sizeable gambling establishment requires a constant flow of money and information (for example, syndicate wire services providing up-to-date betting odds) throughout the organizational apparatus. It requires arrangements to insulate the operation from detection and provide law-enforcement immunity to the higher-echelon participants. The President's Crime Commission conveys something of the complexity of these illicit business operations:

> Money is filtered from the small operator who takes the customer's bet, through persons who pick up money and slips, to second-echelon figures in charge of particular districts, and then into one of several main offices. The profits that eventually accrue to organization leaders move through channels so complex that even persons who work in the betting operation do not know or cannot prove the identity of the leader. Increasing use of the telephone for lottery and sports betting has facilitated systems in which the bookmaker may not know the identity of the second-echelon person to whom he calls in the day's bets. Organization not only creates greater efficiency and enlarges markets, it also provides a systematized method of corrupting the law enforcement process by centralizing procedures for the payment of graft.[77]

The coordination of a large number of persons in successful gambling operations is particularly crucial in fixing the outcome of sporting events. Vincent Teresa provides an example from the world of horse racing:

> It required paying off exercise boys and stable hands to leave areas where horses were to be drugged. It meant reaching the right jockeys and cultivating the right owners. It meant dealing with the right people to obtain the most effective drugs. It also meant warning New England bookmakers working for the Office—so they would not get hurt by the heavy betting. . . .[78]

In addition, there is a complicated "layoff" betting system to insure against severe losses. For instance, more money may be wagered on one horse than a small bookmaker could pay off if that horse won. The operator ensures against this possibility by betting some money himself on that horse through still larger bookmakers, who in turn may hedge against losses up through a network of regional and national layoff men who will take bets from various gambling operations across the country. The syndicate may also use some of these huge gambling profits as loansharking capital to hook independent bet-taking operators and thus coerce them into becoming part of the syndicate gambling operation. Indeed, "anyone whose independent operation becomes successful is likely to receive a visit from an organization representative who convinces the independent, through fear or promise of greater profit, to share his revenue with the organization."[79] One sociologist has estimated that 95 percent of all bookmakers and lottery operators in the United States are either members of syndicates or nonmembers who pay a share of their profits ("sharecrop") to syndicate members.[80]

Yet because of the ignorance of the organizational nature of the commercial bet-taking business and the ambivalent public sentiments toward gambling, the fiction is maintained that no one is really hurt very much by such illegal operations. Consequently, society tends to shield the participants: witnesses to testify against these illicit businessmen are scarce; policemen are likely to ignore bookmakers as long as operations are not too flagrant; judges slap their wrists with petty fines that amount to little more than a "license tax" to do business; and the higher-echelon participants remain mostly immune to arrest and conviction.

What seems clear is that the most troublesome problem with gambling is not the activity itself but the *illicit organizational network* behind it. Although the legalization of all forms of gambling and sports betting would certainly be no panacea, and legalized gambling would still be vulnerable to infiltration by organized crime, a strong case can be made for this means of providing some legitimate economic competition to organized crime (a process partly underway as revenue-starved states and near-bankrupt cities seek new sources of economic vitality). But it will take more ingenuity and business acumen than typically displayed in the meager services and taxable winnings of most state gambling lotteries to cripple the gambling operations of criminal syndicates.

It is rather hypocritical of the dominant white establishment, however, to continue to harass ghetto blacks and Puerto Ricans who prefer the numbers game while the government advertises on television the fun of playing Empire Sweepstakes or betting on the horses at legal off-track betting parlors conveniently scattered throughout New York City. Such legal duplicity deepens the cynicism and alienation of blacks and Puerto Ricans who contend that whites rig the law for their form of gambling (including the stock market, commodity speculation, and church bingo) but criminalize the ghetto dweller's preferred kind of game. Recently, the New Jersey edition of *The New York Times* ran a story of a forty-man police raid of a Puerto Rican numbers operation in East Harlem.[81] The lengthy article detailed the arrest of thirteen people and the confiscation of several thousands of dollars worth of equipment. Below the news story a black-boarded box appeared— a daily feature in this edition—containing this information:

> The winning New Jersey
> daily lottery number yesterday was:
> 25113

A study conducted by a Washington-based group of civil rights lawyers found that over 70 percent of all persons arrested in the United States on gambling charges are black, although blacks comprise only about 12 percent of the population. The report documented the "unequal and unfairly discriminatory administration of criminal laws concerning gambling" in cities across the nation and commented:

> Among the illegal games, [numbers] is the Police Department's primary target, and it is a game favored in Washington's black community. Viewed by many as the ghetto's stock market, black people ask why some lotteries are tolerated or even legalized, while the lottery they favor is legal nowhere.[82]

In an era when former convicted bookmaker Jimmy ("the Greek") Snyder provides the weekly point spread on football games over national television, when synagogues sponsor popular "Las Vegas Nights," and when Atlantic City builds gambling casinos, it is unlikely that the illegality of the numbers game will endure much longer.

Although it is beyond the scope of this chapter to examine the philosophical and thorny issues (e.g., freedom and self-determination, the extent of government regulatory controls) involved in decriminalization of various illicit but consensual transactions among willing adults ("victimless crimes"), it would seem wise to reevaluate our traditional prohibitionist policies.[83] The removal or narrowing of criminal sanctions from usury, drugs, prostitution, and pornography, for example, would have many benefits. It would permit the serious exploration of alternative social, economic, and medical policies to mitigate the most troublesome aspects of these forms of social deviance. Decriminalization would permit those persons who need or desire such services to bypass the criminal black market and its nefarious side effects: corruption and illegal police practices, disease, secondary crimes (e.g., violence and addict theft), diversion of scarce enforcement resources from other serious crime problems, cynicism and disrespect for the legal system, and the enrichment of organized crime. *It is not a matter of whether such products and services will be provided but who will provide them and under what conditions—legal or illegal.* Moreover, the provision of legitimate alternatives might reduce the cultural myopia and moral hypocrisies that accompany our current legal policies toward "vice." Rufus King perceptively comments on some of the cultural blinders and dysfunctional consequences from our Mafia fixation, which helps to mystify and distort the real nature of our social and criminal problems:

> Loan-sharking? Isn't that only a pejorative name for usury (as on Wall Street a nicer name for g-mbl-ng is "speculation")? But in most states there is no usury protection for corporations, and in much of the country bankers use "points," discounts, and premiums to push interest above usury limits. Even assuming the Mafia were making risky loans to people who can't borrow from Household Finance, why not? If anyone, banker or hoodlum, collects debts by physical violence, that becomes the crime of assault. And don't landlords, aided by all the righteous majesty of the law, sometimes inflict comparable trauma when they throw delinquent rent-payers and their families into the street? . . .
>
> The "dope fiend" mythology is a full fifty years older than that of the Mafia.

Yet the truth is that our drug laws and exaggerated enforcement policies, unique in the Western world, have given the United States alone a major drug "problem." We are the only target for smugglers, and the only nation seriously committed to "war" on this front. And we are a laughingstock: bribing and bullying the Turks to give up their poppy-growing ways is as ridiculous as a Turkish campaign in Kentucky to free Istanbul of deadly cigarette tobacco. . . .

And all the odious army of narks has ever done is drive prices up, subsidize the world black market, and tighten the street pusher's cruel monopoly. Until medical and health authorities grow brave enough to return to their responsibilities in the field, the drug peddler's services might even be defended as humanitarian. He is only doing what doctors do in other civilized countries.[84]

A FRACTURED PERSPECTIVE

With a notable exception or two, systematic firsthand empirical research on contemporary organized crime by social scientists has been practically nil. Most of what is known has been pieced together from a few government informers, police intelligence reports, and information secured through wiretaps and electronic bugs. In-depth analyses of the ramifications of organized crime are mostly tucked away in scholarly journals or buried in disparate government reports. Consequently, public knowledge of organized crime is sketchy, fragmented, and stereotypical. Even among some government officials—and I suspect sociologists too—there is still a tendency to perceive organized crime apart from other social problems in America and as only a "tiny part" of the larger crime problem. Probably few Americans recognize the pervasiveness of organized crime in their lives and its impact on the welfare of the society: the economic losses and malfunctioning of our economic system; the contribution to poverty, despair, fear, and violence; the partial nullification of legal government; and the subtle erosion of a free society.

> Popular representations of the scope of organized crime too often convey to the uninitiated the impression that these criminal groups operate in a separate world of crime that victimizes principally the greedy and the amoral, the seekers of a "fast buck," the persons who deserve what they get. Organized crime is therefore bracketed in a separate compartment as a phenomenon that certainly deserves attention sometime, but need not occupy a position of priority and significance, considering the wealth of other social and criminal problems.[85]

The belief, for example, that organized crime is a phenomenon unrelated to conventional "street crimes"—which generate most of the alarm and anxiety in the general public—helps to obscure our understanding of the larger impact of organized crime. It is criminal syndicates that have mostly controlled the importation and wholesale distribution of narcotics that, together with counterproductive prohibitionist laws and police activity, compel most addicts to engage in burglary, robbery, and larceny to pay the exorbitant black-market prices. And it is the "fences" aligned with organized crime groups who allow thieves to convert their booty into cash. Organized crime has also been known to promote bank robberies, hijacking, arson and burglaries, sometimes in cooperation with individual professional criminals.

Moreover, the activities of organized crime have been an important factor in the desperation, poverty, and despair of the ghetto poor. An investigating commission appointed by Governor Richard J. Hughes to study the cause of the 1967 Newark, New Jersey riot reported that a major contributing factor was the loss of confidence in the police because of law-enforcement corruption in gambling. The National Advisory Commission on Civil Disorders noted that organized crime activities, together with poverty and violence, foster the cynical lesson that the path to success is through criminal means:

> With the father absent and the mother working, many ghetto children spend the bulk of their time on the streets—the streets of a crime-ridden, violence-prone and poverty-stricken world. The image of success in this world is not that of the "solid citizen," the responsible husband and father, but rather that of the "hustler" who takes care of himself by exploiting others. The dope sellers and the numbers runners are the "successful" men because their earnings far outstrip those men who try to climb the economic ladder in honest ways.
>
> Young people in the ghetto are acutely conscious of a system which appears to offer rewards to those who illegally exploit others, and failure to those who struggle under traditional responsibilities. Under these circumstances, many adopt exploitation and the "hustle" as a way of life, disclaiming both work and marriage in favor of casual and temporary liaisons. This pattern reinforces itself from one generation to the next, creating a "culture of poverty" and an ingrained cynicism about society and its institutions.[86]

While government agencies pour millions of dollars into the ghetto, much of it winds up in the hands of the syndicate racketeers. The Chairman of the New York State Joint Legislative Committee on Crime estimated that in one recent year "$223,000,000 was siphoned out of the Central Harlem, South Bronx, and Bedford-Stuyvesant ghettos by numbers bankers and narcotics pushers . . . while Federal, state and city welfare funds pumped into the same communities totaled $272,000,000."[87] In parts of Westchester County, New York, organized crime has been reportedly an effective stumbling block to further progress in areas of housing-code enforcement, urban renewal, school integration, and drug control. The perpetuation of slum conditions and the decline of a community are apparently viewed as in the best financial interests of the syndicate. As one organized crime member has put it: "You make more money out of a Harlem than a Scarsdale"—the latter, a rich New York suburban community.[88]

Yet it is also clear that many ghetto dwellers are ambivalent toward organized crime. Many of the criminal activities—gambling, prostitution, loansharking, selling and buying stolen merchandise—are not necessarily viewed as socially harmful (a view shared by many Americans). Drug trafficking, however, is more widely despised. Heroin addiction, for example, is often thought to be a conspiracy on the part of the white establishment to kill off or control ("chemically imprison") rebellious young blacks or Puerto Ricans. While assigning most of the blame to *outside* social forces— especially the Italian-American syndicates for importing drugs and the white-controlled police for permitting their sale in the ghetto community— there is still frequently a begrudging admiration for successful black and Puerto Rican drug "pushers." In answer to the question of why so many ghetto dwellers are sympathetic to and even envious of their peers who have achieved success in organized crime, Ianni says:

> First of all, organized crime is accurately viewed by them in many ways as merely one end of the American business and industrial structure and, as such, is viewed more as a business venture than as a moral sin. Although organized crime is an illicit enterprise, it follows many of the same rules as the American business system. Ghetto dwellers view organized crime from the same perspective many Americans adopt when they regard the American system of business enterprise. That is, they envy it and criticize it at the same time. The line between sharp business practice or successful political machination and crime is thin and can scarcely be distinguished by many Americans.[89]

Further, as Ianni points out, it is the "poverty and powerlessness" of this vast underclass struggling for survival that helps shape the moral climate which fosters acceptance of syndicate activities in the ghetto:

> Like most Americans living in our consumer society, ghetto dwellers are hungry for money and for the goods and services it can procure. They have accepted the American achievement model of striving for success and security. Yet they are cut off from many legitimate ways of obtaining financial security, and, at the same time, they have fewer ways than white Americans to achieve the psychological security that can reduce the incidence of crime. When a man is financially secure, is happy and secure in his work, has a stable family life and lives in a stable community, he has little reason to consider criminal activity as a vocational possibility. But Blacks and Puerto Ricans like other ethnics before them see organized crime as one of the few routes to success, to financial and thus psychological security, open to them. In every society, criminals tend to develop when social conditions seem to offer no other way of escaping bondage. Poverty and powerlessness are at the root of both community acceptance of organized crime and recruitment into its networks. Conditions of poverty also nurture community desire for the services organized criminal operations provide. Escapism accounts in part for both widespread drug use and numbers gambling; the resentment poverty and powerlessness brings in the

subordinated population makes drugs and gambling attractive as mechanisms of rebellion. Organized crime is esteemed for the very reason that society outlaws it.[90]

PROSPECTS

The federal government is currently involved in a spirited if faltering "war" against organized crime. Under the direction of the Department of Justice, so-called strike forces—consisting of centralized teams of federal lawyers and investigators from several different federal agencies—have fanned out across the nation zeroing in on syndicate operations in a number of major cities during the past several years. Although many persons have been arrested and convicted, including some alleged bosses of major Italian-American crime "families," there is no evidence that these illicit enterprises have suffered irreparable damage.[91] Their activities continue to flourish, and there appears to be no shortage of aspiring talent to fill the vacated positions at the top. Much like any modern sizable business, but unlike the criminal gangs of the past, the successful criminal syndicate operates regardless of changes in individual personnel. As G. Robert Blakey points out, no one individual is indispensable: "The killing of Jessie, for example, ended the James gang; the deportation of Luciano merely resulted in the leadership passing to Frank Costello."[92]

These periodic crusades undoubtedly are appreciated by a large segment of the public, as were the investigations into organized crime over the last thirty years stemming from the Kefauver and McClellan Senate committee hearings in the 1950s and 1960s. However, the difficulties in achieving any significant and lasting results from these well-intentioned efforts are not well understood by the American public.

In the face of the latest federal crusade against organized crime, some of the higher-level participants in the well-established criminal syndicates are likely to tighten up their security defenses, to strengthen their arrangements to secure immunity from law enforcement, to resort to legal evasive tactics, to exercise more caution, and perhaps even to retrench further in certain high-risk areas. Convictions of some mostly low-ranking members of these illicit enterprises, temporarily disrupting certain operations, are highly probable. But if our analysis is essentially correct, the prospects of delivering a deathblow to the activities of organized crime in the near future are unlikely. This assertion is not put forth as a counsel of despair, nor is it meant to imply that there are no concrete steps that might be taken to curb more effectively the operations of organized crime in America. Rather it is a plea for the recognition of the interrelatedness of these criminal activities with much of the American way of life and for a more realistic assessment of the magnitude of the task in launching any "war" on organized crime.

As long as we attempt to blame organized crime on individually mal-adjusted "foreigners" and ignore the complicity of law enforcement and political officials; as long as we persist in equating "sinful" moral behavior with crime and thereby make illegal the activity in which significant segments of the American public wish to indulge; as long as businessmen show little interest in persons with whom they do business and are willing to purchase "bargain" (stolen) merchandise; as long as we accord a higher value to the symbols of individual success than to the means of their attainment, and invite all comers to compete for these rewards but restrict the opportunities for their realization from various segments of the population; as long as our culture rewards and encourages exploitative acquisitive behavior—in short, as long as we cling to various myths and cherish certain cultural values, legal policies, and social practices, large-scale syndicated crime is likely to continue to flourish in America. When we are willing to sacrifice and modify selected portions of the American way, only then will our attempts to cope with organized crime have any meaningful chance of success. We cannot, in Walter Lippmann's words, continue to defy the devil with a wooden sword.

FOOTNOTES

1 Dwight C. Smith, Jr., "Mafia: The Prototypical Alien Conspiracy," *Annals*, 423 (January 1976), p. 76.
2 Donald R. Cressey, "Methodological Problems in the Study of Organized Crime as a Social Problem," *Annals*, 374 (November 1967), pp. 104–105.
3 Gus Tyler, "The Roots of Organized Crime," *Crime & Delinquency*, 8 (October 1962), p. 334.
4 Herbert A. Bloch and Gilbert Geis, *Man, Crime, and Society*, Random House, New York, 1962, pp. 244–245.
5 Daniel Bell, "Crime as an American Way of Life: A Queer Ladder of Social Mobility," *The End of Ideology*, Free Press, New York, 1965, p. 128.
6 Herbert L. Packer, *The Limits of the Criminal Sanction*, Stanford University Press, Stanford, Calif., 1968, p. 279.
7 Thomas C. Schelling, "Economic Analysis and Organized Crime," in John E. Conklin (ed.), *The Crime Establishment*, Prentice-Hall, Englewood Cliffs, N.J., 1973, p. 81.
8 Peter Maas, *The Valachi Papers*, G. P. Putnam's, New York, 1968, p. 274. See also Donald R. Cressey, *Theft of the Nation*, Harper & Row, New York, 1969, pp. 77–91; New York State Commission on Investigation, "The Loan-Shark Racket," in Francis A. J. Ianni and Elizabeth Reuss-Ianni (eds.), *The Crime Society: Organized Crime and Corruption in America*, New American Library, New York, 1976, pp. 201–227.
9 Quoted in Nicholas Pileggi, "The Mafia: Serving Your Community Since 1890," *New York*, July 24, 1972, p. 46.
10 Pileggi, "The Mafia," p. 46.

11 Vincent Teresa with Thomas C. Renner, *My Life in the Mafia*, Fawcett, Greenwich, Conn., 1974, p. 142.
12 Roy R. Silver, "Loan-Shark Victim's Ordeal Described," *The New York Times*, Oct. 5, 1973, p. 34.
13 Lowell L. Kuehn, "Syndicated Crime in America," in Edward Sagarin and Fred Montanino (eds.), *Deviants: Voluntary Actors in a Hostile World*, General Learning Press, Morristown, N.J., 1977, p. 165.
14 Maas, *The Valachi Papers*, p. 159.
15 President's Commission on Law Enforcement and Administration of Justice, *Task Force Report: Crime and Its Impact—An Assessment*, U.S. Government Printing Office, Washington, D.C., 1967, p. 43.
16 Francis A. J. Ianni, *Black Mafia*, Simon and Schuster, New York, 1974, p. 11.
17 "Cigarette Smuggling Fills Coffers of N.Y. Mob," *Syracuse Post-Standard*, Feb. 24, 1975, pp. 1, 3.
18 "Cigarette Smuggling Fills Coffers of N.Y. Mob," p. 1.
19 Charles H. McCaghy, *Deviant Behavior*, Macmillan, New York, 1976, p. 232.
20 President's Commission on Law Enforcement and Administration of Justice, *The Challenge of Crime in a Free Society*, U.S. Government Printing Office, Washington, D.C., 1967, pp. 189–191. See also "How the Mafia Invades Business," *U.S. News and World Report*, June 13, 1977, pp. 21–23; Gus Tyler, "The Crime Corporation," in Abraham S. Blumberg (ed.), *Current Perspectives on Criminal Behavior*, Knopf, New York, 1974, pp. 204–205; Denny F. Pace and Jimmie C. Styles, *Organized Crime*, Prentice-Hall, Englewood Cliffs, N.J., 1975, pp. 181–211.
21 President's Commission, *The Challenge of Crime in a Free Society*, p. 190.
22 Maas, *The Valachi Papers*, pp. 274–275.
23 Pileggi, "The Mafia," p. 46.
24 "The Mafia: Big, Bad and Booming," *Time*, May 16, 1977, p. 40.
25 "Pan Am Gets a Big Discount," *The New York Times*, June 2, 1974, p. 3E.
26 Ralph C. Thomas, "Organized Crime in the Construction Industry," *Crime & Delinquency*, 23 (July 1977), p. 309.
27 Robert K. Woetzel, "The Genesis of Crime," *Current History*, 52 (June 1967), p. 323.
28 Gus Tyler, "An Interdisciplinary Attack on Organized Crime," *Annals*, 347 (May 1963), pp. 107–108. See also Frederic D. Homer, *Guns and Garlic*, Purdue University Studies, West Lafayette, Ind., 1974, Ch. 2; Dwight C. Smith, Jr., *The Mafia Mystique*, Basic Books, New York, 1975; Joseph L. Albini, *The American Mafia: Genesis of a Legend*, Appleton-Century-Crofts, New York, 1971, Ch. 5.
29 Quoted in Francis A. J. Ianni and Elizabeth Reuss-Ianni, "The Godfather Is Going Out of Business," *Psychology Today*, 9 (December 1975), p. 88. See also Humbert S. Nelli, *The Business of Crime: Italians and Syndicate Crime in the United States*, Oxford University Press, New York, 1976; Francis A. J. Ianni with Elizabeth Reuss-Ianni, *A Family Business*, New American Library, New York, 1973.
30 McCaghy, *Deviant Behavior*, p. 239.
31 Cressey, *Theft of the Nation*, pp. 35–47. For a contrary view, see Alan A. Block,

"History and the Study of Organized Crime," *Urban Life*, 6 (January 1978), pp. 455–471; Smith, Jr., *The Mafia Mystique*.

32 Bloch and Geis, *Man, Crime, and Society*, pp. 220–221. See also Charlotte Curtis, "Pal Joey—A Study in Gangster Chic," in Nicholas Gage (ed.), *Mafia, U.S.A.*, Dell, New York, 1972, pp. 251–255.

33 President's Commission, *The Challenge of Crime in a Free Society*, p. 188.

34 Ralph Salerno and John S. Tompkins, *The Crime Confederation*, Doubleday, Garden City, N.Y., 1969, p. 199.

35 Salerno and Tompkins, *The Crime Confederation*, pp. 201–202.

36 *Newsweek*, Apr. 5, 1971, p. 23. See also Tom Buckley, "The Mafia Tries a New Tune," *Harper's* (August 1971), pp. 46–56.

37 See Stewart Holbrook, *Age of the Moguls*, Doubleday, Garden City, N.Y., 1953.

38 Martin Luther King, Jr., "Beyond the Los Angeles Riots," *Saturday Review*, Nov. 13, 1965, p. 34.

39 Salerno and Tompkins, *The Crime Confederation*, p. 376.

40 Salerno and Tompkins, *The Crime Confederation*, p. 378.

41 Martin R. Haskell and Lewis Yablonsky, *Criminology: Crime and Criminality*, Rand McNally, Chicago, 1978, p. 157.

42 Quoted in Salerno and Tompkins, *The Crime Confederation*, p. 379.

43 Quoted in Richard A. Cloward and Lloyd E. Ohlin, *Delinquency and Opportunity*, Free Press, New York, 1960, p. 201.

44 Quoted in Cloward and Ohlin, *Delinquency and Opportunity*, p. 201. See also Lena Williams, "Numbers Game Is Still Thriving Despite the OTB," *The New York Times*, Apr. 25, 1978, pp. 35, 65.

45 Ianni, *Black Mafia*, pp. 13–14. Copyright © 1974 by Francis A. J. Ianni. Reprinted by permission of Simon & Schuster, a Division of Gulf and Western Corporation.

46 Henry S. Ruth, Jr., "Why Organized Crime Thrives," *Annals*, 374, (November 1967), p. 119.

47 Quoted in Ruth, Jr., "Why Organized Crime Thrives," p. 119.

48 Quoted in Ruth, Jr., "Why Organized Crime Thrives," p. 121.

49 See Alexander Heard, *The Costs of Democracy*, University of North Carolina Press, Chapel Hill, N.C., 1960, pp. 154–168; John A. Gardiner and David J. Olson (eds.), *Theft of the City: Readings on Corruption in Urban America*, Indiana University Press, Bloomington, Ind., 1974.

50 Maas, *The Valachi Papers*, pp. 272–273. See also John A. Gardiner, "Wincanton: The Politics of Corruption," in Jack D. Douglas and John M. Johnson (eds.), *Official Deviance*, Lippincott, Philadelphia, 1977, pp. 50–69.

51 See Cressey, *Theft of the Nation*, pp. 78–80; Walter Goodman, "A Good Friend at City Hall," in Gage (ed.), *Mafia, U.S.A.*, pp. 259–279.

52 Norton Mockridge and Robert H. Prall, *The Big Fix*, Henry Holt, New York, 1954.

53 Sandy Smith, "The Mob," *Life*, Dec. 6, 1968, p. 40. See also Robert Davis, "Braasch, 18 Others Guilty in Police Shakedown Trial," *Chicago Tribune*, Oct. 6, 1973.

54 Smith, "The Mob," p. 40.

55 See Special Senate Committee to Investigate Organized Crime in Interstate

Commerce (Kefauver Committee), *Third Interim Report*, U.S. Senate Report No. 307, 82nd Congress, 1st Session, U.S. Government Printing Office, Washington, D.C., 1951, pp. 338–339.

56 Ralph Salerno, "Organized Crime," *Crime & Delinquency*, 15 (July 1969), pp. 338–339.

57 *Newsweek*, Dec. 29, 1969, pp. 21–22.

58 *Newsweek*, Jan. 19, 1970, p. 23. See also Thomas A. Hoge, "New Jersey—The Friendly State," in Gage (ed.), *Mafia, U.S.A.*, pp. 280–289; Ron Porambo, "An Autopsy of Newark," in Gardiner and Olson (eds.), *Theft of the City*, pp. 85–96.

59 Ruth, Jr., "Why Organized Crime Thrives," p. 120.

60 Quoted in Cloward and Ohlin, *Delinquency and Opportunity*, p. 200. See also Lawrence W. Sherman (ed.), *Police Corruption*, Anchor, Doubleday, Garden City, N.Y., 1974.

61 Kuehn, "Syndicated Crime in America," p. 184. See also William J. Chambliss, "Vice, Corruption, Bureaucracy and Power," in Douglas and Johnson (eds.), *Official Deviance*, pp. 306–329.

62 Haskell and Yablonsky, *Criminology: Crime and Criminality*, pp. 160–161. See also Knapp Commission, "Police Corruption in New York City," in Gardiner and Olson (eds.), *Theft of the City*, pp. 175–191; Peter K. Manning and Lawrence J. Redlinger, "The Invitational Edges of Corruption," in Douglas and Johnson (eds.), *Official Deviance*, pp. 284–305.

63 Cressey, *Theft of the Nation*, p. 263.

64 Quoted in Cressey, *Theft of the Nation*, p. 267. See also Nicholas Gage, "Organized Crime in Court," in Gardiner and Olson (eds.), *Theft of the City*, pp. 165–174.

65 Ruth, Jr., "Why Organized Crime Thrives," pp. 121–122.

66 Caroline Rand Herron, "Boston Was Burning," *The New York Times*, Oct. 23, 1977, p. 4E.

67 Herron, "Boston Was Burning," p. 4E.

68 Kuehn, "Syndicated Crime in America," p. 181.

69 Jack Nelson and Bill Hazlett, "Teamsters' Ties to Mafia—and to White House," *Los Angeles Times*, May 31, 1973, pp. 1, 22–24.

70 *Newsweek*, Aug. 23, 1976, p. 38.

71 Ianni, *Black Mafia*, pp. 217–219.

72 Cressey, *Theft of the Nation*, p. 282.

73 Cressey, *Theft of the Nation*, p. 281.

74 President's Commission, *The Challenge of Crime in a Free Society*, p. 191.

75 Cressey, "Methodological Problems in the Study of Organized Crime as a Social Problem," pp. 105, 108.

76 Cressey, "Methodological Problems in the Study of Organized Crime as a Social Problem," p. 108.

77 President's Commission, *The Challenge of Crime in a Free Society*, p. 189.

78 Teresa and Renner, *My Life in the Mafia*, p. 161.

79 President's Commission, *The Challenge of Crime in a Free Society*, p. 188.

80 Cressey, *Theft of the Nation*, p. 119. In New York City, however, recent studies indicate that with the emergence of legal off-track horse betting and the shift of illegal bookmaking toward other sporting events, there has been a significant

increase in the number of competing independent operators largely free of syndicate control. See Peter Kihss, "Mob's Role Discounted in Gambling," *The New York Times*, June 26, 1978, p. 1A.

81   Cited in Francis A. J. Ianni, "New Mafia: Black, Hispanic and Italian Styles," *Society*, 11 (March/April 1974), pp. 36–37.

82   Paul Delany, "Legality Sought For the Numbers," *The New York Times*, Sept. 7, 1973, p. 11.

83   See Edwin M. Schur and Hugo A. Bedau, *Victimless Crimes: Two Sides of a Controversy*, Prentice-Hall, Englewood Cliffs, N.J., 1974; Gilbert Geis, *One Eyed Justice*, Drake, New York, 1974; Alexander B. Smith and Harriet Pollack, *Some Sins Are Not Crimes*, Franklin Watts, New York, 1975.

84   Rufus King, "Looking For the Lost Mafia," *Harper's*, (January 1977), pp. 74–75.

85   Ruth, Jr., "Why Organized Crime Thrives," p. 116. See also Conklin (ed.), *The Crime Establishment*, pp. 1–2.

86   *Report of the National Advisory Commission on Civil Disorders*, U.S. Government Printing Office, Washington, D.C., 1968, pp. 129–130.

87   Salerno and Tompkins, *The Crime Confederation*, p. 272.

88   Quoted in Ruth, Jr., "Why Organized Crime Thrives," p. 118. See also New York State Crime Committee, "Organized Crime in the Ghetto," in Gardiner and Olson (eds.), *Theft of the City*, pp. 372–381.

89   Ianni, *Black Mafia*, pp. 324–325.

90   Ianni, *Black Mafia*, p. 325. Copyright © 1974 by Francis A. J. Ianni. Reprinted by permission of Simon & Schuster, a Division of Gulf and Western Corporation.

91   See U.S. Comptroller General, *War on Organized Crime Faltering—Federal Strike Forces Not Getting the Job Done*, Washington, D.C., 1977.

92   G. Robert Blakey, "Organized Crime in the United States," *Current History*, 52 (June 1967), p. 329.

Chapter 5

Drugs and the Medicalization of Human Problems

The concern about the use of illegal drugs by young people has overshadowed the tremendous increase in the use of *legal* drugs in America. Although the nation has witnessed a news media blitzkrieg on the problems of heroin, cocaine, LSD, and marijuana, the media have paid much less attention to the consequences of psychoactive drugs (tranquilizers, sedatives, stimulants, mood-elevators, antidepressants) available by prescription or administered involuntarily. Since the 1930s, the pharmacological industry has synthesized and manufactured thousands of new kinds of psychoactive drugs, which has contributed to a major change in drug-taking patterns in America. Social scientists, however, have only recently begun to examine seriously the vast ramifications of this proliferating drug technology on the culture and structure of American life.

While there are potentially enormous human benefits to be derived from the application of chemistry, it is also clear that there are profound risks in this growing tendency to prescribe or coercively administer mood-altering drugs—especially for the creation of a society that is responsive to human needs. And with the development of this powerful chemical technology, an increasing barrage of social criticism has appeared warning of the dangers from this "drug revolution." Moral entrepreneurs and incipient social movements posing alternative values have begun to challenge the dominant view that medical drug use is the most effective and humane way to deal with not only persons considered deviant but also the varied kinds of existential discomfort in the modern world. This chapter explores some of these challenges to the dominant medical and psychiatric view of human behavior and the growing conflict over conceptions of conformity, deviance, and legal drug abuse in America.

DRUG ABUSE: JUST WHAT THE DOCTOR ORDERED?

Particularly disturbing to many observers is the now widespread use of mood-altering drugs for what might be called the "human problems of living." People are becoming less and less willing to accept psychological discomfort and anguish—the normal trials and tribulations of life—as a natural consequence of human existence. It would appear that much of the medical profession, in fact, has come to view loneliness, anxiety, conflict, or unhappiness as symptoms of "psychic distress," an ailment to be corrected, eliminated, or "cured" with drugs. A recent medical-journal drug advertisement asks: "What Makes A Woman Cry? A man? Another woman? Three kids? No kids at all? Wrinkles? You name it . . . If she is depressed, consider Pertofane."[1]

Physicians and the pharmacological industry have combined to hold out the promise of putting an end to personal distress through chemistry. Drug manufacturers seeking new markets and bigger profits urge everyone to feel better fast ("relief is only a swallow away"), and attempt to persuade physicians and the public that *unpleasant human feelings are abnormal—* an "illness" that should be corrected with drugs. The drug industry cajoles and pampers the 180,000 physicians in America. The large pharmaceutical firms provide not only plentiful free samples, but spend over $1 billion annually on advertising directed solely to physicians—over $5,000 per doctor per year.[2] An advertisement for a tranquilizer in the *Journal of the American College Health Association*, for example, shows a worried young college woman with books in arm. The caption reads: "Exposure to new friends and other influences may force her to re-evaluate herself and her goals. . . . Her newly stimulated intellectual curiosity may make her more sensitive to and apprehensive about national and world conditions." The ad suggests that Librium "can help her get back on her feet." To define normal interpersonal relationships and anxiety as medical and psychiatric problems; to prescribe tranquilizers for the normal problems and stresses involved in the exposure to new ideas in college—is not this kind of pseudoscientific labeling itself, asks psychologist J. Maurice Rogers, a socially irresponsible form of "drug abuse"?[3]

In the United States, doctor-patient visits reportedly last an average of 14 minutes. In about two-thirds of these contacts, the physician prescribes a drug (one-third of them a mood-altering medication).[4] These statistics would suggest that the medical profession is severely drug-dependent. In 1975, for example, doctors wrote 61 million prescriptions for Valium alone, a tranquilizer prescribed for an emotional state vaguely described as anxiety. It is now not only the biggest-selling tranquilizer but the most extensively prescribed drug of any kind in the world, with an estimated 15 percent of the American population taking it, especially women. According to some estimates, at least one-third of all American adults have used minor tranquilizers, with sales growing at the rate of 5 to 6 million prescriptions a year.[5]

From an examination of advertisements for Valium, Librium, and other tranquilizers, it would appear that females are not only the weaker sex but also the sicker sex. They are the subjects in the great majority of these medical-journal ads. According to feminist Deborah Larned, women are so often portrayed in a humdrum domestic setting that "domestic unhappiness" has become a new kind of pseudomedical disorder. The haggard and irritable mother suffers from "housewife's syndrome," signaling the need for a mood-altering drug remedy:

> In a typical Valium ad, a middle-aged woman in a rumpled housecoat and slippers is slouched in a chair surrounded by an ill-made bed, a broom, and pile of laundry. WEARINESS WITHOUT CAUSE, the headline reads. The woman has "psychic tension with depressive symptomatology." Aside from the obvious implication that difficulty with housework may be a sign of mental disorder necessitating chemotherapy, there is the suggestion that the woman's reluctance to do these tasks stems from nothing but "psychic tension." The text goes on: "When the patient complains of fatigue, and you can find no organic cause, you recognize that it may serve her as a means of *avoiding responsibilities* or facing an emotional problem."[6]

Larned contends that such tranquilizer ads come perilously close to a kind of "political pacification" by suggesting that it is psychiatrically acceptable and medically ethical to prescribe drugs that depress the central nervous system so that females may more willingly accept their traditional role "responsibilities." What such "complaining" housewives need, Larned angrily suggests, is not a dose of chemicals but a large dose of women's liberation. And as Robert Seidenberg has wryly noted, perhaps a more useful recommendation by the physician would be to use the prescription money "as a down payment on an electric dishwasher, or a more radical change in life style," instead of suggesting that the woman be *tranquilized* into accepting her life as it is.[7]

One of the most blatantly exploitive attempts to redefine everyday anxiety situations as a form of "mental illness" featured a two-page medical-journal advertisement for Serentil, a powerful tranquilizer. (This drug has been used to treat mental disorders such as schizophrenia with such possible side effects as vomiting, dizziness, rash, and a variety of cardiovascular ailments.) Pictured in the ad was the face of an anguished woman with the bold caption: FOR THE ANXIETY THAT COMES FROM NOT FITTING IN. The ad suggested the use of Serentil for such patients as

> . . . the newcomer in town who can't make friends and the organization man who can't adjust to altered status within his company, the woman who can't get along with her new daughter-in-law, the executive who can't accept retirement. . . .[8]

In fine print the ad cautioned that while no causal connection has been demonstrated, "several sudden and unexpected deaths apparently due to cardiac arrest have occurred in patients . . . while taking the drug."

Over three-quarters of advertising in the *Journal of the American Medical Association* is paid for by pharmaceutical companies. In fact, the AMA derives over half of its funds from the drug industry, prompting this indictment of the medical profession by U.S. Senator Mike Gravel:

> The profession, especially its supposed leading organization, the American Medical Association, deserves ethical and moral blame for developing a severe drug-dependence problem of its own. Apparently for no better reason than money, the AMA publishes even the most aggressively exploitive ads, including those that are patently in violation of the association's own stated policy on drug advertising. There has been no major effort undertaken to unite the profession against the pharmaceutical industry, and anyone suggesting to the AMA that doctors should receive their information on drugs solely from unbiased scientific sources is likely to receive the answer that such a step would mean higher subscription rates for the journal.[9]

THE MEDICAL MODEL OF HUMAN PROBLEMS

The tremendous increase in the use of legal mood-altering drugs is symptomatic of the vast hegemony of the reigning medical model of human behavior. This medical perspective tends to locate the source of a person's troubles—as well as the place of treatment—in the *individual* rather than in the structural flaws of the society or in the patient's immediate social environment. The prescription of a drug by a physician, especially, places the definition of the problem as legitimately within the medical arena of health and illness, strengthening the belief that the problem is basically physiological and located within the body (or, to a lesser degree, in the individual's mind).

In recent decades, the powerful medical profession has widened its jurisdiction to cover more and more kinds of "societal ills" and troubling personal behavior which formerly were not considered to be within the sphere of medical diagnosis, understanding, and treatment (e.g., political deviance, poverty, drinking habits, obesity, violence, delinquency, sexual behavior, misbehavior, learning problems, heroin addiction, anxiety, sadness, rage). Rather than locating the source of the distress, for example, in blocked economic opportunities, in repressive institutions, or in frustrated human needs, the medical model tends to search for more individual defects, such as biological malfunctions (biochemical, neurological, nutritional, or other organic conditions) or psychopathological traits in the person.

Peter Schrag illustrates the alarming ease with which officials in the mental-health, social-service, or criminal-justice systems apply such medical labels and drug "remedies" to behavior they designate as deviant:

> In New York, a mother of three, desperate to find housing for her family, gets into a shouting match with a public-housing official; the police are called and the woman is shipped to a mental-health clinic, where she is diagnosed as a paranoid schizophrenic and drugged; her children are sent to a juvenile home. In Southern California, a group of school children who disturb their teachers with their adolescent energy are sent to the school doctor, who instructs that they take the psychostimulant Ritalin to help them sit quietly in class. In San Francisco, an unemployed schoolteacher appears at a hospital personnel office looking for a job. "The next thing I knew," she says, "I was being held for observation because they decided I was dangerous to myself and others." The ex-teacher was given antidepressants and was allowed to go home three days later only after promising to continue to take her pills; she was also compelled to pay a $225 bill for her "treatment."[10]

When such medical definitions of human problems become dominant, however, other competing definitions are ignored and alternative modes of intervention closed. The problem becomes *individualized, depoliticized,* and entrusted to medical specialists, thereby often removing it from the arena of public debate. Medically prescribed "remedies" to alleviate the disorders of personal adjustment thus become the focus of public policies, rather than the kinds of fundamental social changes and reforms that might more effectively alleviate the stress-producing social conditions.[11]

Even more frightening to civil libertarians is the threat to individual freedom and self-responsibility posed by this facile use of medical language to characterize departures from dominant social norms. Once the deviant is assigned the status of "patient" and becomes the object of "treatment," constitutional protections of due process and the right to privacy are often effectively bypassed. Since the treatment is ostensibly for the person's own good, no humane and normal person could rightfully object to curing such "sick" people; and the complaining patient who protests such coercive treatment is only demonstrating how sick he or she really is. The sometimes tragic result of such absolutist logic is dramatically evident in the confinement and eventual death of an "eccentric" named Robert Friedman, whom the police arrested in Chicago for trying to panhandle a dime in a bus station:

> Friedman had supported himself most of his life and had never been in trouble; but when the cops discovered that he was carrying nearly $25,000 in cash, all of it his own, he was immediately sent to a psychiatric ward for observation, and heavily drugged with tranquilizers. Five days later, acting on the recommendation of a Cuban-born psychiatrist, who spoke only in broken English and who labeled Friedman "schizophrenic," a judge committed Friedman to a mental hospital to protect him from people who, the judge said, might be after his cash. Friedman begged the judge to release him and order the money returned. Until he was laid off a few months before, he had worked steadily as a clerk-stenographer; the rent on his apartment was paid; he had been convicted of no crime; he even promised to stop panhandling and put his money back in a bank. A devout Jew, what he most wanted was to go to Israel and, eventually, to get married. The judge committed him because "letting you go would mean you would be unable to take care of yourself."
>
> Friedman would never be a free man again, nor would he ever again see his money. When he died fourteen months later, more than half of it was gone. The State of Illinois had taken $800 a month for his treatment—largely drugs administered against his will; legal fees took another $5,000. . . . More important, the drugging and brutality of the hospitalization had turned Friedman into a pathetic shell who defecated on himself, ran naked around the hospital corridors, and could no longer understand what was happening to him. When he learned of Friedman's condition, even the judge who committed him was shocked; he allowed Friedman to be released to a nursing home, but by then he could no longer function. When he died a few months later, the official cause of death was listed as cardiac arrest brought on by pneumonia. He was forty-four.[12]

MASKING SOCIAL PROBLEMS AND MEDICALIZING SOCIAL DEVIANCE

The vast prestige and credibility of medical science and chemical technology may function to obscure the causes of not only personal problems but also complex social problems, thereby indirectly perpetuating oppressive social conditions. For instance, Dr. Henry Brill, a former Superintendent of Pilgrim State Hospital in New York, has suggested that "crime in the streets" is a form of "pathological aggression." He put forth psychopharmacology as the solution. Several years ago, a distinguished social psychologist even seriously proposed a pill to solve the problem of war! And today in many of our inner-city ghettos we offer the black heroin addict an equally addicting licit drug—methadone—a Band-Aid remedy, argues David Lewis, instead of the kinds of deep-seated reforms in American life that might more effectively deal with the crippling despair and bleak future that confronts him.[13] As David Bazelon, Chief Justice of the U.S. Circuit Court of Appeals for the District of Columbia, recently asked: "What can psychiatry offer a beleaguered mother with no income, bad housing, and children who lack rudimentary care? . . . Should she be treated with antidepressants for her depression, tranquilizers for her hallucinations and therapy for her alcoholism? One does not need to be a psychiatrist to see that treatment is doomed to failure unless the conditions fostering such disabilities are ameliorated."[14]

What problems do we create—and what failures do we hide—when we tranquilize so-called "hyperactive" school kids who "cause trouble"? In Omaha, Nebraska, school officials discovered that between 5 and 10 percent of the 62,000 elementary school children were being given medically prescribed amphetamines (such as Ritalin and Dexedrine) to control their fidgety restlessness or lack of attention in the classroom. Grade school children in the city were carrying potentially dangerous drugs in their pockets and lunch pails. According to the assistant school superintendent, "They were trading pills on the school grounds. One kid would say, 'Here, you try my yellow one, and I'll try your pink one.'"[15]

Perhaps as many as 1 million school children in America have been diagnosed as "hyperactive" or suffering from "minimal brain dysfunction" or other equally vague syndromes and been drugged with amphetamine-type drugs, often for several years and sometimes without any medical examination. According to studies by several critics, many of these children are not really hyperactive at all or suffering from any organic disorder.[16] These and other stigmatizing labels are pinned on normal children who simply refuse to submit to what their teachers or parents consider obligatory school and family routines. Wholesale medication thus becomes a convenient tool for enforcing behavioral conformity, masking the inadequacies of teachers or parents by blaming their victims. In such an atmosphere, disruptiveness easily becomes translated into sickness, nonconformity is dealt with by "treatment," and all school and family demands and practices are justified. Moreover, not only does such drugging often brand children as "troublemakers," but in many cases it causes them to suffer from headaches, dizziness, loss of appetite, insomnia, nightmares, hallucinations, weight loss, a permanent stunting of growth, and other serious ailments.

Central to the major thrust of this humanist critique is the conviction that by delegating the management of disturbed and disturbing people to drugs, we make it easier for *others* to cope or to control such persons; but we also divert attention from the behavior of relatives, officials, employers, teachers, nurses, institutional attendants, or other persons whose actions contribute to the anxiety or unhappiness of the troublesome individual. The readiness to turn to drugs for "therapy" may diminish pressures to seek more fundamental approaches to the sources of the individual's distress, which may reside in racist and sexist institutions, in the alienation produced by our organization of work, in persistent structural unemployment, in the way we socialize and constrain our young people, or in the lack of meaningful roles for the aged.

Moreover, the adverse side effects of this propensity to turn to drugs are sometimes horrendous. A young woman describes her frightening experiences under the influence of the institutionally administered heavy tranquilizer Thorazine:

> My tongue was so fuzzy, so thick, I could barely speak. Always I needed water and even with it my loose tongue often could not shape the words. It was so hard to think, the effort was so great; more often than not I would fall into a stupor of not caring or I would go to sleep. . . . I could not focus my blurred eyes to read and I always fell asleep at a film. People's voices came through filtered, strange. They could not penetrate my Thorazine fog; and I could not escape my drug prison.
>
> Yet to detail the physical suffering caused by these drugs is to touch only on one aspect of the pain they cause. Psychologically and emotionally they are devastating. They cause sensations—drowsiness, disorientation, shakiness, dry mouth, blurred vision, inability to concentrate—that would be enough to unnerve the strongest among us. . . . It is common practice among psychiatrists *not* to inform their patients that the disturbing things they are experiencing are drug induced. . . . My hands would shake as I held a coffee cup, my legs would beat a wild tattoo on the floor, and sometimes I would fall asleep in the middle of a conversation. I *knew* I was deteriorating, going slowly, surely insane. No one thought it necessary to advise me otherwise. "But why do you *think* people are looking at you strangely?" Dr. Sternfeld would ask. Why indeed?[17]

A young man describes his conception of the real meaning behind the textbook euphemisms that clinically describe a patient as experiencing a "state of indifference or apathy, with a drowsy feeling and motor retardation":

> After 10 days or so, the effects of the Prolixin began building up in my system and my body started going through pure hell. It's very hard to describe the effects of this drug and others like it, that's why we use strange words like "zombie." But in my case the experience became sheer torture. Different muscles began twitching. My mouth was like very dry cotton no matter how much water I drank. My tongue became all swollen up. My entire body felt like it was being twisted up in contortions inside by some unseen wringer. . . . But most disturbing of all was that I feared that all these excruciating experiences were in my mind, or caused by my mind—a sign of my supposed sickness. . . .[18]

Nelson Cruikshank, President of the National Council of Senior Citizens, points out that in nursing homes "exclusive use of tranquilizers can quickly reduce an ambulatory patient to a zombie, confining the patient to a chair or bed, causing the patient's muscles to atrophy from inaction, and causing general health to deteriorate quickly."[19] The long-term use of heavy tranquilizers like Thorazine to treat and manage elderly patients considered "mentally ill" in state hospitals has resulted in the recent discovery of a *physician-induced* condition known as tardive dyskinesia, unknown before the use of this drug. This disabling and disfiguring condition is a central nervous system disorder that has produced serious, irreversible neurological damage to thousands of patients. Its symptoms include:

> . . . involuntary movements especially affecting the lips and tongue, hands and fingers, and body posture. Speech may be seriously affected, the face may become distorted and subject to uncontrolled expressions, and sustained normal posture may become impossible.[20]

Such treatment of old people as useless cast-offs, to be kept drugged and out of sight until death relieves them of their misery, is symptomatic of what Phillip Slater calls the "Toilet Assumption" in dealing with troublesome problems in America:

> Our ideas about institutionalizing the aged, psychotic, retarded and infirm are based on a pattern of thought that we might call the Toilet Assumption—the notion that unwanted matter, unwanted difficulties, unwanted complexities and obstacles will disappear if they're removed from our immediate field of vision. . . . Our approach to social problems is to decrease their visibility: out of sight, out of mind. . . . The result of our social efforts has been to remove the underlying problems of our society farther and farther from daily experience and daily consciousness, and hence to decrease, in the mass of the population, the knowledge, skill, and motivation necessary to deal with them.[21]

Certainly the use of drugs provides a simple, low-cost, and efficient way to *manage* the elderly, the disturbed, and other troublesome persons, although there is no convincing evidence that psychoactive drugs are successful in ameliorating the causes of the person's disturbance or "curing" anybody of anything. But in terms of human and social costs, such self-perpetuating drug strategies are often highly destructive of human support systems. As psychologist Arnold Bernstein and sociologist Henry Lennard argue, we numb both our humanity and our social inventiveness by this blanket use of tranquilizers in nursing homes or hospitals to pacify elderly persons who have been isolated from their children and neighborhood. A group's ability to devise strategies of human relatedness atrophies— erodes—when we constantly reach for the prescription pad to deal with a middle-aged woman who is distressed over her daughter's rebellion, suffers from beatings by her husband, or experiences the loss of a loved one. When a person dies, for example, physicians commonly prescribe tranquilizers for the next of kin to deal with their "psychic distress." This heavy sedation may allow the grieving person to fulfill his or her social obligations at the funeral and other ritual occasions. But such medication also may deny the person the therapeutic function of openly expressing grief and may make it difficult for other relatives to share fully their empathy and closeness to resolve this inevitable and ultimate human experience. "Psychic distress most often is a condition of human existence. . . . [H]uman beings incapable of psychic distress would be robots or automatons, devoid of sensibility and responsiveness."[22]

POLITICAL CONTROL IN THE NAME OF HEALTH AND ILLNESS

There is also the even more ominous danger that drugs administered by the powerful to sedate, numb, restrict, and diminish social activity can become a potent instrument for political control—especially when directed at protesters, social activists, and prisoners. Casting "enemy deviants" into the sick role, to be dealt with through drug "therapy," is a powerful way for dominant groups in society to maintain conformity and the status quo. By defining the deviant's "behavioral disorder" as a symptom of illness, the *willful*, intentional quality of his social dissidence is diminished. Such seemingly merciful medical labels thus serve not only to reduce the responsibility of the deviant for his actions—calling for control through medical supervision or enforced therapy instead of criminal sanctions—but also to reduce the likelihood that such potentially contagious political behavior will be taken seriously and spread.

Clearly, designations of illness, disease, or behavior disorder can easily support dominant moral values, institutions, and political interests. Recall the nineteenth-century Victorian concept of masturbation: a form of illness and addiction requiring medical treatment. Or consider the racist conceptualization of the disease of drapetomania, an illness of the mind, formulated by the distinguished New Orleans physician, Samuel Cartwright, in 1851. His medical findings were reported in the prestigious *New Orleans Medical and Surgical Journal*. The disease of drapetomania afflicted only slaves. Its major symptom: running away.[23]

In the Soviet Union, the practice of incarcerating in prison hospitals outspoken political dissidents, drugged and diagnosed as suffering from "sluggish schizophrenia," offers chilling evidence that the right to dissent and the right to be different can become emasculated in a "therapeutic state." This new drug psychotechnology, together with neurosurgery and behavior modification, has obvious and dangerous implications for totalitarian control beyond Orwell's wildest dreams of *1984* or the terror of *One Flew over the Cuckoo's Nest*.[24]

The use of drugs as a means of social control is now commonplace in American prisons, which are often viewed as convenient laboratories to test the latest behavior-modifying drugs. Inmates who show "disrespect for authority" or highly politicized inmates who harbor "subversive beliefs" are considered particularly dangerous and sometimes become the research subjects of this powerful psychodrug technology. To control or terrorize troublesome inmates, drugs may even be administered that make the prisoner feel that he or she is dying:

> In one California prison, for example, the drug Anectine has been used to induce sensations of extreme terror, suffocation and imminent death in rebellious inmates. During these cataclysmic episodes, the authorities scream recriminations at the victim and warn him to reform or face further "treatment." Sexual deviance and stealing, as well as outbursts of physical violence, are "indications" for Anectine. Prolixin, also used in some prisons, is described by E. R. Squibb, its manufacturer, as a "highly potent behavior modifier with a markedly extended duration of effect." Prisoners protesting its use in testimony before the California State Committee on Penal Institutions said that it turns men into "somnambulists, robots and vegetables." Squibb allows that possible adverse side effects include a catatonic-like state, impotence, glaucoma and symptoms resembling Parkinsonian or a palsy-like syndrome along with the facial grimaces of encephalitis, which "persist after drug withdrawal, and in some patients appear to be irreversible." Other drug "therapies" include the use of anti-testosterones, which chemically castrate the victim.[25]

SOCIAL EXPECTATIONS AND CHEMICAL REMEDIES

In addition to the concern with the political uses of forced drugging and the possible erosion of civil liberties under the guise of medical treatment, a growing number of social critics are beginning to warn of the injurious consequences of the *conventional* reliance on medication throughout the general population. As noted earlier, many humanists particularly deplore the now ubiquitous use of psychoactive drugs simply to meet heightened expectations of social fulfillment in modern complex societies. Bernstein and Lennard contend that one of the major reasons people flock to doctor's offices is the high value our culture places on "mood, appearance or performance."[26] (An estimated 60 percent of the patients in a general practitioner's office or clinic are there for conditions with no apparent physical symptom.) People are troubled because they find it difficult to meet current social expectations concerning what they ought to be, ought to feel, or ought to get out of life. They're not as popular, successful, happy, thin, beautiful, or energetic as they feel they should be, while television commercials implore them to "look better, feel younger," "grab for all the gusto you can get," and "calm those jangled nerves." For more and more people, drugs obtained from the pharmacist hold out the promise of instant relief for psychological pains, just as we have Rolaids in America for instant relief of indigestion and Revlon for instant beauty and youth. Within a 24- to 36-

hour period, an estimated 50 to 80 percent of American adults will have consumed one or more "medical drugs."[27] As Irving Zola notes, the American pharmacological cafeteria provides drugs for nearly every mood:

> to help us sleep or keep us awake
> to enhance our appetite or decrease it
> to tone down our energy level or to increase it
> to relieve our depression or stimulate our interest.[28]

One of the most disturbing consequences of this easy access to psychoactive drugs, however, is that it may bamboozle the user—and the social web of persons around him—delude him or her into believing that personal problems have chemical solutions. Most humanist critics, of course, recognize that some mood-altering drugs may be useful and desirable for short-term relief. Drugs may enable some persons to muddle through immediate crises or assist some individuals to run the daily gauntlet of a stress-laden society. Yet the risks are great, these critics contend, that such "treatment" may become self-perpetuating and counterproductive. Convinced that there is a pill for every problem, people may never learn how to cope effectively with their world, how to seek nonmedical solutions, how to deal creatively with the real sources of their anxiety and misery. (The faith that persons would accomplish these humanist goals without drugs, however, would doubtless strike many sociological skeptics and drug promoters as not only idealistic but probably unrealistic.)

THE HIDDEN ADDICTION

The potential for abuse of these popular psychoactive drugs is considerable—a social reality that many advocates of a more drug-free life-style are beginning to publicize. For example, while the U.S. Drug Enforcement Administration declares war on narcotics and cocaine, a government report released in 1977 by the National Institute on Drug Abuse discovered that the tranquilizer Valium is now associated with "drug abuse crises" more often than heroin or any other drug.[29] Statistics provided by more than 1,200 hospital emergency rooms, crisis centers, and medical examiners in twenty-three metropolitan areas show that Valium was associated with 10 percent of all drug abuse cases reported, higher than the level for any other single drug—legal or illegal. Four percent of all deaths reported in the survey were associated with this prescription tranquilizer.

In fact, medical experts estimate that there may be over 1 million tranquilizer and barbiturate *addicts* in the United States. (Both these types of drugs can be physically addicting as well as habitually desired.) Yet police do not harass most of these drug addicts, ransack their apartments, or try to apprehend and arrest them. Few of them languish in jails and prisons.

Indeed, hardly anyone really views them as addicts. These heavy users of barbiturates and sedativelike drugs are victims of what Moffett and Chambers refer to as "the hidden addiction."[30]

In contrast to the majority of heroin addicts, these addicts are typically older, and are more likely to be Caucasian, from the middle and upper classes, and better-educated. They are seldom involved in conventional street crimes, and although they are more common than heroin addicts, their addiction is systematically protected and hidden from legal authorities—indeed from most everyone:

> In fact, the addiction is often hidden from the *addict himself*. Though heavy barbiturate users are addicted in precisely the same way that chronic heroin users are addicted, and though their drug has much the same effects that heroin does, society grants their behavior an aura of respectability. They do not think of themselves as "pill junkies." And almost no one else does either.[31]

Society does not stigmatize and scorn these kinds of respectable drug addicts. Unlike most poor heroin addicts, they are able to secure their "fix" without having to shoplift, burglarize, peddle drugs, or prostitute themselves. The average cost of feeding their habit is only about $3 a day, with the drug attained easily through their doctor's prescription at the corner pharmacy.

These socially approved addicts tend to become physically addicted later in life, having used barbiturates or tranquilizers initially for medical or quasi-medical reasons: to calm their anxiety, cope with tension, or to induce sleep. Yet such deceptively harmless capsules and "sleeping pills," it appears, share many of the same pharmacological effects as heroin—the "killer drug" in the rhetoric of law-enforcement officials. Barbiturate withdrawal, in fact, is often even more severe. For chronic, heavy users who become addicted, withdrawal from the drug can cause convulsions and psychotic symptoms:

> The individual first appears anxious and then shows a progressive weakness accompanied by dizziness and distortion of perception. Nausea, vomiting, and a drop in blood pressure are common. In severe cases, convulsions and delirium or a major psychotic episode may occur. Usually an individual will have one or two convulsions during the first forty-eight hours and then become psychotic on the second or third night. Withdrawal from barbiturates is more dangerous for the user than withdrawal from any of the other drugs. . . .[32]

Although there are no reliable figures, some medical authorities estimate that there may be tens of thousands of barbiturate deaths annually from overdose, resulting in fatal respiratory failure or cardiac arrest. When barbiturates are used with alcohol, a frequent combination, the interaction of the two drugs can be extremely dangerous. Barbiturates are reportedly involved in three-quarters of all drug-connected suicides in the United States. Infants born to mothers addicted to barbiturates, like infants born to mothers addicted to heroin, are also addicted; the babies must be painfully weaned from the drug, which sometimes results in the death of the infant. By any criterion, barbiturates must rank along with alcohol and cigarettes as one of the leading causes of drug-linked fatalities in the nation.[33]

It would appear that the decision to allow *some* addicts legal access to dangerous drugs bears very little relationship to the potential risks of harm to either the individual or the society. Clearly, young lower-class ghetto blacks, Puerto Ricans, or Chicanos, who dominate the media image of heroin users, lack the power, respectability, and more savory image of white, upper-middle-class housewives. As Erich Goode points out, if the heroin user takes his drug of choice in conjunction with a hedonistic language of "getting high" and "taking off"—though more frequently, if addicted, simply to stop feeling sick—he risks imprisonment and the stigmatizing label of "criminal deviant," "dope fiend," or "junkie." If a lawyer uses her preferred drug within a medical-therapeutic rhetoric and her habit helps support a multibillion dollar drug industry, she will be allowed to continue her addiction unmolested by legal authorities. The barbiturate addict will associate mainly with physicians, pharmacies, and hospitals; the heroin addict with police, prosecutors, and 6- by 9-foot prison cages.[34] (While most humanist critics have no desire to see barbiturate addicts treated as criminals, which would only compound their problems, the selective application of the criminal label is seen as mystifying, hypocritical, unjust, and symbolic of the power of dominant groups in the society.)

Not only does the widespread use of legal drugs create a climate of tolerance for all kinds of drug use, but a significant proportion of this abundant supply of amphetamines, barbiturates, and tranquilizers is siphoned off into the black market. Barbiturates, for example, may be taken by young people to get "high" or "stoned" on several hundred milligrams of powerful, quick-acting "nemies" and "yellow-jackets" (Nembutal) or "seckies" and "red devils" (Seconal). Although some of these drugs may be stolen, a significant proportion are simply obtained from prescribing physicians, a practice which is sometimes particularly lucrative. For example, the head of California's Division of Medical Quality estimates that "between 500 and 1000 of the state's licensed physicians are 'drug-pusher doctors' who will prescribe virtually anything in return for a fee and earn up to $1000 a day."[35] One reporter describes the physical appearance of some street users of barbiturates and other "downers," whose intoxication appears to create a cloudy, stupefying dreamlike state—obliterating the user's awareness of the immediate surroundings—but sometimes worse:

> [L]ook at their eyes. Chances are they'll be heavy, sleepy looking, blinking in slow motion stop and go. There won't be much conversation. Most of the kids

in the group you watch will probably have taken some combination of barbiturates and amphetamines. If they're lucky, they'll feel balanced on the kind of thin edge of consciousness you experience just before dropping off to sleep. If not, they'll be genuinely drowsy, depressed, and in ill temper. Strangely, despite their general depression, they'll be jittery, easily excitable, slightly paranoid. If any of the kids are really strung out on pills . . . they'll look and act like maniacs. They'll be confused, argumentative, and violent.[36]

Nearly all the barbiturates sold illegally on the street are manufactured by pharmaceutical companies, whose profit-oriented policies and often stringent resistance to tighter governmental controls, many critics contend, must share some of the responsibility for the widespread availability of a drug that can produce (like heroin) addiction and death from overdose. As one observer pointedly notes: "The almost exclusive emphasis of 'drug education' campaigns on illegal drugs would seem to be entirely misplaced."[37] In 1978, Peter Bourne, President Carter's special assistant on drug abuse, declared that "more persons die from barbiturates than all other drugs put together," prompting an extensive federal government study to consider the possibility of banning all barbiturate prescriptions except for hospitalized persons.[38]

CORPORATE RESPONSIBILITY

Introduction into the common "pain-pill-pleasure" view of things starts early in life, perhaps in part through the television bombardment of children by drug companies advertising vitamins. Sandwiched in between Bugs Bunny cartoons and the Flintstones, these vitamin ads, some critics feel, may possibly establish behavior patterns that could become precedents for taking pills to solve problems. As social scientist Arthur Berger observes, the implicit message sent to the children is: "Don't worry if you don't eat properly, if you fill yourself up with junk foods, candy, and soda pop, etc., for we have a solution to your difficulties—a nice pill that looks like an M&M or little animal."

> Thus the child was told he could gratify his impulses and escape from their consequences because of the magic of vitamin pills. Not only does the pill "make up" for his inadequacies, it also tastes and looks like candy. Children's vitamins serve to socialize the American child and prepare him for his role as an adult "pill-popper." It is rather distressing to know that these pills were taken off children's programs only because of the strength of protest from aroused and angered parents.[39]

The drug industry has not always been that morally sensitive to the consequences of its sales campaigns. Indeed, some corporate conceptions of the limits of company responsibility remind one of the satirical popular song written by Tom Lehrer dedicated to the American rocket experts:

Once they are up who cares where they come down
That's not my department, says Werner von Braun.

As medical sociologist Irving Zola points out, such sentiments have implications far exceeding that of rocketry. "That's not my department" has provided a protective shield for many medical scientists, pharmacologists, and corporate executives—a convenient argument to deny moral accountability for the adverse consequences and possible abuses of their burgeoning biochemical technology and aggressive sales policies.[40]

Consider as a case in point the practice of some large multinational drug corporations. They have hardly been zealous in communicating accurately and effectively the potential dangers of various psychoactive drugs—especially at the expense of their profits.[41] And when government control and scrutiny jeopardize their economic investment, some of these large pharmaceutical firms have simply dumped hazardous drugs onto other countries that lack such regulatory controls. Milton Silverman, a pharmacologist, recently testified before a Senate committee that U.S. drug companies in Latin America are partly responsible for the deaths and injuries of many people because they do not fully disclose to foreign doctors the potential dangers of some drugs and because they exaggerate their effectiveness. In a detailed comparison of twenty-eight separate prescription drugs, Silverman discovered "glaring inconsistencies" in the promotion of antidepressants, antibiotics, oral contraceptives, and other drugs. "I find great difficulty," he says, "in understanding how a company can describe one of its products as dangerous in San Diego but safe a few miles across the border in Tijuana." According to Silverman, Latin American doctors "have told of the cases of permanent brain damage caused by excessive use of antipsychotic tranquilizers—and sometimes by tranquilizers given to control bed-wetting or nail-biting in children." In U.S. pharmaceutical manuals, he notes, the list of "warnings and possible adverse reactions is lengthy and detailed. The potential hazards published in the Latin American volumes are usually minimized, glossed over, or totally ignored. In some cases not a single danger is disclosed."[42] Senator J. Glenn Beall, chairman of the Senate committee before which Silverman brought these charges, said that the federal government could not intervene in the matter because the jurisdiction of the Food and Drug Administration did not cover corporations that package and label drugs outside the country.

Even when the jurisdiction of federal regulatory agencies does cover drugs sold within the country, concern seldom extends beyond a narrow focus on the possible physical health and safety hazards of these pharmacological products. The psychological and social consequences are essentially ignored, especially as they relate to the workplace. Yet during the last two decades, psychoactive drugs have become an integral part of workers' attempts to cope with job stress, sometimes with the tacit support or even pressures from employers and supervisors. Use of amphetamine-type pep pills and tranquilizers is common among auto workers, professional athletes, telephone operators, waitresses, Chicano field hands, factory workers, airline stewardesses, and workers in many other occupations as they attempt to meet deadlines, production quotas, and performance standards.[43] Interviews with Bell System telephone operators, for instance, confirm that a large number, perhaps a majority, survive on Valium and Librium. According to a Communications Workers Union report: "the pressure applied to these employees has led to unnecessary absence because of nervous sickness or nervous breakdown, widespread use of tranquilizers and a large turnover in the traffic operating force."[44]

In the lead smelting industry, private physicians regularly prescribe Valium to enable workers to cope with "irritability" that many medical experts feel is caused by lead poisoning.[45] In some factories workers routinely deal with the strain caused by job stress and industrial noise by tranquilizing themselves. Yet according to Carl Chambers, head of an independent consulting firm in Washington, "It's hard to tell who does the encouraging and who looks the other way."[46] A former assembly-line worker at the Ford auto plant commented: "If stimulants help get the job done . . . management will look the other way. If a guy knocks over his toolbox and five hundred reds fall out, everybody will be embarrassed, but unless it formally gets to the upper levels of management, they'll be pragmatic about it."[47]

Although conditions in the trucking industry appear to have improved in recent years (it is now against official policy to use on-the-job drugs, at least in the major trucking companies), one driver testified before a Senate committee in the early 1970s that "possibly 90 percent of the drivers on long-line operations take pills [amphetamines]. They don't take them just to get hopped up. They take them so they can drive without running over people on the road."

> It is either take a pill and go or quit. They tell you if you can't take it, you can quit. When you ask off, the first thing a [management] guy says is, "What's the matter, can't you take it?" This is not an exception. This is a condition of employment. . . .
> The things that they put on the bulletin boards at these terminals, everything they say to you is apparently aimed at dominating you completely. This does away with a lot of a man's self-confidence. It puts him in a state of anxiety. When he climbs behind the wheel, he doesn't know whether he can do the job right or not. He is never told. . . . He is going from clock to clock, panic-stricken. If you can't make the run in the fog, the rain, ice conditions, they are always ready to tell you if you can't make it, we can hire a man that can.[48]

Perhaps the most insidious consequence of such job-connected drug use is that the oppressive work conditions become not only more tolerable but *legitimatized* and *normalized*. As Schrag points out, whether such drug-

induced manipulation of the individual occurs from voluntary self-medica-
tion or from pressures from supervisors; whether it be the "boss-intimidated
truck driver who takes speed to finish his run, the auto workers who pop
Bennies and Black Beauties to get through the night shift," or the physician
who prescribes Valium to deal with worker "irritability," the results are the
same: the status quo is reinforced.[49] By complying with the demands and
impositions of the work setting, the worker's ability to perceive alternatives
diminishes. The hope for a more humane organization of work conditions
that would significantly reduce stress becomes a fading dream.

BRAVE NEW WORLD

Who should decide what our public policies should be regarding psychoactive drugs? What kinds of drugs should be administered, by whom, to
whom, toward what goals, and in quest of what values? Regardless of how
we resolve these difficult questions, humanistically oriented social scientists
are beginning to examine critically the medical model of human behavior
that individualizes and depoliticizes social problems, that offers a drug for
every psychological discomfort, and that labels persons as medical patients
who deviate from conventional social standards or who are not perpetually
happy, tranquil, and anxiety-free.

Yet the development of a society more responsive to human needs, one
that would not necessitate continual reliance on psychoactive drugs, does
not appear very likely in the immediate future. Today, few of our institutions and social arrangements are adequate to the complexities of living in
the modern world—the boring and stress-inducing jobs, deadening and
alienating schools, prolongation of adolescence, heightened expectations
and fragile marriages, poverty amidst affluence, and social turmoil in our
cities. Family, neighborhood, and community can no longer provide the effective control and supportive functions they once did. The traditional mechanisms for resolving social problems and dealing with troublesome persons
and problems of living have eroded in a rapidly changing, urban, industrial
society. Consequently, well-intentioned medical practitioners, whether or
not they share the dominant and often mystifying conceptions of illness,
health, and deviance, find they have few immediate and effective options
to deal with individual distress and complex social problems—to deal with
the disturbed and the difficult, the belligerent, the economically superflu-
ous, the aged, and the socially marginal. And thus drugs are increasingly
thrown into the breach, as physicians and other medical specialists respond
to pressures to "do something."

But as Schrag points out, this dependence on drugs to deal with personal crises, although understandable, functions to *maintain* the very social
system that helps generate such personal problems. The "side effects" of

drugs are not only biological and psychological but are also social, political, and ideological.

> Perhaps it is the fault of the system, the economy, the whole society; perhaps it would be better if we left this person alone; but the system can't be changed, and this person needs help now. . . . [T]he pain is immediate, the disturbance is real, the institution can't function with this man acting up, his family is not safe. Thorazine for peace, Prolixin for safety, behavior mod for institutional order. By the time the system changes, if indeed it ever does, he'll have failed in school, lost his job, murdered his children. *Every pill makes it less likely that the system ever will change.*[50]

Thus we witness on the one hand, the accelerating use of legal drugs to shore up our ineffective and badly battered social institutions; and on the other, the massive use of mood-altering drugs by increasing numbers of persons as they try to escape, blot out, or transcend—at least temporarily— the discontent that pervades much of our impersonal and bureaucratic society.

Aldous Huxley, who deplored the effects of an imaginary happy pill in his satire, *Brave New World*, nonetheless concluded that it seems "very unlikely . . . that humanity at large will ever be able to dispense with artificial paradises."[51] Whatever the truth of Huxley's contention, chemical alteration of human consciousness is becoming a fact of life. Advances in this proliferating drug technology recently prompted psychiatrist Arnold Mandell to claim: "You name the psychic state you want, and I can put you there."[52] And the Office of Health Economics in London in their report *Medicine in the 1990's—A Technological Forecast* predicted that "it is likely that every individual will be taking psychotropic [mind-altering] medicines either continuously or at intervals."[53]

Hence it would seem essential that our society place high on the public agenda for vigorous debate and research the dangers and benefits of this drug culture so deeply ingrained in American life. Although the federal government and the medical profession are showing increased concern with the medical effectiveness of barbiturates and tranquilizers, and may possibly impose tighter controls, the immediate prospects of a far-reaching debate are unlikely. The use of psychoactive drugs to deal with complex social problems and disturbing individuals is now deeply entrenched. And the stakes are high: personal careers, research funds, treatment centers, corporate profits, and entire bureaucratic organizations have a vested interest in institutionalizing drug use and medicalizing certain forms of social deviance.

Moreover, the media-celebrated successes of the antibiotic "wonder drugs" and "miracles of chemistry," along with the widespread drug treatment of chronically mentally ill patients, have helped to legitimize this increasing medical intervention and the supremacy of deterministic conceptions of human behavior. The prestige and power of the medical profession and the pharmaceutical industry are immense. And thus the scattered chorus of voices from some feminists, liberal academicians, civil libertarians, humanist social critics, and dissident members of the medical and drug-treatment establishment seem, as yet, relatively powerless to reverse or alter fundamentally this unrelenting quest for chemical solutions to every disturbing feeling and feature of contemporary life.

FOOTNOTES

1   Cited in J. Maurice Rogers, "Drug Abuse—Just What the Doctor Ordered," *Psychology Today*, 5 (September 1971), p. 16.
2   Peter Schrag, *Mind Control*, Pantheon Books, New York, 1978, p. 122.
3   Rogers, "Drug Abuse—Just What the Doctor Ordered," p. 18.
4   Arnold Bernstein and Henry L. Lennard, "Drugs, Doctors and Junkies," *Society*, 10 (May/June 1973), p. 22.
5   Schrag, *Mind Control*, p. 136. See also Gilbert Cant, "Valiumania," *The New York Times Magazine*, Feb. 1, 1976, pp. 34–44.
6   Deborah Larned, "The Selling of Valium," *Ms.*, November 1975, p. 32.
7   Quoted in Mike Gravel, "Corporate Pushers," in David E. Smith and Donald R. Wesson (eds.), *Uppers and Downers*, Prentice-Hall, Englewood Cliffs, N.J., 1973, p. 128. See Robert Seidenberg, "Drug Advertising and Perception of Mental Illness," *Mental Hygiene*, 55 (January 1971), pp. 21–31.
8   Quoted in Schrag, *Mind Control*, p. 114. See also Gravel, "Corporate Pushers," p. 127.
9   Gravel, "Corporate Pushers," p. 129. See also Gaylord Nelson, "Advertising and the National Health," *Journal of Drug Issues*, 6 (Winter 1976), pp. 28–33; John Patterson, "The Impact of Promotion on Physicians' Prescribing Patterns," *Journal of Drug Issues*, 6 (Winter 1976), pp. 13–20.
10   Peter Schrag, "Mind Control," *Playboy* (May 1978), p. 138.
11   See Renee C. Fox, "The Medicalization and Demedicalization of American Society," *Daedalus*, 106 (Winter 1977), pp. 9–22; Ivan Illich, *Medical Nemesis*, Pantheon Books, New York, 1976; Peter Conrad and Joseph W. Schneider, *From Badness to Sickness: A Sociology of Deviance and Social Control*, Mosby, St. Louis, forthcoming.
12   Schrag, *Mind Control*, pp. 83–84. Copyright © 1978 by Peter Schrag. Reprinted by permission of Pantheon Books, a Division of Random House, Inc.
13   David L. Lewis, "Color It Black: The Failure of Drug Abuse Policy," *Social Policy*, 7 (March/April 1976), pp. 26–32. See also Dorothy Nelkin, *Methadone Maintenance: A Technological Fix*, George Braziller, New York, 1973.
14   Quoted in Schrag, *Mind Control*, p. 237.
15   Quoted in Henry L. Lennard et al., *Mystification and Drug Misuse*, Harper & Row, New York, 1972, p. 32.
16   See Peter Schrag and Diane Divoky, *The Myth of the Hyperactive Child*, Pantheon Books, New York, 1975; Peter Conrad, "The Discovery of Hyperkinesis:

Notes on the Medicalization of Deviant Behavior," *Social Problems*, 23 (October 1975), pp. 12–21; Peter Conrad, *Identifying Hyperactive Children: The Medicalization of Deviant Behavior*, D.C. Heath, Lexington, Mass., 1976.

17   Quoted in Schrag, *Mind Control*, pp. 108–109.

18   Quoted in Schrag, *Mind Control*, p. 109. See Senate Subcommittee to Investigate Juvenile Delinquency, *Drugs in Institutions: Hearings Before the Subcommittee to Investigate Juvenile Delinquency*, U.S. Government Printing Office, Washington, D.C., 1977, pp. 14–15, 33; Theodore Van Puten, "Why Do Schizophrenic Patients Refuse to Take Their Drugs?" *Archives of General Psychiatry*, 31 (July 1974), p. 70.

19   Quoted in Rogers, "Drug Abuse—Just What the Doctor Ordered," p. 18.

20   Bernstein and Lennard, "Drugs, Doctors and Junkies," p. 24.

21   Philip Slater, *The Pursuit of Loneliness*, rev. ed., Beacon Press, Boston, 1976, pp. 21–22.

22   Bernstein and Lennard, "Drugs, Doctors and Junkies," pp. 16, 22.

23   Samuel A. Cartwright, "Report on the Diseases and Physical Peculiarities of the Negro Race," *New Orleans Medical and Surgical Journal*, 7 (May 1851), pp. 691–715.

24   See Sidney Bloch and Peter Reddaway, *Psychiatric Terror*, Basic Books, New York, 1977; Nicholas Kitterie, *The Right to Be Different*, Penguin Books, Baltimore, 1973; Stephen Chorover, "Big Brother and Psychotechnology," *Psychology Today*, 6 (October 1973), pp. 43–54; Samuel Chavkin, *The Mind Stealers: Psychosurgery and Mind Control*, Houghton Mifflin, Boston, 1978.

25   David Rorvik, "Behavior Control: Big Brother Comes," *Intellectual Digest*, 4 (January 1974), p. 18. See also Wayne Sage, "Crime and the Clockwork Lemon," *Human Behavior*, 3 (September 1974), pp. 16–25; Jessica Mitford, *Kind and Usual Punishment: The Prison Business*, Knopf, New York, 1973.

26   Bernstein and Lennard, "Drugs, Doctors and Junkies," p. 16.

27   Irving K. Zola, "Medicine as an Institution of Social Control," *Sociological Review*, 20 (November 1972), p. 497. See also Glen D. Mellinger et al., "An Overview of Psychotherapeutic Drug Use in the United States," in Eric Josephson and Eleanor E. Carroll (eds.), *Drug Use: Epidemiological and Sociological Approaches*, Halsted Press, New York, 1974, pp. 333–366; Hugh J. Parry et al., "National Patterns of Psychotherapeutic Drug Use," *Archives of General Psychiatry*, 28 (June 1973), pp. 769–783.

28   Zola, "Medicine as an Institution of Social Control," p. 495.

29   Associated Press, *Syracuse Post-Dispatch*, July 9, 1976, p. 3. See also "Study Finds Valium Most Abused Drug; Many Deaths Cited," *The New York Times*, Oct. 19, 1975, p. 63.

30   Arthur D. Moffett and Carl D. Chambers, "The Hidden Addiction," *Social Work*, 15 (July 1970), pp. 54–59.

31   Erich Goode, *Drugs in American Society*, Knopf, New York, 1972, p. 155.

32   William Bates and Betty Crowther, "Drug Abuse," in Edward Sagarin and Fred Montanino (eds.), *Deviants: Voluntary Actors in a Hostile World*, General Learning Press, Morristown, N.J., 1977, pp. 275–276.

33   Goode, *Drugs in American Society*, pp. 151–155.

34   Goode, *Drugs in American Society*, p. 227.

35 *Behavior Today*, Mar. 20, 1978, p. 7.

36 Lucian K. Truscott, "The Return to Cool," *The Village Voice*, June 19, 1971, p. 9. See also the collection of articles in Smith and Wesson (eds.), *Uppers and Downers;* Lester Grinspoon and Peter Hedblom, *The Speed Culture: Amphetamine Use and Abuse in America*, Harvard University Press, Cambridge, Mass., 1975.

37 Erich Goode, *Drugs in American Society*, p. 156. See also James M. Graham, "Amphetamine Politics on Capitol Hill," *Transaction*, 9 (January 1972), pp. 14–22, 53.

38 *The New York Times Briefing Papers for Public Affairs*, vol. II, 1978, p. 11.

39 Arthur Asa Berger, "Drug Advertising and the 'Pain, Pill, Pleasure' Model," *Journal of Drug Issues*, 4 (Summer 1974), p. 210.

40 Irving K. Zola, "In the Name of Health and Illness: On Some Socio-Political Consequences of Medical Influence," *Social Science and Medicine*, 9 (February 1975), p. 83.

41 See Schrag, *Mind Control*, pp. 122–126; Milton Silverman and Phillip R. Lee, *Pills, Profits and Politics*, University of California Press, Berkeley, Calif., 1974; Sanford J. Ungar, "'Get Away With What You Can,'" in Robert L. Heilbroner et al., *In the Name of Profit*, Warner, New York, 1973; James S. Turner, *The Chemical Feast*, Grossman, New York, 1970.

42 Quoted in Elbert W. Stewart, *Sociology: The Human Science*, McGraw-Hill, New York, 1978, p. 264. See also Milton Silverman, *The Drugging of the Americas*, University of California Press, Berkeley, Calif., 1976.

43 Schrag, *Mind Control*, 139–142. See also Carl D. Chambers et al., *Chemical Coping: A Report on Legal Drug Abuse in the United States*, Halsted Press, New York, 1975.

44 Quoted in Schrag, *Mind Control*, p. 139.

45 Schrag, *Mind Control*, p. 141.

46 Quoted in Schrag, *Mind Control*, p. 141.

47 Quoted in Schrag, *Mind Control*, p. 142.

48 Quoted in Schrag, *Mind Control*, pp. 139–140. See U.S. Senate Subcommittee on Alcoholism and Narcotics, *Amphetamine Abuse Among Truckdrivers*, U.S. Government Printing Office, Washington, D.C., 1972, p. 14.

49 Schrag, *Mind Control*, p. 142.

50 Schrag, *Mind Control*, p. 253. Italics added. Copyright © 1978 by Peter Schrag. Reprinted by permission of Pantheon Books, a Division of Random House, Inc.

51 Quoted in Joel Fort and Christopher T. Cory, *American Drugstore*, Little, Brown, Boston, 1975, p. 9.

52 *Behavior Today*, Jan. 23, 1978, p. 7. See also Ronald R. Fieve, *Moodswing: The Third Revolution in Psychiatry*, William Morrow, New York, 1975.

53 Quoted in Rogers, "Drug Abuse—Just What the Doctor Ordered," p. 24.

Demystifying Drinking Behavior

What happens to you when you drink? Do you become more happy, mean, sexy, aggressive, sullen? Consider the observations of this party-goer:

> Not long ago I went to what promised to be a dull party. But after everyone had had a few drinks, things warmed up. One young woman did a remarkable belly dance. A married man seemed to forget his wife was present and tried to persuade a young girl to accompany him to a darkened bedroom. Another man insulted someone on whom a good part of his livelihood depended. And most of the other guests danced and talked and laughed with more enthusiasm and less restraint than they would have if only tea had been served.[1]

As the writer comments, it was a good, lively party. And the following day undoubtedly many of those guests who had misbehaved apologized to their host and were forgiven. "After all, they had been drinking, and we all know that people are not responsible for their behavior when they are drunk."[2] Such beliefs about the powerful ability of alcohol to unleash our primitive impulses are widespread. In Santa Barbara, California, a news report describes what happened at a youth dance:

> Six youths were arrested, car windows were smashed and several persons suf-
> fered minor injuries at midnight Friday when students from two rival high
> schools here rioted at a crowded dance at the city Recreational Center. . . .
> [The] assistant youth supervisor was struck in the face as she attempted to turn
> on bright lights on the dance floor after fighting started. . . . A dozen policemen
> responded to a call for help from recreation officials at the auditorium filled
> with more than 1,100 students.[3]

In answer to a news reporter's question of what caused the riot, a police lieutenant gave this readily accepted explanation: "A few of the boys evidently
had been drinking."

Finally, consider this sexual incident involving a young teaching assistant and a college student:

> At a small party in the instructor's apartment, Betty, a junior, became intoxi-
> cated and the teacher had intercourse with her after the party. He thought little
> more about it, and was surprised and very distressed to be summoned by the
> dean two days later. There he learned that the girl had gone to the dean, stat-
> ing that she had been attacked and forced into relations when her inebriated
> state made it impossible for her to protest effectively. The teacher stated that
> he had in no way used force, and that he believed that the girl had been an active
> participant.[4]

While such an unfortunate episode after "a good night's fun" may be treated
as the exception, few readers will probably be surprised that "if it is a really
good party some of the participants can usually be counted upon to become
'drunk enough' to do things that are truly 'out-of-character.'"[5] As "everyone knows" the psychopharmacological potency of alcohol can radically
alter our social behavior. Liquor, it is widely recognized, can make us temporarily immune to those internalized constraints ("inhibitions") that ordinarily channel our behavior in socially acceptable ways.

Yet there is increasing skepticism among many social scientists toward
these traditional notions that it is the alcohol that directly causes such deviant behavior. According to a cross-cultural survey of drunken behavior
by psychologist Craig MacAndrew and anthropologist Robert Edgerton,
drinking alcohol does not in itself cause persons to become more verbally
aggressive, violent, sexually promiscuous, morose, maudlin, or euphoric
than they would be if sober. From a review of studies of drunken behavior
in many different societies, these two social scientists maintain that there
is no convincing evidence that alcohol directly causes the social and moral
behavioral changes commonly believed.[6]

Such a view, of course, goes against centuries of conventional wisdom
embodied not only in popular beliefs but also in medical and scientific views,
which typically claim that alcohol "depresses the uppermost level of the
brain—the center of inhibitions, restraint and judgment."[7] The drinker,

most medical scientists contend, is "disinhibited" because of the "toxic assault" of alcohol on the "higher brain centers." Under the influence of this intoxicating beverage, people shed their inhibitions and behave in an impulsive manner that they normally would not if sober:

> Since alcohol depresses the powers of judgment, drinking may release inhibitions. . . . As far as sexual behavior is concerned, it is well-known that alcohol reduces the inhibitions of individuals and removes the controls. The individual becomes careless and will often do things under the influence of alcohol that he would not do if his judgment were not impaired. Therefore, impairment of the judgment by alcohol may cause sexual behavior that would not occur were he not exposed to the loss of control that alcohol brings about.[8]

Two leading authorities on alcohol write:

> The apparent "stimulation" from alcohol is the result of the lower brain centers being released from higher brain controls. This reduces inhibitions, and behavior which is untoward when the individual is sober becomes acceptable. For example . . . an always proper, ladylike woman may become obscene and promiscuous when intoxicated.[9]

There is, of course, well-documented and universal evidence that alcohol has certain *physical* effects on the human body. If a person drinks enough, his sensorimotor responses will be significantly incapacitated: his reaction time will slow down, and he'll have difficulty coordinating his movements (as when operating a car or machinery). If the person's blood-alcohol level increases sufficiently, she'll have difficulty walking straight and her speech will thicken and slur; if she consumes enough, she'll pass out. Although the speed with which such effects occur will depend partly upon body weight, amount of food in the stomach, and type of alcoholic beverage, all such physiological changes invariably occur among humans— male or female—in any society.[10] Yet the same cannot be claimed for changes in *social* behavior.

THE DIVERSITY AND SELECTIVITY OF DRUNKEN BEHAVIOR

MacAndrew and Edgerton observe that social behavior under the influence of alcohol ("drunken comportment") is highly *variable* in different drinking cultures. For example, the Urubu Indians of Brazil, a ferocious group of machete-wielding headhunters when sober, sing and dance with their neighboring tribal enemies when drunk during peace talks.[11] Yet the powerful qualities of alcohol can no more explain this reversal of behavior than they can illuminate the rather consistent behavior of the Aritamans of Northern Colombia. When these somber, controlled, and almost morose people drink their favorite rum potion, they become even more reserved and morose: "All communication stops and gloominess sets in."[12]

The diversity of drunken behavior among the same people in different situations is particularly striking in South Africa. Within the tradition-bound tribal villages, native beer parties are typically associated with a behavior "free of rancor" and lacking in physical violence; a "proper sense of decorum" is maintained throughout the festivities. Yet upon migration to the urban slums of Johannesburg, the same beer drinking among these up-rooted people frequently results in violent quarrels, stabbings, and brawls. "While the beverage of the South African Bantu has not changed, the circumstances surrounding its consumption most certainly have. And as these circumstances have changed, so, too, has their drunken comportment."[13]

Among the Lepchas, a Mongolian tribe in the Sikkim Himalayas, incest taboos of intricate complexity are strictly enforced. For example, a man may not have sex with his wife's mother or elder sisters, the wife of his wife's older brother, the wives of his sons and younger brothers, and so on, including restrictions through nine generations on the father's side and four on the mother's side of the family. Despite these extensive incest taboos, the Lepchas are extremely sexually permissive. Sex is the major source of recreation and a constant topic of conversation. Adultery is widespread and causes no quarrels between spouses. Children as young as ten and twelve engage in sexual activity and continue to have vigorous intercourse well into old age. On the night of the annual rice harvest festival, when everyone gets intoxicated on the native drink *chi*, wild sexual abandonment in the fields is not only permissible but encouraged and practiced (the belief being that the more couples that copulate, the more plentiful the harvest will be). Yet notwithstanding this culturally sanctioned sexual license, in which anyone may sleep with anyone else except the tabooed relatives, the incest rules are rigidly observed. The Lepchas feel a sense of horror toward incest, fearing that a single act of incestuous intercourse will bring calamity to the entire village. Thus even when persons are extremely drunk and the social norms otherwise encourage rampant promiscuity, the taboos are never violated.[14]

Among the Camba Indians of Eastern Bolivia, a tribe that stresses harmonious interpersonal relationships and a strict puritanical approach to sex, many people drink themselves into a state of unconsciousness at festivities that last several days. The Camba consume a potent brew that is 89 percent ethyl alcohol (about 180 proof) and which is drunk *undiluted!* Yet at no time is there any evidence that such drunkenness leads to an increase in sexual activity, verbal or physical aggression, obscene joking, clowning, maudlin sentimentality, or whatever. Indeed, like the Aritamans of Northern Colombia, *no one is disinhibited at all.* Not only does alcohol "fail to produce tidal waves of aggression and sexuality, it does not even produce ripples."[15] If humans are allegedly "out of control"—the higher centers of their brain anesthetized by alcohol, which dissolves inhibitions—such totally restrained drunken comportment among the puritanical Camba is difficult to explain.

A growing body of social scientific research supports these cross-cultural observations. How people morally *behave* when inebriated and their subjective *experience* of being drunk depend upon the interaction of many factors, which are not simply a function of specific biochemical reactions induced by the pharmacological properties of alcohol. As with any psychoactive drug, the kinds of social behavior and subjective feelings that occur when drinking reflect the interaction of personality characteristics, experience with alcohol, mood, social expectations, and the social setting. To understand more fully alcohol-related behavior we must examine this phenomenon within a social and cultural context.[16]

Particularly crucial are the social definitions surrounding alcohol: what a society conveys to its members regarding drinking and drunkenness—the social *meanings* imputed to behavior "under the influence" in the culture and subcultures in which people participate. As Edwin Lemert emphasizes, pharmacological generalizations about the effects of alcohol must take into account the particular cultural milieu in which the behavior occurs:

> [I]n one study of the function of alcohol in a primitive Mexican culture located in the mountains of Chiapas few of the more extreme types of behavior which arise in connection with intoxication in our culture were found to occur. There, in the state of feeling high, native men could play guitars or handle a machete with perfect safety. In extreme intoxication there seemed to be less interference with speech than that observable in inebriation in our culture, and even in stuporous states the natives carried through with familiar routines and transacted complicated business of which later they had no memory. There seemed to be very little vomiting after overindulgence, and there was little evidence of hang-overs beyond mild tremors and shakiness. Little fighting arose in drinking parties, and there was no evidence of lowered inhibition in erotic behavior. These people typically drank for the sense of warmth it induced and as a prelude to sleep.[17]

The tremendous variability in drunken comportment in cultures across the world is only one kind of evidence that suggests the crucial importance of social factors in shaping alcohol-related behavior and experiences. It is also clear that within a given society people are *situationally selective* in the inhibitions they shed—if any—when drinking. In every society there exists a tacit understanding as to which transgressions of social rules will be tolerated and which will not. In no society does "anything go" when drunk (as seen in the scrupulous adherence to incest rules among the promiscuous Lepchas). Altered behavior may occur but usually *within certain socially sanctioned limits*.[18] There is a permissible zone or range of allowable behavior. Most people seem implicitly to know about how much they can get away with in different situations. Even with the same consumption of alcohol, many drinkers will act with much more restraint at a formal and sedate cocktail party than at a raucous fraternity party.

Except in rare cases most ordinary drunk people normally retain certain controls in different social situations and circumstances. For example, the drunken comportment of the Irish countryman in his pub is strikingly different from his equally intoxicated behavior during an Irish wake. In the United States, a financially distraught but normally law-abiding upper-middle-class citizen doesn't hold up a service station when drunk. (A conventional criminal offender may use alcohol to bolster his nerve, but the alcohol doesn't *make* him commit the robbery). A female college student may become maudlinly sentimental at a fraternity party and even bare her soul—but she will not bare her breasts, especially when faculty guests are present. A drunken tavern brawler may slug any man who seeks to restrain him but hold his punches when the would-be peacemaker is a woman or a priest. This kind of selectivity in the objects of drunken verbal, violent, or sexual aggression clearly challenges the contention that alcohol renders inoperative our internal moral controls.

Finally, haven't we all witnessed persons who behave much the same way in certain situations when either sober or drunk? Such persons may be inappropriately amorous, belligerent, vulgar, or withdrawn—both with and without alcohol. Indeed, isn't it part of the popular folklore in certain drinking circles that even when heavily drinking some persons can "really hold their liquor," seemingly exhibiting no significant changes in their social comportment when drunk?

Thus it would appear that the answer to the question "Why do they act the way they do?"—especially in deviant behavior for the worse—cannot be adequately explained by the potent mystical qualities of alcohol. The popular biochemical explanation given for misconduct—"I was drunk"—although socially significant is really not a satisfactory explanation. The selectivity in the distinctive patterns (time, place, and object) of drunken behavior and the existence of certain limits beyond which most people do not normally go when drunk would appear to invalidate the contention that when a person is drunk an alcohol-induced brain paralysis allows the drinker's "uninhibited impulses" to take over. Instead, a growing number of social scientists maintain that "letting go" is *learned* behavior and would agree with MacAndrew and Edgerton that at least in part "the way people comport themselves when they are drunk is determined not by alcohol's toxic assault upon the seat of moral judgment, conscience, or the like, but by what their society makes of and imparts to them concerning the state of drunkenness."[19]

The importance of the *social expectations* we learn to associate with alcohol is quite evident, for example, in the party trick sometimes played on unsuspecting youngsters who are informed that the fruit punch contains the forbidden booze:

> A rather common practical joke is to tell young teenagers that the harmless punch at the party is spiked. Almost invariably a certain number of them will exhibit classic drunken symptoms. They act sillier than they'd normally act, they say things they might ordinarily hold back, they feel ill and stagger just a bit and they have a fine, uninhibited time. From having watched adults, movies, and television, the kids know how alcohol "makes" Americans act at a party, so they get high on fruit juice, sugar and club soda.[20]

Americans acquire these shared understandings of the nature of drunken conduct and permissible uninhibited behavior from many sources: (1) watching role models while drunk and imitating them, (2) trial-and-error testing of social limits while drunk, and (3) through the mass media, jokes, stories, and everyday social interactions.[21] But whatever the sources of socialization—peers, parents or television comedians—these collective beliefs may take on the character of a self-fulfilling prophecy; such widespread mythology may generate its own kind of validating "evidence." It is reported that one impoverished New York City host began his cocktail parties with martinis, but refilled his guests' drinks from a pitcher of water as the party wore on. Most of the guests were unmindful of the substitution and the host remarked: "the parties got wilder and wilder the more they drank."[22] As sociologist W. I. Thomas once observed: situations defined as real are real in their consequences. Or as MacAndrew and Edgerton put the point:

> *Over the course of socialization, people learn about drunkenness what their society "knows" about drunkenness; and, accepting and acting upon the understandings thus imparted to them, they become the living confirmation of their society's teachings.*[23]

CALLING TIME OUT

If alcohol does not narcotize our moral control centers, unshackling our primitive impulses in the straightforward manner often assumed, what is the function of such popular beliefs that alcohol causes us to lose our inhibitions? According to MacAndrew and Edgerton, such a belief in many societies permits its members to call "time out" from social responsibility. The socially available excuse "I was drunk" enables us to *excuse social behavior that we would otherwise ordinarily condemn.* The drunken person, we feel, is not the "real person." Thus the drinker may not be held to the same degree of accountability that would occur if the person were sober.

MacAndrew and Edgerton contend that we all need some occasional relief from strict liability and the psychic pressures of always conforming to social rules:

> People do things accidentally, inadvertently, while under duress, and so on, and to deny persons the right ever to plead one or another such defense would be much the same as to deny an engine its necessary lubricants. In both cases, the result would be disastrous.[24]

In many societies around the world alcohol is used in this fashion to permit temporary exemptions from the unrelenting demands for conformity. The culture supplies us with a socially acceptable set of rationalizations to justify and account for our lapses from social propriety. In short, we are provided with excuses to act badly—within limits—by pleading that we were temporarily "not ourselves." As Sam Blum points out, in everyday life we may make use of a plea of temporary insanity ("I just got so angry I didn't realize what I was saying") to win forgiveness for our deviant behavior. So, too, we often use drunkenness for this purpose:

> In no society can human beings tolerate unceasing responsibility. No one but a saint could do what is righteous and just at all times. All of us, from time to time, do act badly; and in order for a society, an organization, a family, a friendship, to endure, individuals must be provided with excuses to act badly (though always within limits), yet be forgiven.[25]

The reason alcohol is so well suited for this function is the obvious physical effects of alcohol. The warm sensations of feeling "high," the staggered gait, the clumsy movements, the slurred speech, the poorly executed tasks—all are beyond the drinker's ability to overcome and control by sheer willpower. From an awareness of these highly visible effects on our bodily behavior it is an easy step to presume that liquor also channels our social behavior in ways beyond our power to control. Thus we are easily persuaded not to judge the person's behavior in a way that we would were his supposedly critical moral faculties intact. Though obviously there are limits beyond which the argument "I was drunk" will not excuse the offender, the widespread belief in the power of alcohol appears to reduce the severity of the social judgment and reaction to the deviant behavior (even resulting in a reduced penalty for homicide in some societies).

Robert Edgerton provides a contemporary example of the operation of such "time out" functions from an incident that he witnessed in a restaurant:

> A middle-class man of about forty-five was losing a fairly nasty argument with his two teen-aged children. The teen-agers were attacking him for being authoritarian and not treating them like human beings. After a while the father got up from the table and went into the bar, where, as many diners noted, he had a couple of fast drinks; he returned to the table carrying two more drinks,

which he gulped down in dramatic fashion. And literally ten seconds after-ward he put on a display of anger that quieted not only his kids but the rest of the restaurant as well.

Five minutes later he had grown maudlin and was singing "Happy Birth-day," and not much later he was weeping and proclaiming, "You've got to for-give me. I'm your father and I love you. . . . I'm sorry for having embarrassed you in front of all these people. But I work so hard and I'm so tired and the booze got to me."

I doubt . . . that his children completely accepted the idea that their father was innocent of responsibility for the scene he had just created, but at least they said, "We understand."[26]

Whether the father in this incident intentionally used the excuse of alco-holic impairment of his judgment to act in a way that he desired is difficult to determine. Yet the man was certainly able to berate his children in an ob-noxious manner that he knew would be unacceptable public behavior. Seemingly "out of control," the father was able to shout down his sons and to squelch an argument that he had obviously been losing. But by fortifying himself with a few quick drinks before he launched into his tirade, the father provided himself with the social mechanism to remove responsibility for his behavior and still allow for the possibility of forgiveness. In short, he was able to use the socially provided license—"drunkenness"—to engage in certain kinds of deviant behavior without fear of severe sanction.

Certainly it is quite possible that many persons calculatingly exploit and manipulate the deviance-mitigating consequences of behavior "under the influence" to get away with behavior for which they would otherwise be severely reprimanded, ostracized, or harshly punished. Unsuccessful seduc-tion that culminates in rape but is explained away through the excuse "I was drunk, I didn't know what I was doing" is only one example of the so-cially available vocabulary of justification that our culture provides to as-sailants to absolve them or at least make more understandable their sexual assaults.

Not only rapists may offer such accounts, but also "child molesters." Since such sexual activity (for example, fondling the genitals of young chil-dren) provokes public moral outrage and disgust, few such adults are will-ing to confess to *intentional* sexual behavior with children. In an attempt to sustain an image of themselves as normal, apprehended offenders com-monly *disavow* their deviant behavior, admitting the acts, but denying re-sponsibility and the damaging characterization by blaming their actions on drinking. It is better to be portrayed as having a "drinking problem"—a more socially acceptable kind of problem—than be stigmatized as a fiend-ish "child molester," as the comments of these offenders indicate:

—If you been drinking a lot your passions get aroused.
—I was intoxicated and I couldn't account for myself.

—I was drunk. I didn't realize their age and I was half blind. I've always been a drinker. [The victims in this case were six and seven years old.]

—Drinking is the reason. I could always get women. I can't figure it out. A man's mind doesn't function right when he's got liquor on it.

—If I were sober it never would have happened.

—I have an alcohol drinking problem, not a sex problem.[27]

Even the legal consequences of drinking-connected theft or homicide may at least be partially softened by the belief that alcohol numbs our internal social controls. The Pennsylvania Supreme Court in 1975, for example, ruled that a person's state of "intoxication" or "drug influence" must be taken into account in assessing the intent to commit a criminal act. This judicial decision involved a man accused of committing a burglary during which the homeowner was killed. The defense lawyer, however, argued that the defendant had "no recollection" of the events because he had drunk a quart of wine and swallowed an "LSD-type pill." In this state of intoxication, the lawyer contended, the man lacked the capacity to commit a burglary or any other crime. Not all judges apparently find such an argument wholly convincing. In a bitter dissent, three associate justices of the court pointed out "that all a criminal needs now to carry out a successful robbery or burglary would be a revolver in one hand and a quart of liquor in the other."[28]

Despite the likelihood that some persons take advantage of the blame-removing or mitigating effects of drunkenness to engage in troublesome behavior with relative impunity, it is more likely that most people actually *believe* that they were not fully responsible for their misconduct. Socialized into the prevailing beliefs about the powerful biochemical effects of "demon rum," beliefs reinforced by often observable alcohol-induced bodily changes, drinkers are probably quite sincere in their conviction that they were simply "not themselves." Although most people may not typically put on drunken acts, such "time out" interludes do permit drinkers to use such occasions to fulfill certain desires and communicate important feelings. Consider, for example, this wife who is willing to cause a scene at a party to let her philandering husband know how she feels about his adulterous affairs with other women:

A woman arrived a bit late at a party, matched drinks with her husband for awhile and became visibly drunk. She knocked over her Martini, flicked ashes on the floor and then approached the husband of one of her friends, and insisted that he dance with her and put on such a demonstration of nuzzling and rubbing against the embarrassed man that he finally had to hold her away.

"Oh," she said in her loudest voice, "you're the faithful type." Then to the room at large she launched into a long, loud speech punctuated with four-letter words concerning her husband's interest in ladies other than herself. It took her distressed husband quite a while to get her into another room, where she fell onto a bed and went to sleep. Her husband returned to the living room and explained to the hostess and to anyone else who would listen that they'd been to an earlier party, where his wife had started drinking; furthermore she had been up late with the baby, so the liquor hit her really hard. And everybody was glad to accept his explanation. The next day the woman called the hostess, apologized and repeated the excuse, which was accepted again.[29]

Probably the willingness of the distressed woman to create such a scene—embarrassing both herself and her husband—was aided by her implicit knowledge that "people will understand; I'm drunk."

ALCOHOL AND SUBTERRANEAN VALUES

In advanced industrial societies, there are two major competing value orientations. A formal, more official set of values governs in large measure our workaday world: sobriety, deferred gratification, self-control, hard work, security, productivity, restraint, discipline—the values of the *work ethic*. Existing along side of—and frequently in competition or conflict with—these more bureaucratic and puritanical formal values is a set of *subterranean values*. These values typically come to the fore during our leisure time and emphasize short-run hedonistic pleasures, thrills, excitement, risk taking, adventure, spontaneity, aggressive (and often violent) notions of masculinity, and a disdain for work.[30]

However, as Jock Young points out, the process of socialization into the dominant work ethic frequently evokes guilt and anxiety feelings in many adults when they indulge in the uninhibited expression of these subterranean values. The person is "unable to let himself go fully, release himself from bondage of the performance ethic and enter unambivalently into the world of 'play.'"[31] Drinking occasions, therefore, help to facilitate the release of certain internalized inhibitions in modern industrial societies. Yet, as we have argued, drinking does not indiscriminately release asocial aggressive and sexual animalistic urges. But rather, drinking leads to a social arena in which these expressive *values* may dominate, usually temporarily, superseding for the moment the formal norms of the office, factory, and classroom.

Drunken episodes during our leisure time are not merely "escapes from reality." They are rather escapes into *alternative* kinds of social reality—with their own social norms of appropriate and inappropriate behavior. However ambivalently dominant conventional groups may view such drinking behavior, the world of subterranean values is as real as the world of adding machines, assembly lines, and IBM. The social roles and expectations associated with drinking in neighborhood taverns, in after-hours clubs, and during the Saturday night disco fever are as real and meaningful to the participants as are the social norms related to budget reports, inventory counts, and term papers attended to by bureaucrats, clerks, and college students.[32]

Particularly in complex industrial societies, alcohol serves as a *vehicle*— a transitional bridge—from the boredom, restraint, alienation, and discipline of bureaucratic work and formal school settings into a more spontaneous, expressive, hedonistic world of excitement, conviviality, flirtatious sociability, and sometimes passion and violence.[33] There are, of course, many kinds of institutionalized occasions in American society that serve as transitional bridges to the expression of subterranean values: New Year's Eve, Christmas office parties, a night out "on the town," outdoor rock concerts, the spring-vacation migration of college students to Florida, conventions, fiestas, cruise ships, vacation resorts, and weekend social parties. All of these occasions often function as partial "moral holidays" during which the participants may call "time out" from some of the usual restraining norms of everyday life.[34] An integral part of these ceremonially arranged periods of release, during which many of the normal social rules and penalties may be suspended or eased, is usually some kind of mood-altering chemical lubricant. As Aldous Huxley has noted, alcohol along with other kinds of psychoactive drugs frequently serve as a "Door in the Wall" to this subterranean reality:

> That humanity at large will ever be able to dispense with Artificial Paradise seems very unlikely. Most men and women lead lives at the worst so painful, at the best so monotonous, poor, and limited that the urge to escape, the longing to transcend themselves if only for a few moments, is and has always been one of the principal appetites of the soul. Art and religion, carnivals and saturnalia, dancing and listening to oratory—all these have served . . . as Doors in the Wall. And for private, for everyday use, there have always been chemical intoxicants. All the vegetable sedatives and narcotics, all the euphorics that grow on trees, the hallucinogens that ripen berries or can be squeezed from roots—all, without exception, have been known and systematically used by human beings from time immemorial. And to these natural modifiers of consciousness, modern science has added its quota of synthetics—chloral, for example, and benzedrine, the bromides, and the barbiturates. Most of these modifiers of consciousness cannot now be taken except under doctor's orders, or else illegally and at considerable risk. For unrestricted use the West has permitted only alcohol and tobacco. All the other chemical Doors in the Wall are labelled Dope, and their unauthorized takers are Fiends.[35]

In America, social drinking is approved by most groups—even occasional drunkenness by some—as long as the accompanying behavior remains within socially sanctioned limits and the alcoholic "beverage" (drug) is used in a way that is considered ancillary and subordinate to the dominant world of work: a "place to relax and refresh oneself before the inevitable return to 'reality.'"[36] Or as Paul Roman expresses this pragmatic justification for alcohol use among workers who have "earned" their right to imbibe:

"Evening cocktail parties and the weekend drinking are seen as useful 'unwinding' to reward the individual for work completed and 'rewind' him for work ahead."[37] Whether it be a midweek respite in the neighborhood tavern, a thank-god-it's-Friday barroom bash, or a swinging singles' weekend discotheque, these institutionalized drinking occasions represent but a temporary sojourn from the dominant formal values of productivity, work, and Monday morning. In fact, the ritualized use of alcohol is often an integral part of the workaday world, evident in the two-martini business luncheon so prominent (and tax-deductible) in the world of sales and commerce. Hosting and attending cocktail parties may not only enhance status and solidarity among old business friends but also provide settings for meeting potential clients and making business contacts.

Alcohol appears to serve similar functions in modern industrial Japan, where it is a universal ice-breaker, especially in business situations. According to some observers, alcohol in fact performs almost a "therapeutic" function by providing an occasion for a controlled release from the tight constraints and discipline of the business world. As one foreign diplomat comments: "Alcohol here plays the role of psychiatry in the West. I think the country would explode without it."[38]

Although alcoholic abuse in the form of prolonged work absence and reduced efficiency ("problem drinking") is a serious concern in American industry, most patterns of social drinking do not threaten the basic bureaucratic system of production, the materialistic rewards system, and the expectation of conventional work as a means of achieving these rewards. Similarly with caffeine, cigarettes, prescription or over-the-counter sedatives, stimulants, and tranquilizers. When long-haul truck drivers, students cramming for exams, assembly-line workers, secretaries, or executives use these drugs in moderation, they tend to be viewed as enabling the user to work more efficiently, or at least helping to cope with the strains and tensions produced by deadlines, production quotas, and the demands of industry, office, and classroom.

There are other kinds of mood-altering drugs, however, such as LSD, heroin, cocaine (and until very recently in most of America, marijuana), which many people view as supporting life-styles and values that *threaten* the dominant system of bureaucratic production and materialistic rewards. For many conventional groups, these "dangerous drugs" stereotypically linked with bohemian, radical, or lower-class subcultures symbolize a rejection of competitive materialistic success and conventional status striving; indeed, they suggest a repudiation of the entire bureaucratic ethos of structured time schedules, deferred gratification, and restraint. Hippies and "cool" drug users, for instance, are often seen as rejecting the work ethic, wallowing in a drug-induced ecstasy of play, thrills, and sexuality—an undiluted and *continuous* subterranean experience unearned by hard work and

sacrifice. Such enemy deviants and their psychedelic drug of choice thus
evoke not only moral indignation but often vigorous suppression:

> But other drugs, in the hands of groups who disdain the ethic of productivity,
> are utilized as vehicles to more radical accentuations of subterranean reality.
> It is drug use of this kind that is most actively repressed by the forces of social
> order. For it is not drugtaking *per se* but the culture of drugtakers which is
> reacted against: not the notion of changing consciousness but the type of con-
> sciousness that is socially generated.[39]

CULTURAL AMBIVALENCE

America lacks a consistent general cultural orientation toward alcohol. In
some situations, for example, it is not always exactly clear what is permissible or forbidden when drinking. Moreover, whether it be popular beliefs
about "making" a girl ("candy is dandy, but liquor is quicker") or making
a sale, a rich mixture of fact and folklore, guilt and fantasy, and moral uncertainty surrounds the subject of the mystical powers of alcohol.

Clearly, America is preoccupied with alcohol, either as a source of
pleasure or distress, and this is evident in the rich cultural vocabulary linked
to drinking activities. There are cocktail dresses, beer blasts, and happy
hours. We hit the bottle, bend the elbow, and go on the wagon. We sip or
gulp before-dinner drinks, table wines, or after-dinner cordials. We get
loaded, bombed, smashed, and plastered, and sail three sheets to the wind—
and then suffer from hangovers and the morning after. Beer, wine, and
liquor advertisers spend over $250 million annually urging us to "grab for
all the gusto," to interrupt our workaday world temporarily for fun and re-
laxation ("It's Miller time"), or to purchase illusions of sex and sophistica-
tion with Black Velvet and Chivas Regal. And in many communities, we
seldom visit a friend, eat at a fancy restaurant, or attend a party without
being offered a drink.

Our cultural heritage is riddled by deep conflicts, contradictions, and
anxieties concerning the use and abuse of alcohol. From the puritanical
substitution of grape juice for wine in the communion cup to national Prohibition and the current suppression of liquor advertisements (but not beer
or wine) on television, from *in loco parentis* college rules banning alcohol
to 3.2 beer flowing in student unions, disagreements about the effects and
control of this troubling beverage have precipitated raging political conflicts and launched social movements. Whether it be hatchet-wielding Carry
Nation battling saloon keepers, evangelists preaching the message of Alcoholics Anonymous, or advertising account-executives serving the $27 bil-
lion dollar alcohol industry—important political, business, and moral
entrepreneurial careers have been built upon the suppression, sale, and
regulation of alcohol.

The persistent *ambivalence* toward alcohol in contemporary American society is in part a legacy of these social conflicts and competing vested interests. This lingering uncertainty about the evil and beneficent effects of alcohol also reflects the *dual potential* of this ancient intoxicant: to harm millions of persons through drunken accidents, damaged health, and ruined lives as well as to enhance sociability and sexual pleasure, ease social awkwardness, relieve tension and anxiety, increase self-confidence, and make more enjoyable a variety of otherwise dull events; and for some drinkers, to extricate them temporarily from the monotony and existential pains of everyday life into a more subterranean world of hedonistic adventure, exquisite fantasy, and joyous barroom brawls. Perhaps W. C. Fields best captured the ambivalence so many Americans feel about alcohol when he remarked, "A woman drove me to drink, and I never even wrote to thank her."

This cultural ambivalence, however, is also a result of the vast religious, ethnic, and life-style diversity in the American people. Unlike the small homogeneous primitive societies surveyed by MacAndrew and Edgerton, the United States contains not only teetotaling groups but a multitude of heterogeneous drinking subcultures: merchant seamen, Puerto Rican inner-city dwellers, orthodox Jews, Irish-Catholic FBI agents, proper Bostonians, Ivy League college fraternities, uprooted urban Indians, and skid-row tramps. Each of these social groups may hold different—sometimes radically divergent—conceptions of when, why and how to drink and what is appropriate or reprehensible drinking or drunken comportment.[40]

Although all of these imbibing groups may believe that alcohol can disinhibit, their distinctive life-styles, group norms, and shared beliefs may provide different images of what it means to be drunk, what is permissible and desirable behavior to get away with, and what is normal or deviant drinking behavior. Thus, in America there is no one single and consistent pattern of drunken comportment. Nor is it always clear exactly what social and moral behavior the explanation "I was drunk" will excuse. As MacAndrew and Edgerton conclude:

> Because our society's teachings are neither clear nor consistent, we lack unanimity of understanding; and where unanimity of understanding is lacking we would argue that uniformity of practice is out of the question. Thus, although we all know that in our society the state of drunkenness carries with it an "increased freedom to be one's other self," the limits are vague and only sporadically enforced, and hence what (if anything) the plea of drunkenness will excuse in any specific case is similarly indeterminant. In such a situation, our formulation would lead us to expect that what people actually do when they are drunk will vary enormously; and this is precisely what we find when we look around us.[41]

Yet despite these highly diverse patterns of behavior among American drinkers, the knowledge that alcohol is not the all-powerful social and moral disinhibitor it is commonly thought to be may offer certain insights. We may be able to learn something of the drinker's needs, desires, frustrations, and feelings. As Blum observes:

> If it was not the spirit in the bottle that slapped the hostess on the behind but the spirit in the man, we can be pretty sure that the slap was intended either as a gesture of disrespect or as an intimacy. If we believe that it was the inebriate's own choice to sing "Raindrops Keep Falling on My Head" as loudly as possible at two in the morning outside his crankiest neighbor's bedroom window, we can be pretty certain that he is doing so not because of the liquor he has drunk but because of long-restrained anger.
>
> For people of all backgrounds, drinking can be an attempt to reach other human beings, for getting high together is, in a fashion, to embark on an adventure. It is to say, "We don't know where the alcohol will take us, but let's go together."[42]

Furthermore, even heavy drinking permits a variety of *rewarding* social roles, especially for persons who have few other marks of distinction. One can play the role of "the clown," "the jokester," "the good Joe," and especially "the drinker"—a guy who can drink everyone else under the table and who is considered in some circles a "real man." In some elite private colleges, students who do not measure up to their own or other's expectations in their academic work may still carve out a reputation for themselves as the "best drinker." A Stanford University student writes:

> At stag parties, games are concocted to determine how drinkers stand against one another. "Thumper," for example, is a round-robin type of game where the individual who makes a mistake must gulp down a drink. . . . Many parties dispense with any such ritual and "get directly to the matter at hand"; that is, they have "chugging" or "chug-a-lug" contests in which the goal is merely to discover who can drink the most the fastest. I maintain that those individuals who engage in this sort of activity the most eagerly are trying to excel in the area of drinking because they have no other area in which they feel they can succeed. Such an individual would rather be known as the best drinker than just an average student or athlete.[43]

Basing their work on a study of male college students and working-class men, David McClelland and his associates theorize that the excessive male drinker very frequently is a person with an intense need for *personal power* who uses drinking as the way to express his feelings. Although there are alternative ways for persons who are concerned with personal power to express their needs, heavy drinking—especially in a fraternity party or barroom situation—often leads to fantasies of special strength, sexual daring, of being "big, strong and influential" and having vast impact on others:

> When heavy drinking accentuates his sense of power, this leads to more drinking, drunkenness, fights, accidents, marital discord and sexual exploits. Among college students David Winter identified a stud cluster of activities in which drinking is associated with sexual conquests and high-powered motorcycles or cars.[44]

If, as many scientists contend, intoxication affects to some degree our judgment of the consequences of risks and dangers, it is not surprising that some men with intense needs of personalized power cannot drink safely. This risk of serious alcohol abuse is particularly evident in cultures and groups that stress machismo values of strength and daring but provide frequent situations that challenge and undercut a male's sense of personal power and self-worth. For men whose male prowess has been threatened, the use of liquor in certain settings that encourage heavy drinking is apt to lead to frequent drunkenness, occasional violence, high-speed reckless driving, and "to all those personal-power actions that can destroy themselves and others."[45] In such ways then do the personality characteristics of the drinker, the value orientations and sex-role expectations dominant in the culture or subculture, and the situational pressures and expectations of the drinking setting interrelate with the pharmacological effects of alcohol to shape drunken behavior.

THE ALCOHOLIC SICK ROLE

Heavy or excessive drinking is often associated with the deviant drinking role of the "alcoholic." Although there is a vast literature on this topic, unvalidated theories, inconclusive studies, and widely divergent opinions exist in the scientific community as to the precise meaning and causes of alcoholism. It is not our intention here to discuss these competing viewpoints and varied definitions of "heavy drinker," "problem drinker," and "alcoholic." It is quite possible that there are many different combinations of biological, psychological, and sociocultural factors involved in the origin and development of this complex phenomenon called alcoholism. There is, for example, increasing evidence that although a drinker may become physiologically addicted to alcohol, the extent of drinking and the personal and social disruption necessary to confer the label of alcoholic or problem drinker on a person are highly variable in different groups, communities, and societies. Much depends upon local sentiments toward drinking and drinking customs. In a national study of drinking practices among American men, Cahalan and Room found that more extensive drinking is necessary to get a man in trouble (with his wife, friends, police, on the job, and so forth) in "wetter" communities, where greater tolerance for heavy drinking exists, than in communities where there is less alcoholic consumption and more hostility toward drinking. In other words, the "dryer" the community, the *less* drinking it took to get men in trouble and evoke an image of "problem drinker."[46]

Moreover, the speed with which the deviant label is assigned, the swiftness with which the alcoholic addiction occurs, the behavior displayed while addicted, and the possibilities of recovery and return to "normality" are all at least partially shaped by the shared beliefs regarding alcoholism and the social strains, pressures, and expectations that engulf the drinker. For instance, family pressures may create intolerably stressful situations that encourage drift into this deviant drinking role. "The wife who treats her heavy-drinking husband as 'inadequate' may squeeze him into an 'alcoholic role.'"[47] To buttress his feelings of masculinity, the husband may drown his sense of inadequacy in still heavier drinking, which is often regarded as a sign of manliness. Yet such heavy alcoholic consumption may further impair his sexual relations and occupational performance—two major criteria of male status—thereby aggravating the husband's sense of inadequacy in a self-defeating vicious circle.

The crucial significance of social beliefs and pressures in shaping behavior can also be seen in the perspective of Alocholics Anonymous, a large self-help organization of persons who have experienced serious problems with drinking. According to this group's doctrine, alcoholics are persons who have a kind of physiological allergy to alcohol. Such persons are considered incapable of drinking in moderation and cannot stop drinking even when it results in the destruction of the alcoholic's life and the lives of those around him. "Once an alcoholic, always an alcoholic," A.A. contends: there are no "former alcoholics," only *sober* alcoholics. Alcoholics are persons who cannot drink at all—ever. The official publication of Alcoholics Anonymous describes their belief in this persistent indwelling condition of alcoholism:

> We learned that we have to fully concede to our innermost selves that we were alcoholics. . . . The delusion that we are like other people . . . has to be smashed. We alcoholics are men and women who have lost the ability to control our drinking. We know that no real alcoholic *ever* recovers control. . . . We have seen the truth demonstrated again and again. "Once an alcoholic, always an alcoholic."[48]

Thus, lifelong permanent abstinence is required even though some current scientific studies (bitterly contested by A.A.) suggest that a large proportion—perhaps even a majority—of treated alcoholics can resume moderate social drinking without any destructive consequences.[49]

In many Western industrial societies, there are deeply ambivalent attitudes toward persons considered alcoholics. Feelings of pity and compassion alternate and mingle with attitudes of disgust, shame, and contempt. The alcoholic may be viewed simultaneously as both weak-willed and sick.[50] Since there is still a social stigma or derogatory connotation attached to this alcoholic identity in America—partly a legacy of the cultural value placed on self-control—most heavy drinkers in our society initially resist such self-definitions and attempt to stave off the efforts of others to pin such a deviant label on them. (Although prolonged heavy drinking can result in physiological addiction and acute physical illness and misery, recent evidence shows that chronic heavy drinking does not inevitably result in addiction and that many drinkers are apparently neither miserable nor ill during long periods of steady heavy drinking.)[51]

Moreover, the intimate friends and close relatives of the heavy drinker are also reluctant to define the person's drinking habits as symptomatic of alcoholism. Even when the drinker becomes involved in occasional and visible disturbing drinking incidents, the "intimates of drinkers (and drinkers themselves) take great pains to deny or underplay the signs of their heavy drinking."[52] The alcohol-related trouble is commonly viewed as only a temporary aberration out of character with the real personality of the drinker.

This tendency to delay conferral of the alcoholic label may in part derive from the popular view of alcoholism as an "all-or-nothing" kind of disease. Either the drinker is or is not afflicted by the ailment. But in reality the road from social drinker to compulsive alcoholic represents more of a continuum. There is no clear-cut, universal, and uniform syndrome of behavioral characteristics to mark off the alcoholic from the normal heavy drinker. Consequently, "people who drink heavily have no guideposts along the way to determine just where they are in regard to alcoholism and neither do the people closest to them."[53]

The attempt to normalize heavy drinking in many social groups, withholding and disavowing the deviant label of alcoholic, is also aided by the culturally supported role of social drinker. As noted previously, this socially rewarding drinking role in America is associated with many positive personal traits: not only a person who is sociable, gregarious, and fun-loving but, if a male, someone who is also very manly. Although the differences in the amount of alcohol consumed by the heavy "social drinker" and the "alcoholic" may be miniscule, the popular cultural differentiation between these two drinking roles is vast.

Another important reason for the reluctance of persons close to the heavy drinker to assign him or her to this deviant role is the degrading and extreme stereotypes of the behavior and life-style of an alcoholic in America, characteristics which the typical heavy drinker may lack:

"He can't be an alcoholic," the wife of a heavy drinker will say to herself, "because he's not like *those* people"—meaning the cultural stereotype of the alcoholic is someone whose life is totally dominated and completely destroyed by the consumption of liquor. It is the belligerent or the tragic-comic falling down drunk. It is the man or woman whose failure to perform on the job or even the ability to hold down a job is due to intoxication or the pursuit thereof. The alcoholic, according to this view, is the man . . . or woman whose family life is in shambles, whose spouse and children have become alienated, frustrated, bitter, or have departed for their own protection. From social isolation, unemployment, divorce, and complete and catastrophic failure, skid row is only a short step.[54]

Thus the awareness and final judgment that someone close to you is an alcoholic represents a long, vacillating, and often tortuous process. It involves disbelief, skepticism, accommodation to embarrassing drunken episodes, humiliation, shame, "cover-ups," guilt, rationalizations, hostility, and denial—until the person's drinking becomes too blatantly extreme, troublesome, outrageous, and disruptive to tolerate any longer. This common tendency by close friends and intimate relatives to "conventionalize" the deviant behavior and thereby help sustain the person in heavy drinking is evident in the remarks of this woman, who for years vacillated between rejection and tolerance of her alcoholic brother:

The drug-taker . . . usually finds himself quickly . . . shunned in polite society, hitting bottom fast and . . . available early for treatment or isolation. The alcoholic addict, unfortunately, can go on year after year, increasing his addiction while everybody smiles, approves, and offers him another drink.[55]

Regardless of what multidimensional factors may be involved in the originating causes and persistance of alcoholism, a worthy hypothesis for systematic research is that some significant proportion of persons in America who become labeled alcoholics may be *attracted* to this social role at some stage during their drinking troubles.[56] Although there is still a lingering moral disdain in our society for persons who cannot control their drinking, educational campaigns and most physicians increasingly portray the alcoholic as the victim of a "disease" and cast him or her into the *sick role*.[57] The medical definition that underlies this conception presumes that such "compulsive drinkers" do not enjoy their drinking, that they are temporarily not their "real selves," but are driven by forces beyond their control. Such a view of problem drinking as "illness" encourages expressions of humanitarian and therapeutic concern, rather than moral indignation and punishment.

Consequently, as some drinker's life problems intensify, intolerably aggravated by heavy drinking, the designation of the person as a sick alcoholic may offer certain advantages to the drinker. No one really expects alcoholics to perform even close to their abilities or to meet normal adult obligations or to measure up to culturally prescribed standards of success and adequacy as a man or a woman. This sick role therefore may function to *excuse* the drinker from failure in job and career, from ineptitude as a husband or father, or from shortcomings as a wife or mother.

Certainly the reasons for the attraction of the alcoholic sick role are often subtle and may operate below the ordinary threshold of the drinker's consciousness; that is, probably very few persons defined as alcoholics can easily verbalize the advantages of such culturally defined "helplessness." Yet implicit knowledge—reinforced by expert medical opinion—of the responsibility-removing consequences of this vaguely defined "disease" provides at least some relief from the pains of social reality. This alcoholic box thus offers an immediate *individual* "solution" to the irreconcilable conflicts and impossible situations in the alcohol user's marriage, family, job, financial problems, entanglements with the law, or other areas of personal stress.

As Jock Young argues, for many addicts—alcohol and heroin—the "benefits of sickness are greater than the pains of freedom."[58] And with the progressive onset of tangible, visible symptoms of ill-health, for example, expanded blackouts (memory losses) and withdrawal distress (i.e., acute trembling or the "shakes," restlessness, and physical weakness), the drinker's belief that he or she is *really* sick finds increasing confirmation. Whether the problem drinker identifies the source of the sickness as psychological in origin or merely physiological or both, he may surrender his ability to make a choice regarding drinking in the light of his perceived illness.

To be sick is to be unable to manage drinking through sheer volition, since the person is presumably suffering from a medically defined pathological ailment lodged within the individual. The "significant others"—close friends, relatives, spouse—surrounding the troubled drinker may also share such a conception. Although friends and relatives may admonish the drinker to "shape up," stop drinking, and seek treatment, unwittingly they also may reinforce the social *expectations* that accompany the sick role: that the problem drinker is not responsible for his or her behavior and that he or she will undoubtedly continue to engage in deviant drinking practices. With bated breath we await the next binge or relapse, communicating our pessimism. As Roman and Trice point out, "we are not surprised to see a drunk alcoholic and we marvel with amazement when we see a sober one."[59]

Thus the drinker's ability to control alcoholic consumption further diminishes, and performance on the job or in marriage increasingly deteriorates from the protracted drinking. The mutual interaction of stress, drug dependence, social expectations, and deterministic beliefs may take on the character of a self-fulfilling prophecy. The drinker becomes progressively engulfed—and for some, entrapped—in the bittersweet and partly socially created role of an alcoholic. Especially for problem drinkers who believe that their alcoholic dependence is irreversible, permanent, or fated, such mystifying beliefs, as Sagarin and Montanino note, may imprison the chronic drinker in this alcoholic condition:

> [T]here is in addiction both voluntarism and some degree of involuntarism, the former being greater in earlier stages. The involuntarism that develops in the course of addiction takes on the form of psychological and physiological dependence. Yet such a condition is not irreversible, not beyond correction, and is far from hopeless. Only the definition of it in terms of irreversibility can possibly make it so. It is not an easy task, but the addict and the alcoholic, in the last analysis, have freedom of choice: whether to inject the next dose, whether to take the next drink. One can say no, face up to the responsibility of accounting for one's own state of existence, and do something about it. Or one can continue to deny this responsibility, pointing to forces, both interpersonal and social as well as psychological, that impinge on and impel a person to continue. This is to succumb to an escape from responsibility. If this is sometimes an easier alternative, it is also one that proves detrimental and dysfunctional not only for the individuals and intimate others around them but for the society of which they remain a part.[60]

Unfortunately, even when the alcoholic seeks treatment, those who *individualize* the drinker's problems through the medical vocabulary of illness and therapy often do not examine the possible sources of personal stress resulting from repressive conditions affecting the family, the workplace or minority groups. The tendency to isolate the alcoholic's problems in this clinical and strictly "pathological" manner—whether the alcoholic is a college-educated woman trapped in the boring, banal, and unrewarding role of housekeeper or a poor black man who has given up hope of ever finding work again when laid off at age forty-five—may divert concern from the removal of the basic stress-producing social arrangements.

This brief discussion of the possible attractions of the sick role for some alcoholics—perhaps only a small minority—is not meant to deny the reality of physiologically induced illness that can occur from chronic heavy drinking or the varied responses of alcoholics to their misery. Nor do we wish to discount the benefits of disease and sick-role designations for helping many drinkers to cope more effectively with their alcohol-related problems and for instituting more humanitarian responses instead of jailing drunken derelicts. Certainly the considerable success of Alcoholics Anonymous and other kinds of treatment programs has demonstrated the positive value of medical labels. But, rather, we wish to emphasize the importance of sociocultural factors in the development, persistence, and definition of chronic drinking problems and the crucial significance of deterministic beliefs and other people's reactions and expectations.

Research and knowledge of the diverse causes of compulsive and destructive drinking are still in a primitive state. But whatever future studies reveal, it seems likely that the social *meanings* imputed to alcohol and drunken comportment—the shared beliefs and expectations—as well as the structural strains and social pressures in the society will be found deeply implicated in these troubling drinking patterns.

FOOTNOTES

1 Sam Blum, "Why We 'Let Go' When We Drink," *Redbook*, May, 1970, p. 96.
2 Blum, "Why We 'Let Go' When We Drink," p. 96.
3 Quoted in Craig MacAndrew and Robert B. Edgerton, *Drunken Comportment: A Social Explanation*, Aldine, Chicago, 1969, p. 4.
4 Group for the Advancement of Psychiatry, Committee on the College Student, *Sex and the College Student*, Atheneum, New York, 1966, p. 95, quoted in MacAndrew and Edgerton, *Drunken Comportment*, p. 4.
5 MacAndrew and Edgerton, *Drunken Comportment*, p. 3.
6 MacAndrew and Edgerton, *Drunken Comportment*.
7 Leon A. Greenberg, "Alcohol in the Body," *Scientific American*, 189 (December 1953), p. 88.
8 Marvin Block, *Alcoholism: Its Facets and Phases*, John Day, New York, 1965, pp. 219–220, quoted in MacAndrew and Edgerton, *Drunken Comportment*, p. 7.
9 Morris Chafetz and Harold W. Demone, *Alcoholism and Society*, Oxford University Press, New York, 1962, p. 9, quoted in MacAndrew and Edgerton, *Drunken Comportment*, pp. 6–7. See also Morris Chafetz, *Why Drinking Can Be Good For You*, Stein and Day, New York, 1976, p. 16.
10 See Ben Morgan Jones and Oscar A. Parsons, "Getting High, Coming Down," *Psychology Today*, 8 (January 1975), pp. 53–58.
11 MacAndrew and Edgerton, *Drunken Comportment*, pp. 57–60.
12 Gerado Reichel-Dolmatoff and Alicia Reichel-Dolmatoff, *The People of Aritama*, Routledge & Kegan Paul, London, 1961, p. 197, quoted in MacAndrew and Edgerton, *Drunken Comportment*, p. 24.
13 MacAndrew and Edgerton, *Drunken Comportment*, p. 53.
14 MacAndrew and Edgerton, *Drunken Comportment*, pp. 78–82.
15 MacAndrew and Edgerton, *Drunken Comportment*, p. 33.
16 See Robin Room, "Normative Perspectives on Alcohol Use and Problems," *Journal of Drug Issues*, 5 (Fall 1975), pp. 358–368; Jock Young, *The Drugtakers*, Paladin, London, 1971; Richard H. Blum and Associates, *Society and Drugs*, Jossey-Bass, San Francisco, 1969; Erich Goode, *Drugs in American Society*, Knopf, New York, 1972, Ch. 1.
17 Edwin Lemert, *Social Pathology*, McGraw-Hill, New York, 1951, p. 341, quoted in Young, *The Drugtakers*, p. 39. See also Edwin Lemert, *Human Deviance, Social Problems, and Social Control*, Prentice-Hall, Englewood Cliffs, N.J., 1972, Ch. 12, "Sociocultural Research on Drinking"; Richard Stivers, "Culture and Alcoholism," in Ralph E. Tarter and A. Arthur Sugerman (eds.), *Alcoholism*, Addison-Wesley, Reading, Mass., 1976, pp. 573–602; Robert F. Bales, "Cultural Differences in Rates of Alcoholism," in Raymond G. McCarthy (ed.), *Drinking and Intoxication*, Free Press, Glencoe, Ill., 1959, pp. 263–277; Ephraim

M. Mizruchi and Robert Perrucci, "Prescription, Proscription and Permissiveness: Aspects of Norms and Deviant Drinking Behavior," in George L. Maddox (ed.), *The Domesticated Drug: Drinking Among Collegians*, College and University Press, New Haven, Conn., 1970, pp. 234–253.

18 See MacAndrew and Edgerton, *Drunken Comportment*, Ch. 4.

19 MacAndrew and Edgerton, *Drunken Comportment*, p. 165.

20 Blum, "Why We 'Let Go' When We Drink," pp. 145–146.

21 See Morton Issacs, "Stereotyping by Children of the Effects of Drinking on Adults," *Journal of Studies on Alcohol*, 38 (May 1977), pp. 913–921.

22 Quoted in Joel Fort and Christopher T. Cory, *American Drugstore*, Little, Brown, Boston, 1975, p. 29. See also Ira H. Cisin, "Formal and Informal Social Controls over Drinking," in John A. Ewing and Beatrice A. Rouse (eds.), *Drinking: Alcohol in American Society—Issues and Current Research*, Nelson-Hall, Chicago, 1978, p. 151.

23 MacAndrew and Edgerton, *Drunken Comportment*, p. 88. See also James D. Orcutt, "Toward a Sociological Theory of Drug Effects: A Comparison of Marijuana and Alcohol," *Sociology and Social Research*, 56 (January 1972), pp. 242–253; Howard S. Becker, "Consciousness, Power, and Drug Effects: An Exploration of the Social Bases of Drug-Induced Experiences," *Journal of Health and Social Behavior*, 8 (September 1967), pp. 163–176; John Auld, "Cannabis, Alcohol, and the Management of Intoxication," in Paul E. Rock (ed.), *Drugs and Politics*, Transaction Books, New Brunswick, N.J., 1977, pp. 261–268.

24 MacAndrew and Edgerton, *Drunken Comportment*, p. 167. For a general discussion of social vocabularies of justification and excuse, see Gresham M. Sykes and David Matza, "Techniques of Neutralization: A Theory of Delinquency," *American Sociological Review*, 22 (December 1957), pp. 664–670; Marvin B. Scott and Stanford M. Lyman, "Accounts," *American Sociological Review*, 33 (February 1968), pp. 46–62.

25 Blum, "Why We 'Let Go' When We Drink," p. 146.

26 Quoted in Blum "Why We 'Let Go' When We Drink," p. 146.

27 Charles H. McCaghy, "Drinking and Deviance Disavowal," *Social Problems*, 16 (Summer 1968), p. 48.

28 Quoted in Robert B. Edgerton, *Deviance: A Cross-Cultural Perspective*, Cummings, Menlo Park, Calif., 1976, p. 60.

29 Blum, "Why We 'Let Go' When We Drink," p. 146. See also Phillip A. Dennis, "The Role of the Drunk in an Oaxacan Village," *American Anthropologist*, 77 (December 1975), pp. 856–863.

30 See Young, *The Drugtakers*, Ch. 6; David Matza and Gresham Sykes, "Juvenile Delinquency and Subterranean Values," *American Sociological Review*, 26 (October 1961), pp. 712–719.

31 Young, *The Drugtakers*, p. 133.

32 See, for example, Julian B. Roebuck and Wolfgang Frese, *The Rendezvous: A Case Study of an After-Hours Club*, Free Press, New York, 1976; Sherri Cavan, *Liquor License: An Ethnography of Bar Behavior*, Aldine, Chicago, 1966; E. E. LeMasters, *Blue Collar Aristocrats: Life Styles at a Working Class Tavern*, University of Wisconsin Press, Madison, Wis., 1975.

33 Young, *The Drugtakers*, p. 135. See also Dennis Brissett, "Toward an Inter-
    actionist Understanding of Heavy Drinking," *Pacific Sociological Review*, 21
    (January 1978), p. 11; Alexander D. Blumenstiel, "The Sociology of Good
    Times," in George Psathas (ed.), *Phenomenological Sociology*, Wiley, New
    York, 1973, pp. 187–215.
34 Cavan, *Liquor License*, p. 236.
35 Quoted in Young, *The Drugtakers*, pp. 135–136.
36 Young, *The Drugtakers*, p. 137.
37 Paul M. Roman, "Settings for Successful Deviance among Middle- and Upper-
    Level Employees," in Clifton D. Bryant (ed.), *Deviant Behavior*, Rand McNally,
    Chicago, 1974, p. 113.
38 *Behavior Today*, Jan. 2, 1978, p. 7.
39 Young, *The Drugtakers*, p. 137.
40 See, for example, the collection of articles in Maddox (ed.), *The Domesticated
    Drug;* David J. Pittman and Charles R. Snyder (eds.), *Society, Culture, and
    Drinking Patterns*, Wiley, New York, 1962. Also, Richard Stivers, *A Hair of
    the Dog: Irish Drinking and American Stereotype*, Penn State University Press,
    University Park, Pa., 1977; James P. Spradley, *You Owe Yourself a Drunk:
    An Ethnology of Urban Nomads*, Little, Brown, Boston, 1970; Richard Jessor
    et al., *Society, Personality, and Deviant Behavior: A Study of a Tri-Ethnic
    Community*, Holt, Rinehart, & Winston, New York, 1968.
41 MacAndrew and Edgerton, *Drunken Comportment*, p. 172.
42 Blum, "Why We 'Let Go' When We Drink," pp. 146–147.
43 Quoted in Robert D. Russell, "College Drinking: Students See It Many Ways,"
    in Maddox (ed.), *The Domesticated Drug*, p. 193. For a discussion of the posi-
    tive functions of heavy drinking for establishing a meaningful sense of individual
    identity, see Brissett, "Toward an Interactionist Understanding of Heavy Drink-
    ing," pp. 9–10.
44 David C. McClelland, "The Power of Positive Drinking," *Psychology Today*,
    4 (January 1971), p. 78.
45 McClelland, "The Power of Positive Drinking," p. 79. See also David C.
    McClelland et al.,*The Drinking Man*, Free Press, New York, 1972; Sharon C.
    Wilsnack, "The Needs of the Female Drinker: Dependency, Power, or What?"
    in Morris E. Chafetz (ed.), *Proceedings of the Second Annual Alcoholism
    Conference of the National Institute on Alcohol Abuse and Alcoholism*, Na-
    tional Institute on Mental Health, Washington, D.C., 1973, pp. 65–83.
46 Don Cahalan and Robin Room, *Problem Drinking Among American Men*,
    Rutgers Center of Alcohol Studies, New Brunswick, N.J., 1974, pp. 81–82.
47 Young, *The Drugtakers*, p. 115.
48 Quoted in Erich Goode, *Deviant Behavior*, Prentice-Hall, Englewood Cliffs,
    N.J., 1978, p. 98. See also Harrison M. Trice and Paul M. Roman, "Delabeling,
    Relabeling, and Alcoholics Anonymous," in Earl Rubington and Martin S.
    Weinberg (eds.), *Deviance*, Macmillan, New York, 1978, pp. 476–483; Irving
    Gellman, *The Sober Alcoholic*, College and University Press, New Haven,
    Conn., 1964.
49 See David J. Armour et al., *Alcoholism and Treatment*, Wiley-Interscience,
    New York, 1978.

50 See Robin Room, "Drinking and Disease: Comment on 'The Alcohologist's Addiction,'" *Quarterly Journal of Studies on Alcohol*, 33 (December 1972), p. 1050; Harold A. Mulford and Donald E. Miller, "Measuring Public Acceptance of the Alcoholic as a Sick Person," *Quarterly Journal of Studies on Alcohol*, 25 (June 1964), pp. 314–323.

51 Roman, "Settings for Successful Deviance," p. 112. See also Don Cahalan and Ira H. Cisin, "Epidemiological and Social Factors Associated with Drinking Problems," in Tarter and Sugerman (eds.), *Alcoholism*, pp. 543–544; Cahalan and Room, *Problem Drinking Among American Men.*

52 Goode, *Deviant Behavior*, p. 58. See also Joan K. Jackson, "The Adjustment of the Family to Alcoholism," in Saul D. Feldman (ed.), *Deciphering Deviance*, Little, Brown, Boston, 1978, pp. 335–343.

53 Goode, *Deviant Behavior*, p. 58.

54 Goode, *Deviant Behavior*, p. 59.

55 Quoted in Goode, *Deviant Behavior*, p. 63.

56 Young, *The Drugtakers*, pp. 81–89.

57 See Don Cahalan, *Problem Drinkers*, Jossey-Bass, San Francisco, 1970, pp. 1–11; Paul M. Roman and H. M. Trice, "The Sick Role, Labelling Theory, and the Deviant Drinker," *International Journal of Social Psychiatry*, 12 (1968), pp. 245–251; Room, "Drinking and Disease," pp. 1049–1059; Joseph W. Schneider, "Deviant Drinking as Disease: Alcoholism as a Social Accomplishment," *Social Problems*, 25 (April 1978), pp. 361–372.

58 Young, *The Drugtakers*, p. 87.

59 Roman and Trice, "The Sick Role, Labelling Theory, and the Deviant Drinker," p. 246.

60 Edward Sagarin and Fred Montanino (eds.), *Deviants: Voluntary Actors in a Hostile World*, General Learning Press, Morristown, N.J., 1977, p. 13.

Chapter 7

Homosexuality in a Changing Society

During the last decade the study of homosexuality has become more than a subject for detached scholarly research. The battle over the normality, morality, and civil rights of persons with different sexual orientations has become a major public issue, igniting powerful emotions and launching social movements of protest and counterprotest. Although scattered homosexual incidents and expressions of gay pride increasingly appeared in the mass media in the 1970s, two events, in particular, helped to focus public attention on the deprivations imposed on homosexuals and the strong feelings surrounding homosexuality in American society. The first involved the case of a gay Air Force sergeant and winner of a Bronze Star who was involuntarily discharged from the military. Martin Duberman describes the impact of the discovery of the homosexual orientation of this popular and highly rated Air Force instructor:

> If there has ever been a son of midAmerica, it was Leonard Matlovich, tech sergeant, Langley Air Force Base, Hampton, Va. Matlovich believes in God, duty, his country, monogamy, competition and hard work. He volunteered for three tours of duty in Vietnam because "that's where my nation needed me."

He erected an 18-foot flagpole in his front yard. He voted for Goldwater. He always did more than his share on the job, pushing himself to excel—and then took on additional jobs. He was never comfortable with sexuality; in his conservative Catholic family, "anything relating to sex was not discussed." His politics were right-wing: when the Air Force became integrated, he protested being housed with "niggers"; he considered Walter Cronkite a "flaming liberal."

That is, until two years ago when Leonard Matlovich, aged 30, lost his virginity—to a man.

One doesn't want to claim too much for the transforming power of sex—or even of self-acceptance—but if the causes can't be neatly charted, Matlovich today is clearly a different man from the superpatriot of a few years back. He is now deeply ashamed of the stand he took against integration, and his eyes water when he notes the irony that blacks at Langley have formed his chief support group since he publicly came out as a homosexual seven months ago. A sign on his apartment wall reads, "Legalize Freedom." On his front door the placard says, "Trust in God—She will provide."

Some of his values have been modified, not transformed. . . . Seemingly comfortable now with his sexual orientation, he admits that had he the choice—and he is adamant that homosexuals never have the choice—he would rather be straight. . . . He still loves the Air Force and is sure that he will be allowed to serve in it, but not if it means "living a lie."[1]

Subsequently, a court-martial ruled that Sergeant Matlovich, with twelve years of distinguished service, could not remain in the military because of his homosexuality. His sexual orientation was considered more significant than his patriotism, dedication, and abilities. A federal district court judge later upheld the discharge but urged the military to reconsider its policy that homosexuality is in itself evidence of a person's unfitness for service.

But it was the well-publicized actions of singer Anita Bryant in Miami that moved the issue of gay rights to the center of national public controversy in the late 1970s. Bryant, a 36-year-old mother of four children, a television entertainer, and a former Miss America runner-up, led a successful fight to repeal a Dade County civil rights ordinance barring discrimination against homosexuals in housing, jobs, or public accommodations. Acting out of strong religious convictions, Bryant, a born-again Christian, launched a "Save Our Children" campaign to warn citizens of the immorality and dire consequences of permitting homosexual teachers to gain legitimate access to the classrooms of the nation. Thousands of school children, she claimed, were the objects of "recruitment" by homosexuals who cannot have kids of their own: "What these people really want, hidden behind obscure legal phrases, is the legal right to propose to our children that there is an acceptable alternative way of life—that being homosexual or lesbian is not really wrong or illegal."[2]

Gay liberation groups, however, began to fight back, using the national spotlight on Miami to mobilize support for their cause. On television

talk shows and in magazine articles, these activists challenged public stereotypes about the "danger" of homosexuals. Gay leaders publicized the fact
that there is no convincing evidence that an erotic preference for the same
sex is basically caused by seduction of a youth by an older gay man or lesbian woman. Spokesmen cited findings from scientific studies that indicate
that the vast majority of adult homosexuals have no more special interest
in sexual contact with young boys and girls than do most heterosexual
adults; that homosexuality is not a "disease" like measles that can be
"caught" by innocent children; that, in fact, contrary to widespread beliefs,
the overwhelming majority of child molestation cases do not involve homosexuals, but heterosexual offenders.[3] In addition, homosexual activists began to borrow tactics from the black civil rights struggles of the 1960s:
marching, demonstrating, and threatening to organize consumer boycotts
of the Florida citrus industry if it did not stop using antigay crusader Anita
Bryant in orange juice television commercials.

As Anita Bryant's speeches at public rallies became more strident, she
accused these "enemy deviants" of harassment and causing injury to her
public career. In 1978, she went on public record in support of not only
denying homosexuals certain basic civil rights but punishing them severely
for making love with persons of the same sex. Asked by an interviewer if
she favored prosecuting homosexuals as criminal felons, even if a single
homosexual act among consenting adults resulted in a 20-year prison term,
Bryant answered:

> Yes, I think so. Anytime you can water down the law, it just makes it easier for
> immorality to be tolerated. . . . Why make it easier for them? I think it only
> helps to condone it and to make it easier for kids who wouldn't be so concerned
> if it were a misdemeanor, whereas a felony might make them think twice, es-
> pecially the younger ones.[4]

Although not all persons who view gay people as sinful, sick, degenerate,
ǒr criminal would support such harsh penal sanctions—or even any criminal penalties—the moral indignation often animating such absolutist views
is widespread among a sizable proportion of the population.

Despite the persistence of this antipathy toward homosexuality, there
have been some significant changes both attitudinally and legally toward
homosexuals in the United States. Since 1962, for example, nineteen states
have decriminalized private sexual acts and about forty municipalities have
passed limited civil rights ordinances protecting homosexuals in housing
and employment (at least in the eyes of the law, if not always in practice.)[5]
Many younger psychotherapists are also challenging the traditional psychiatric view of homosexuality as a "sickness" or "mental illness." And
after years of court battles, the U.S. Civil Service Commission in 1974
changed its policy that homosexuality automatically disqualifies a person

for government service. Moreover, among *some* young heterosexuals there appears to be a greater moral acceptance of various alternative sexual life-styles. A male college student, for example, upon informing his resident advisor, a young woman, that he was a bisexual was pleasantly surprised by her matter-of-fact reaction: "So what?"

> My next step was to tell my roommates. . . . Their reactions were also, "So what?" This shocked me because they really meant it. I found that my room-mate didn't care, either. . . . In a short time the entire building knew. I assume my suitemates spread the word . . . but people really found out when they came up to me and asked if I was bisexual. I reasoned that they already knew and just wanted confirmation and I told them, "Yes, I am." The general reaction was, "Hey, Wow!" followed by an avalanche of questions of a sincere nature seek-ing honest information. It was this reaction which helped me to find the strength to honestly accept myself as I am.[6]

Yet for the majority of Americans, homosexuality, like bisexuality, is clearly viewed as deviant behavior—devalued and stigmatized. Notwith-standing the increased sexual permissiveness in America, many homosex-uals must still work, love, and live in a hostile and condemnatory social climate. In a survey of public attitudes toward homosexuality based on a nationally representative sample of over 3,000 adults, nearly half of the re-spondents agreed that "homosexuality is a social corruption which can cause the downfall of civilization." Two-thirds of the entire sample indi-cated their dislike of homosexuals ("obscene and vulgar") and supported barring them from government service and medical practice, and three-quarters denied homosexuals the right to be schoolteachers, judges, or ministers. About 60 percent opposed the decriminalization of homosexual acts among consenting adults.[7] (In 1976, the U.S. Supreme Court upheld the constitutionality of state laws that can lead to imprisonment of men and women who engage in homosexual acts.)

Although there has been a growing *tolerance* toward homosexuals in certain social circles and in some large urban centers—a kind of live-and-let-live attitude—genuine *acceptance* of homosexuality as a morally equal, valid, and normal sexual variant is still quite uncommon among the vast majority of conventional heterosexual adults. The soul-searching and an-guished sentiments of this well-educated father of four boys clearly reveal ambivalence and troubled feelings toward homosexuality, and especially a deep-seated dread that one's children might turn out to be homosexuals:

> If I had the power to do so, I would wish homosexuality off the face of this earth. . . . They are different from the rest of us. Homosexuals are different, moreover, in a way that cuts deeper than other kinds of human differences— religious, class, racial—in a way that is, somehow, more fundamental. Cursed

without clear cause, afflicted without apparent cure, they are an affront to our rationality, living evidence of our despair of ever finding a sensible, an explainable, design to the world. One can tolerate homosexuality, a small enough price to be asked to pay for someone else's pain, but accepting it, really accepting it, is another thing altogether. I find I can accept it least of all when I look at my children. There is much my four sons can do in their lives that might cause me anguish, that might make me ashamed of them and of myself as their father. But nothing they could ever do would make me sadder than if any of them were to become a homosexual. For then I should know them condemned to a state of permanent niggerdom among men, their lives, whatever adjustment they might make to their condition, to be lived out as part of the pain of the earth.[8]

It is quite likely that this gnawing fear that parents will lose their children to "them" is a basic component of much antihomosexuality, epitomized in Bryant's emphasis on "saving our children." Parental insecurity, therefore, is probably an important factor in hardening and crystallizing many people's negative feelings toward homosexuals.

DIMENSIONS OF HOMOSEXUALITY

What is a homosexual? How does a person have to act, think, or feel to warrant such a label? In popular discussions on the subject, it is commonly assumed that "everyone knows" what a homosexual (often scornfully referred to as a queer, fag, fairy, pansy, or fruit) is. The assumption, however, of two mutually exclusive and absolute categories—homosexuals and heterosexuals—obscures the fact that people can express same-sex orientations at different moments in their lives and in different situations (for example, in prison, in boarding school, in early adolescent "circle jerks"). And people can express homosexual orientations in many different ways: in sexual preference (whether one prefers to have sex with males or females), in actual physical and genital sexual behavior, in romantic feelings (falling in love), in sexual arousal (the ability to be turned on physically)—all of which may have different consequences for one's self-image as heterosexual, bisexual, or gay. While these various dimensions of sexual expression— *preference*, *behavior*, *emotions*, and *identity*—frequently cluster together, they may also to some degree vary independent of one another. That is, a person may be considered "homosexual" in terms of one characteristic (for instance, the ability to get turned on physically—become erotically aroused— by a person of the same sex) but "heterosexual" in other characteristics (a self-image as "straight" and actual sexual behavior confined exclusively to the opposite sex).

Consider, for example, George, a married truckdriver in his mid-thirties who finds tension release by furtive sexual encounters with males in public restrooms. A Roman Catholic father of seven children, George doesn't want any more kids, but his wife objects to contraceptives:

> My wife doesn't have much outside interest. She doesn't like to go out or take the kids places. But she's an A-1 mother, I'll say that! I guess you'd say she's very nice to get along with—but don't cross her. She gets aggravated with me—I don't know why. . . . Well, you'd have to know my wife. We fight all the time. Anymore, it seems we just don't get along—except when we're apart. Mostly, we argue about the kids. She's afraid of having more. . . . She's afraid to have sex but doesn't believe in birth control. I'd just rather not be around her! I won't suggest having sex anyway—and she just doesn't want it anymore.[9]

In a study of persons in a Midwestern community who seek quick impersonal sex in "tearooms" (public men's rooms), Laud Humphreys found that almost *two-thirds* of such persons are *heterosexually married men*, many of whom resemble George.[10] For frequenters of tearooms who actively perform fellatio on males, George is considered *trade*—heterosexual men who are the passive recipients of oral-genital sex but who will not reciprocate in the same manner. Despite George's regular participation in these brief sexual encounters, he still considers himself heterosexual and quite masculine. Apart from this narrowly confined but frequent sexual contact with males, George has no other involvement in gay subcultures or even any homosexual friends. In answer to Humphreys' query as to how frequently he had intercourse with his wife, George replied: "Not very much the last few years. . . . It's up to her when she feels like giving it to me—which ain't very often."[11] Thus, impersonal orgasms in urinals—often without a word exchanged with the fellator—appear to serve as a kind of substitute for sex with his wife.

As Humphreys points out, with many working-class men like George, any intimate and prolonged adulterous affair which required much time away from home—or patronizing a prostitute which would involve considerable expense—would threaten their shaky marriage, jeopardize their standing as father, and might separate them from their children, a relationship that is extremely important to these men who have few other sources of satisfaction in their lives—either in the marital bed or at work. Often lonely and without any close friends, they "slip off the freeways for a few moments of impersonal sex in a toilet stall."[12]

Or consider the case of Doy, a lower-class adolescent "street hustler," who for money allows men occasionally to perform fellatio on him. Doy, like George, does not define what he does as homosexual; nor does he label his activity as prostitution. Rather, "getting a queer" is simply a quick way of earning extra cash. Doy describes how he got started:

> I went along with these older boys down to the bus station, and they took me along and showed me how it was done . . . they'd go in, get a queer, get blowed

and get paid . . . if it didn't work right, they'd knock him in the head and get their money . . . they showed me how to do it, so I went in too.[13]

Doy and his other adolescent hustler friends deny that any sexual gratification derived from the act is a reason for their willing participation in these business-like sexual encounters. Such sexual behavior is seen, rather, as strictly an expedient means of making some "easy money." As long as the sexual transaction is limited to quick oral-genital fellatio by the customer in a casual pickup situation and is devoid of any visible emotional attachments, there is no apparent threat to the adolescent hustler's self-image as masculine and heterosexual. However, if the fellator suggests any further desires for sexual or emotional involvement, or treats the hustler as if he were a homosexual—especially in front of the boy's peers—the customer risks being beaten up:

> This gay comes up to me in the lobby of the Empress when we was standin' around and starts feelin' me up and callin' me Sweetie and like that . . . and, I just couldn't take none of that there . . . what was he makin' out like I was a queer or somethin' . . . so I jumps him right then and there and we like to of knocked his teeth out.[14]

Such violence helps to protect the boy's self-image as nonhomosexual, to bolster his self-concept as masculine, and most important, to legitimate his heterosexuality and status in the eyes of his adolescent peer group. Yet this hustling activity is typically short-lived for these lower-class boys. With increasing pressures from the dominant sectors of society to settle down, marry, and go to work, most of these peer-oriented hustlers, according to Albert Reiss, move out of such forms of prostitution as they get older. The vast majority enter into steady female relationships, marriage, and conventional jobs, with a few boys gravitating toward more serious delinquent careers.[15]

A very different type of sexual experience is that enjoyed by Don, a thirty-three-year-old successful buyer for a department store who lives with Leslie, another male, in a white, middle-class, suburban community:

> Don and Leslie have been married for seven years. They feel that their marriage represents a lifelong partnership. They emphasize the fact that their marriage represents a sexual commitment of faithfulness, and neither has had a sexual relationship with another person since they began living together.[16]

Don and Leslie practice a stable homosexual life-style of monogamous marriage—without the solemn blessings of the church. Neither of these two men has ever been arrested, visited a psychiatrist, or belonged to any informal or formal homosexual organizations. While they occasionally entertain a few of their mutual, gay friends at small dinner parties, Don and Leslie no longer cruise gay bars for sexual pickups (which is more characteristic of a certain singles life-style among many male—and, less frequently, female—homosexuals); nor do they seek impersonal, momentary sex with strangers in restrooms and steam baths. Both of these otherwise very conventional men, however, carefully present a heterosexual image at their place of work for fear of being fired if their deep affectional and sexual relationship were discovered.

Psychological and sociological studies of homosexuality almost completely ignore relatively well-adjusted couples like Don and Leslie.[17] In their suburban life-style, enjoying a barbecue on the patio of their modest home, they resemble in most respects their suburban neighbors—worrying about crab grass, inflation, job promotion, and Leslie's occasional arthritis. Yet beyond the fact that these two mates have no children—unlike most of their neighbors—Don and Leslie differ in one other fundamental respect: in most of the nation their sexual behavior is the object of public scorn and regarded as criminal, what many law statutes still refer to as "unnatural lascivious acts" or the "unspeakable and abominable crime against nature." (Homosexuals, of course, do nothing in bed that is not also done by many heterosexuals, though such vaguely worded laws are enforced, if at all, only against the former.)

To take one final illustration from the multitude of diverse ways of expressing the human potential for homosexual experience, consider the life of Joan, a very physically attractive and "feminine" twenty-six-year-old editorial assistant in a major publishing firm. For two years Joan has been deeply involved in a serious relationship with her lesbian lover, a fact that she does not attempt to conceal from her few close heterosexual friends. Joan, an open homosexual and very active in women's liberation activities, grows indignant when she hears men contend that all any lesbian needs is a "good, stiff prick"—a real man—to awaken her "true" heterosexual destiny, or that lesbians are so ugly or "masculine" in appearance that they cannot attract men. Actually, until very recently men have played a central part in Joan's sex life. Conforming to typical heterosexual pressures in growing up, she dated boys exclusively during adolescence, and by her early twenties Joan had had intercourse with four different male friends. These sexual experiences, however, were unexciting and unsatisfying, performed largely as a response to peer expectations and sexual pressures from often aggressive males.

Based on *her experiences with men*, Joan insists that she simply prefers women as sexual and emotional partners. Contrary to male mythology, studies reveal that, like Joan, nearly all self-admitted lesbians (90 to 95 percent) have dated males, and a substantial majority (50 to 80 percent) have had sexual intercourse with one or more men.[18] One study, in fact, found that not only were the homosexual women in the sample more likely to have had heterosexual intercourse than the *heterosexual* women (79 percent versus 58 percent), but the homosexual women also had received as many marriage proposals from men as did their heterosexual counterparts (79 percent versus 78 percent).[19] As two researchers point out:

> Far from being rejected by men, lesbians tend to be unsatisfied by them. The fact that their erotic and emotional life is with women is the result of an active choice. They have chosen women over men; they *prefer* women to men. It is difficult for men to understand this, because such a choice would represent a threat to their desirability. The only explanation most would find acceptable would be one that relegates such a choice to the twilight world of psychiatric pathology, an explanation which is ideological—based on a masculine fear—rather than scientific.[20]

From these few examples, it is clear that there are many dimensions to homosexuality. There is no single kind of "homosexual"; and no single dimension (sexual contact, erotic arousal, masturbatory fantasies, romantic feelings, participation in gay subcultures, or self-image) easily sums up the diverse ways of experiencing orientations toward persons of the same sex. The meaning and significance imputed to behavior and emotions are highly variable and, like sexual identities, may shift over a life span. As Alfred Kinsey pointed out over thirty years ago, sexual orientation is more usefully conceived as a *continuum*. In his pioneering studies of sexual behavior of males and females published in 1948 and 1953, Kinsey presented a seven-point heterosexual-homosexual rating scale, which emphasized that homosexuality is a matter of degree. In terms of (1) physical contact involving erotic arousal or orgasm and (2) "psychic response," most people, he noted, range somewhere between the polar extremes of exclusive homosexuality and exclusive heterosexuality:

> [Humans] do not represent two discrete populations, heterosexual and homosexual. The world is not to be divided into sheep and goats. Not all things are black nor all things white. It is a fundamental of taxonomy that nature rarely deals with discrete categories. Only the human mind invents categories and tries to force facts into pigeon-holes. The living world is a continuum in each and every one of its aspects. The sooner we learn this concerning human sexual behavior the sooner we shall reach a sound understanding of the realities of sex.[21]

To a shocked American public, who had assumed that homosexuality was a rare phenomenon, Kinsey reported that although only 4 percent of white American males are exclusively homosexual (never having had any sexual contact with women or having been aroused by them), 37 percent of males have had at least one homosexual experience to the point of orgasm between adolescence and old age. An additional 13 percent of males have experienced erotic physical arousal (sexual urges and desires) by another man short of orgasm. For females, Kinsey found a similar pattern but with considerably small percentages: exclusive homosexuality, about 2 or 3 percent; one or more episodes to the point of orgasm, 13 percent; and homoerotic arousal without orgasm, 7 percent.[22]

Kinsey's work, of course, has been severely criticized for its use of biased and unrepresentative sampling methods. Some critics feel his figures are greatly inflated since Kinsey's subjects were voluntary and highly selective. Moreover, a close examination of Kinsey's data shows a high proportion of these reported homosexual experiences occurred during adolescence and did not reoccur after this teenage period of experimentation. Based on more recent studies, many researchers feel that a 25 percent figure for males who have had homosexual episodes since the onset of puberty would probably more accurately describe male homosexual experiences in contemporary America. A national study conducted in the early 1970s by Morton Hunt, for example, produced estimates of 20 to 25 percent of males with some overt homosexual experience; for females in the sample, the comparable figures were 10 or 11 percent for married women and 20 percent for unmarried women.[23]

Since many persons with homosexual experiences conceal their sexual behavior or identity, there is no easy or reliable way to assess the prevalence of homosexual activity in America using conventional sampling and survey techniques. But Kinsey's classic work and subsequent scientific studies do clearly suggest at least three important points: (1) a considerable proportion of American men and a smaller proportion of women have had some form of homosexual experience and erotic desire toward the same sex; (2) a sizable proportion of these persons *continue* to engage actively in homosexual behavior throughout a significant period in their lives (30 percent of Kinsey's male sample reported at least incidental homosexual experiences over a period of at least three years, and 18 percent had as much homosexual as heterosexual activity or desire during a similar period); and (3) a person's *homosexual orientation is not necessarily a permanent, fixed "condition"* but may change over time. (Half of the males in Kinsey's study who confined their sexual activity exclusively to males for three or more years also had sex with women at another period in their lives.)[24]

THE DIVERSITY OF THE HOMOSEXUAL ROLE

The tendency of most conventional Americans to not only stigmatize homosexual behavior but to see such forbidden behavior as evidence of the *essential* character and pivotal identity of the person—overwhelming all other characteristics—is a perspective that is absent in many societies around the world. In those cultures in which homosexuality is permitted, there may

be a great deal of homosexual *behavior* but not necessarily a clearly defined *role* or societal definition of a person as "a homosexual."[25] In ancient
Greece, for example, it was widely accepted and expected that adult married men would also have a love affair for several years with an adolescent
boy. Upon reaching maturity, the boy in turn would eventually repeat the
culturally approved pattern, taking a new young lover. While exclusive
homosexuality was not approved—all males were expected to marry and
raise a family—romantic feelings toward "beardless, tender and beautiful
youth" were the social norm.[26]

Although *no* society approves of *exclusive* homosexuality as a permanent way of life for the majority of the general population, the social reaction to homosexual activity is remarkably tolerant and morally neutral in
many cultures. Indeed, in *most* societies homosexual behavior has not been
morally condemned for certain segments of the population, and socially approved bisexuality (as in ancient Greece) has been commonplace. In a survey
of seventy-six societies, anthropologists Ford and Beach found that in
forty-nine of them (64 percent) "homosexual activities of one sort or another
are considered normal and socially acceptable for certain members of the
community."[27] As one writer comments:

> [T]he Judeo-Christian model of "normal" sexuality can hardly accommodate
> the evidence that Arab women in certain Red Sea areas take black female
> lovers, that among the Keraki anal intercourse is thought essential to the health
> and character of the growing boy, and that prominent Siwan men in Africa
> lend their sons to each other for purposes of sodomy.[28]

Some societies, however, have severely punished homosexual conduct.
From the brimstone and fire inflicted upon the ancient Sodomites in the
Book of Genesis to the castration, flogging, and burning alive of persons in
bundles of sticks called faggots in the Middle Ages, many Western societies
with a Judeo-Christian tradition have been particularly harsh in their treatment of suspected homosexuals. But by the eighteenth century, European
nations began to soften and liberalize their laws. (Although in Nazi Ger-
many, persecuted homosexuals were required to wear pink triangles, and
nearly a quarter of a million homosexuals were executed in concentration
camps.)[29] Today, the majority of Western nations have no legal restrictions on homosexual activity among consenting adults in private. Even
where such legal restrictions exist, penalties are much less severe than in the
United States, where some state laws still permit prison terms of ten years
to life imprisonment for the crime of making love to someone of the same
sex. (However, such draconian penalties are practically never imposed today, with the trend toward decriminalization, initiated by the state of Illinois in 1962, continuing.)

Central to the concern of this chapter is the belief that the traditional preoccupation by behavioral scientists with the "roots of deviancy" deflects attention away from a fuller understanding of the dynamics, problems, and variable life-styles of homosexuals. To locate the "original and ultimate" causes of homosexual desires, for example, in early childhood experiences or in hormonal and genetic characteristics contributes little to learning how such persons at a particular juncture in their lives come to label themselves as "queer," "homosexual," or "gay," (or even "heterosexual" or "bisexual"). The "roots of homosexuality"—about which there is a profusion of conflicting and unsubstantiated theories—are unlikely to illuminate the social forces that help create the stigma, oppression, and dilemmas that homosexually oriented persons must somehow deal with at various stages in their life cycle.[30]

Moreover, these emergent, changeable, and diverse patterns of homosexuality cannot be adequately understood apart from the dominant cultural values and beliefs and the social reactions to these men and women as they come of age and seek affection and sexual satisfaction. Too often, it is deterministically assumed that homosexual life-styles are merely a continuation or reenactment of the original circumstances that initiated movement along this deviant sexual corridor. While such initial or predisposing factors may be an important component in a particular homosexual lifestyle (and precisely what these factors are is still a scientific mystery), they are only a part of a complex and dynamic process in which elements of both *choice* and *constraint* exist.

Perhaps the most fundamental fact in understanding the problems homosexuals face is the deeply ingrained prejudice against homosexuality that still persists in America. It is this social reality that sets the context in which persons with erotic desires for the same sex must struggle with their identity, deal with feelings of anxiety and guilt, and search out sexual partners. Strategies of deception, "passing," and carefully managed "presentations of self"—part of the identity kit of most gay people—thus become understandable in a society that most homosexuals correctly perceive as basically hostile and discriminatory.

COMING OUT: IN SEARCH OF AN IDENTITY

One of the most significant moments in the gay experience occurs when a person recognizes himself or herself as a homosexual and begins to explore the homosexual community. Although the expression "coming out" has diverse meanings and is sometimes used in the gay liberation movement to refer to "going public"—allowing oneself to be recognized in the heterosexual world as a homosexual—we shall use the phrase to refer to homosexual self-labeling and initial exploration of the homosexual world.

In view of the public scorn and negative associations attached to homosexuals, even the faint suspicion that one's own sexual behavior or attraction may be symptomatic of such a despised creature may precipitate massive feelings of panic and guilt, a sinking feeling that "something is wrong with me," and attempts to deny or explain away the significance of such homosexual stirrings: "I was drunk," "It's just a passing phase," "We were just horsing around," "It doesn't mean anything." A man who had enlisted in the military explains his feelings at the time:

> I started to realize that I felt a sexual attraction for other men. . . . I passed the attraction off as being due to the circumstances—the loneliness and the need for female companionship. . . . I rationalized my feelings as indicating . . . deep friendship. . . . The possibility that I might be gay terrified me.[31]

The tendency to delay definitions of same-sex attractions or behavior as homosexual is especially characteristic of lesbians, who typically "come out" much later than males.[32] Since most lesbians also participate in the same kinds of social behavior as heterosexual girls, and date boys for a long period of time, the recognition of their growing sexual orientation may be obscured. Unlike the more characteristically male tendency (regardless of sexual orientation) to want sex first and love (maybe) later, the conventional socialization of adolescent females (both straight and lesbian) encourages the desire for deep affection first. Young teenage females are apt to prefer expressions of tenderness and physical closeness—hugging and caressing— but to postpone orgasm-inducing sexual acts, if any, until much later in the relationship or a later stage in their lives. (The majority of lesbians typically do not have oral-genital sex with another woman until their early twenties.) Lesbians thus are not necessarily aware or conscious of their affectional and more socially acceptable hugging involvement with another girl as *homosexual*, as evident in this description by a lesbian of her earlier experiences:

> We started out just being friends and then it became something more special. She taught me a lot of things. I love music and she taught me how to listen to it and appreciate it. She liked things I liked, like walking. We read a lot together. We read the Bible, we read verses to each other. We shared things together. We caressed each other and kissed. I think it was a need to have someone there. And I was there and she was there and we just held on to each other.[33]

But with persistent sexual arousal, with continuing homosexual fantasies or activities that induce pleasurable feelings, and with a growing lack of erotic or emotional interest in the opposite sex, it becomes increasingly difficult for the male or female to explain away these same-sex feelings in a society that polarizes humans so sharply into two mutually exclusive categories. Although probably most people have had erotic attractions toward a person of the same sex at least once in their lives—with a significant minority having overt homosexual experiences—only a small proportion of men and women ever identify themselves as being "a homosexual." The process by which this tiny proportion of persons comes to see themselves in this manner is probably due to a combination of many factors, which "come together to bring someone who *suspects* that he or she is gay to gradually *accept* and *incorporate* it into his or her identity."[34]

As the lack of any strong sexual desire or emotional interest in the opposite sex continues and the individual is unable to account for the persistence of the enjoyment from homoerotic feelings and activities, several other experiences may also occur that lead men and women to question their fundamental sexual identity: (1) a gay person, particularly one with whom the neophyte has had a close relationship, may simply inform the latter that he or she *is* gay—that that is the essence of his or her being; (2) the person may discover that there are many attractive and normal-appearing men and women who are homosexual but don't fit the usual negative stereotypes; or (3) the person may have a "deep, significant, meaningful homosexual experience with someone whom one respects and loves."[35] One man recalls one such meaningful episode in his life that helped to crystallize his self-identity:

> I met a straight guy when I was in college. . . . As our friendship developed, I realized that I was falling in love with him and that I had never cared for anyone as deeply as I cared for him. . . . One night we were out drinking with a bunch of guys at a college bar. We both got rather high and when we returned to the dorm I went with him to his room. It was the beginning of a very beautiful night. I walked over to him, put my arms around him, and kissed him. He reciprocated. We eventually masturbated each other to orgasm. He is now married and has a family. This incident led to a fateful resignation that I was irrevocably gay. Due to the beauty of the experience . . . I was able to rid myself of any doubts that I had regarding my being a homosexual as negating the possibility of being a good person.[36]

The development of an intense affectionate relationship with another person is particularly common in the emergence of a lesbian identity. One woman describes her growing intimacy and romantic "drift" into homosexual behavior and subsequent self-identification as a lesbian:

> When I first came to school we were on the same hall. We both had singles. A lot of us used to hang around the floor lounge and talk, and Helen and I got to know each other pretty well. We always used to do things together, go to shows and concerts. She was a movie freak. The next term we got a doublet together, but nothing happened for a long time. She was just someone I got really close to and we shared a lot of our personal feelings with one another. Sometimes we used to hug each other if we were happy or if something really

good happened, but that's all and neither one of us thought anything of it. Then it just happened. We'd hold hands and feel really close to each other. It was nice. I stayed in the city that summer and got a job. We decided to still live in the dorm . . . I really didn't think much about what I might be [sexually]. We never talked about being gay or anything. Anyway nothing really big [i.e., sex] happened for a long time. We just kept getting closer and we were really important to each other. When it did happen, it was nice and seemed natural. We knew we were [lesbian] then, and that was nice too.[37]

A person may experience this crucial sense of "rebirth" in his or her identity without any firsthand contact with the gay subculture. But involvement with other self-defined homosexuals can be extremely significant for a person previously struggling alone with the knowledge of the *symbolic stigma* of homosexuality, which in America brands persons with same-sex orientations as queer, perverted, or mentally disturbed.[38] Through interaction with experienced gay people, persons grappling with the societally tabooed sexual attractions and erotic urges may begin to reconstruct their shameful and devalued identities, gradually forging a more favorable self-image that offers a sense of self-worth and self-esteem:

I had always thought of them as dirty old men that preyed on 10-, 11-, 12-year-old kids, and I found out that they weren't all that way. . . . It was a relief for me 'cause I found out that I wasn't so different from many other people. . . . I thought I was mentally ill. Now I accept it as a way of life, and I don't consider it a mental illness. . . . I consider myself an outcast from general society, but not mentally ill.[39]

Involvement in the gay scene—bars, informal social networks, homosexual organizations, or gay-liberation activities—provides the newcomer to the homosexual world with a vocabulary of motives, understandings and justifications that may help the neophyte cope more effectively with his or her sexual feelings. Through this ideological and emotional support from the gay community, people confused and troubled by the awareness that they are "different" from their heterosexual friends are better able to *neutralize* the social stigma and deal with psychological conflicts from deeply internalized traditional norms. These new perspectives may enable the person to place his or her behavior within the sphere of psychological normality as a morally acceptable, even desirable, alternative life-style—regardless of the oppressive views of the conventional world:

In every other capacity I am as normal or more normal than straight people. Just because I happen to like strawberry ice cream and they like vanilla, doesn't make them right or me right.[40]

Moreover, the diverse homosexual subworlds provide an arena in which the neophyte may find new friends and sexual partners and acquire new possibilities for a meaningful and valued life-style. "The individual moves from a world characterized by secrecy, solitude, ambiguity, and guilt to a subworld where homosexual role-models are available, where homosexuality may be temporarily rendered public, where 'coaches' are willing to guide him into homosexual roles."[41] A young man describes the exhilarating impact of his first contact with the homosexual subculture:

> I knew there were homosexuals, queers and what not; I had read some books, and I was resigned to the fact that I was a foul, dirty person, but I actually wasn't calling myself a homosexual yet. . . . And the time I really caught myself coming out is the time I walked into this bar and saw a whole crowd of groovy, groovy guys. And I said to myself, there was the realization, that not all gay men are dirty old men or idiots, silly queens, but there are just normal looking and acting people. I saw gay society and I said, "Wow, I'm home."[42]

This phase of self-discovery and exploration of the gay world—of recognizing oneself as a homosexual and entering into relationships with other acknowledged homosexuals—is highly variable and may occur at different ages for different individuals. From the first faint awareness of same-sex attraction to the definition that one is a homosexual may involve an interval of a few years or much of one's life.[43] Developing a commitment to a homosexual life-style is neither inevitable, automatic, nor always a simple process. For some individuals the experience is a long, drawn-out, and painful one. And some persons may remain "in the closet" for much of their lives, struggling in privacy with deep-seated feelings of guilt, shame, confusion, and sexual frustration, particularly in small restricted communities where few, if any, opportunities to meet other homosexuals may exist. Yet even when there is knowledge of a well-established and easily accessible gay subculture, many persons may be unable to take advantage of the potential opportunities available. The fear of being recognized by a parent, a heterosexual business associate, the fear of uncertainty, the fear of being beaten up, the fear of trouble with the police and the public degradation of official labeling—all such fears, whether well-grounded in reality or exaggerated—may conspire to keep persons in a hidden cocoon, concealing their secret identity from both the gay and the straight worlds. One young man, extremely distraught and confused about his homosexual orientation, commented upon his inability to return after one visit to a gay club that had been raided by the police:

> I can't relax in clubs. I keep thinking I might see someone from work, or that the police might raid. . . . It's my problem and I've had to live with it for the past seven years, I think of it all the time—every day. I just can't see where it's all going to lead—I wish I was dead.[44]

Certainly not all initial experiences in the gay network of bars, dances, parties, and informal groups are positive ones. Some men and women may experience rejection upon this first tentative encounter with the homosexual community, which highly values sociability, physical attractiveness and youthful appearance. An unattractive, shy, middle-aged or older man, for example, attempting to come out in the gay-bar milieu may experience a double rejection: "a failure in the heterosexual world and a failure in the homosexual world."[45]

But for many persons who enter into the diverse homosexual subcultures, the impact of this experience may have far-reaching effects on their life-adjustment, self-image, and establishment of a new life-style.

MANAGING A STIGMATIZED IDENTITY

"To be a homosexual in our society," writes gay liberationist Dennis Altman, "is to be constantly aware that one bears a stigma."[46] No matter how well one resolves his or her identity after "coming out"—indeed discovering that the sheer sexual aspect of homosexuality is often no "big deal"— gay people in societies like America must, nevertheless, manage their lives with the awareness that many straight people hold them in contempt. And as Altman observes, this knowledge that the majority disapproves of your behavior—often fears and hates "people like you"—can be sometimes disconcerting even for the most well-adjusted gay person.

Perhaps the most fateful choice gay men and women must make is whether to keep their sexual identity hidden from the straight world, even from heterosexuals close to them. In one study of male homosexuals, only about one-fourth (27 percent) of the sample reported that their mother and only one-fifth of their fathers definitely knew of their homosexuality. *Only 10 percent of the respondents felt that most of their heterosexual friends knew or suspected*, and half (52 percent) indicated that "only a few" were aware of their sexual orientation.[47] Thus it appears that most self-admitted homosexuals *pass* as straight in the eyes of the conventional world, despite the popular stereotype that heterosexuals can readily spot a gay man or lesbian woman.

Paradoxically the very decision by most gay persons to conceal their identity from most of the straight world also helps to reinforce the negative stereotypical images that abound in the media and in popular perceptions. Since most heterosexuals are simply unaware that they are having daily firsthand contact with "such people," these crude one-dimensional conceptions of homosexuals (limp-wristed, effeminate, lisping "faggots" and masculine, "butch" lesbians) are slow to change. If the millions of ordinary homosexual men and women who are our workmates, neighbors, relatives, or close acquaintances were to disclose their homosexual identity *en masse*— doctors, lawyers, secretaries, executives, clerks, insurance agents, assembly-line workers, teachers, clergy—most of the stereotypes would be difficult to sustain.

In a society saturated with public contempt and antipathy toward homosexuals, however, secrecy, deception, and pretense are not only under-standable but reflect a perception—often correct—of the possible discrim-ination, exclusion, or ostracism that might confront a particular individual whose sexual life-style suddenly becomes public knowledge. Even when these severe social reactions are unlikely to occur, the uncertainty of what to expect, the belief that the confrontation will be at least awkward, or that one may be treated as a curious sexual object—an erotic oddity—may im-pel gay people to conceal their identity. Consequently, many gays *avoid certain threatening situations* that would heighten their homosexual visi-bility or make it an issue: for example, avoiding gay bars that unsuspecting straights might enter or refraining from a defense of gay rights when such issues pop up in coffee-break discussions. Even if many homosexuals do not fear getting fired from their work for their sexual life-style, they may fear the reactions of their co-workers. As one lesbian explained:

> I work very hard at not letting people at the office know. I don't think I would get fired or anything. It's just the nervousness I know it would start. The other girls look at you curiously. Any touching, even accidental, is taken for a pass. I've had it happen before, when I got careless and let someone know who talked. I got so that I'd wait for the john to be empty before I'd go in. I don't want to go through that again.[48]

Another strategy to evade detection is to *control the information* that one gives off to the straight world. Gay people, for example, may construct fictional heterosexual relationships and present distorted and selective biog-raphies. For the sake of family and straight friends, two males sharing an apartment may live with two single beds in the same room while sleeping in one.[49] Lyman and Scott describe another kind of rearrangement of prop-erty to create a heterosexual impression: "A . . . homosexual might invite someone who suspects his true identity to his bedroom where a seemingly casual and careless display of pictures of female nudes and his baseball cap and glove convey a contradictory impression."[50] The homosexual may also play down or conceal altogether the sexual parts of his life. And this decep-tion requires an alertness to and control over offhand expressions that might betray his secret. As one homosexual remarked: "When I was home watching television with my folks, I'd catch myself saying, 'There's a good looking guy.'"[51] This attempt to manage a disreputable identity through total concealment from heterosexuals may sometimes cause severe per-sonal stress:

> The strain of deceiving my family and friends often became intolerable. It was necessary for me to watch every word I spoke and every gesture that I made in case I gave myself away. When jokes were made about queers I had to laugh with the rest, and when the talk was about women I had to invent conquests of my

own. I hated myself at such moments but there seemed nothing else I could do. My whole life became a lie.[52]

Certainly many, perhaps most, homosexuals who keep a part of themselves hidden except with their gay friends are able most of the time to compartmentalize their lives with minimal strain as they navigate their way through the straight world. Unlike the stigma of the physically handicapped or racial minorities, homosexuality is generally invisible. One's sexual—and even social—life is often easily privatized in the segregated and insulated spheres of a complex urban society. Indeed, a small proportion of homosexuals may spend most of their lives in "gay ghettos," largely cut off from the dominant heterosexual world. Even for the vast majority of homosexuals whose jobs require intensive contact with the conventional world, heterosexual role playing, if considered essential, may become habitual and techniques of coping with interactional problems routinized without much self-consciousness.[53]

While most self-accepting gays with a circle of close homosexual friends and access to sexual partners do not experience the lives of unrelieved misery ("obsessed," "suicidal," "in emotional turmoil') that some writers impute to all homosexuals, the frequent necessity for many gay people to lead a "double life"—especially in certain kinds of jobs and careers—may sometimes induce intense anxiety and distress. Periodic incidents or crisis points may arise where questions of sexual identity become problematic, and the gay person must draw upon all of his or her dramaturgical skills of impression management to maintain a convincing heterosexual front. The public admission by novelist-journalist Merle Miller that he had masqueraded for years as a heterosexual in the straight community prompted this anonymous letter to the editor in the *San Francisco Chronicle*:

> To the Editor—Merle Miller is very lucky that he no longer has to masquerade as a heterosexual. Many of us have to live a masquerade for at least eight hours a day just to earn a living. And living in the web of lies and pretense is not easy.
>
> I am a college-educated, under-30 homosexual working my way up in a large corporation. I do not expect to get too far, though. My career will probably stop at the lower end of middle management. To go any farther I would have to be married, to a woman.
>
> I have been married for the past three years, but to a man. The company considers me single. I certainly would not tell them I am married. Yet marriage is a very significant fact of my life. And it is my biggest problem. Marriage between men is very hard in this world that requires people to seem heterosexual.
>
> For eight hours a day I must pretend that I am single; straight and single. Our kind of marriage does not exist at work. Any upsets, any financial problems, any crises of our marriage do not exist either. I must be very careful not to say anything that would make my roommate and me sound "too" close.
>
> When I was transferred from another city some time ago, I had to hide

the fact that my roommate came along; and then weave a fabric of lies to explain why he was here when I accidentally mentioned him. And we are married! If he had been a woman, the company would have given me extra money to bring him here.

How often people tell me I act like a married man. Most of them find out I am single later on. Then the fun begins. The young women at work think I am a good prospect ("with a bright future"). They expect me to be interested in them—but I am married!

I must join in "stag" talk with the fellows. It is a big bore, but I had better not show it. To satisfy my boss' curiosity about my life I must intimate that a good friend of mine, who happens to be a female, is having an affair with me.

I am trapped in a cage of pretending. I do not look at all different. How is anyone to know I am a homosexual? I do not look one bit different from other respectable, aggressive, married young men.[54]

To live with a stigmatized life-style is not only to suffer from the possible denial of the right to hold certain jobs and have the same opportunities for promotion and success as heterosexuals. In some communities it may even involve the risk of police harassment in public places, blackmail, and "queer baiting" by young males who bolster their own sense of masculinity by beating up "fags." Oppression can take many forms. To be a homosexual also may mean the inability to express your affection publicly by walking hand-in-hand with your lover, especially in the inhospitable social climate of a small Midwestern town. It may mean that if you are in love you cannot share your happiness and jubilant feelings with your parents because of the pain you know it will cause *them*.

To be a homosexual in America is to feel the special sting of "fag stories," or to discover after twenty years of quasi marriage that you may not be permitted to visit your mate dying in a hospital, a privilege reserved for only "the immediate family." Moreover, "when a lesbian loses her partner she can expect little or no comfort from conventional sources of support like neighbors, a priest or a doctor who would try to ease the hurt of a heterosexual faced with bereavement or divorce."[55] In fact, Dennis Altman argues that "it is impossible to be both a self-accepting homosexual and live a conventional life in American society."[56] Even many well-intentioned liberals, he points out, may contribute to a subtle form of oppression; not by blatant persecution or discrimination but by a kind of patronizing tolerance laced with pity and condescension:

Certainly liberals would not wish to see me arrested for sleeping with another man or even for cruising one; they might, of course, send me to their therapist; more likely they will ignore my homosexuality, rather as some liberals will say anything rather than describe a black by his color. The difference between tolerance and acceptance is very considerable, for *tolerance is a gift extended by the superior to the inferior:* "He's very tolerant," one says, which immediately tells us more about the other person's social position than his views. Such an attitude is far different from acceptance, which implies not that one pities others but rather that one accepts the equal validity of their style of life.[57]

Until very recently in America, to be homosexual was also to *internalize* the oppression imposed by heterosexuals: the crushing sense of guilt, shame, and self-hatred. Yet for increasing numbers of young, self-accepting homosexuals today, gay is not only good but angry.

GAY PRIDE: FIGHTING BACK

At 3:00 A.M. on June 27, 1969, the police raided the Stonewall Inn, a popular gay dance bar on Christopher Street in New York City's Greenwich Village. Rather than withdrawing passively—the usual reaction of homosexuals to police raids during the late 1960s—an angry mob of 200 males spontaneously began to battle the invaders. Surging out on to the street, they hurled rocks and bottles at the police and ripped up parking meters as the attempt to expel these gay men from the Inn escalated into a full-scale riot. Thirteen rioters were finally arrested and four policemen injured in the disturbance. The next several nights noisy crowds of homosexuals and sympathizers gathered in nearby Sheridan Square to protest the vice-squad raid, shouting slogans of "gay power," and "I'm a faggot, and I'm proud of it!"[58]

The violent confrontation outside of the Stonewall Inn reflected the pent-up anger and long-simmering frustrations of homosexuals in America. Tired of police harassment and the guilt-ridden docility of previous generations, these gay men exploded; and for the first time in America they momentarily united to fight back against their tormenters. The Stonewall riot ushered in the beginning of a more militant stage in the efforts of gay people to confront directly the prejudice, injustice, and oppression that have plagued homosexuals in our society. While the homophile movement (the emergence of homosexual interest groups) has a much longer history in the United States, its organizational activities were mostly conservative, cautionary, almost secretive, and often somewhat apologetic toward homosexuality. The new gay activists, however, marched openly and proudly "out of the closets," stridently affirming the moral legitimacy and equal validity of their sexual orientation. As one gay liberation publication announced: "We are serving notice that we'll tolerate no more brainwashing or brutalization."[59]

With the stimulus provided by the emerging countercultures and the more sexually permissive climate of the 1960s, the radical political consciousness of the antiwar protests, the black-power struggles, and the women's movement, a small but spirited gay liberation movement spread across America in the 1970s. (Although the gay population has its own share of male chauvinists and racial bigots, the increasing awareness by many radical gays that the heterosexual oppression of homosexuals has many meaningful similarities with the domination of men over women and whites over blacks is evident in Carl Wittman's remark in "The Gay Manifesto" that "chick equals nigger equals queer.")[60] Using some of the tactics and strategies of these earlier protest movements, a number of gay men and women in larger cities began to form loose alliances to pressure for legal and social changes that would permit prideful homosexuals to enjoy the same opportunities as other Americans to live and work without discrimination.

On Gay Liberation Day in 1970, an estimated two to three thousand homosexuals marched proudly in New York's Christopher Street Parade, as did gay marchers in Chicago and Hollywood. On the second anniversary of the Stonewall riots, a crowd twice as large marched down Sixth Avenue in New York. And in Boston, New Orleans, Oakland, and in numerous cities across the country, gay men and women marched both in celebration of their life-style and in active protest against the continuing social, economic, and political disabilities from which they suffer. On June 26, 1978, tens of thousands of homosexual men and women paraded up Fifth Avenue to demand enactment of a New York City ordinance against sex-orientation discrimination, a law supported by Mayor Koch who proclaimed it "Gay and Lesbian Pride Week" and declared that "the state has no place in the bedrooms of the nation."[61]

In addition to the marches, picketing, and political lobbying, other gay groups began to spring up on college campuses, serving as support groups for homosexual students and providing peer counseling and information. In the increasingly permissive sexual environment of college campuses in the 1970s, these small groups sponsored social activities for gay students to ease the feeling of social isolation and offered emotional support for the often traumatic process involved in sexual experimentation and coming out. (Only a tiny minority of self-admitted gay students, however, appear to be active in these groups, with the vast majority of campus homosexuals protecting the privacy of their sexual identity.) By 1978, over 200 gay college organizations had formed, although not without sparking frequent controversy.[62] Many college counselors feared pressures toward premature homosexual commitments, and conservative college administrators worried about the negative reactions of the general public and irate alumni. For example, in 1978 this vitriolic letter to the editor appeared in an Ivy League college alumni magazine in response to the formation of a gay support group on campus:

> Revolting is a mild description of my reaction to the reference to the homosexual student support group on campus. . . . I wanted to vomit. I read unbelievingly that homosexuals were represented at registration; how homosexuals were members of the faculty *and* administration; and how . . . a spokesman for

the homosexuals and one himself, said there were probably 300 homosexuals on the faculty and in the student body! . . .

Homosexuals are dangerous to young people. Those like myself who have served on school boards were given the cold stark facts that homosexuals are as dangerous as repetitive rapists when their unnatural appetites are aroused. The overwhelming medical opinion concludes that homosexuals are sexual perverts; that they are dangerous not only to young children but also to teenagers, who are frequent targets for their unnatural and dangerous sexual activities.

Homosexuality is a disease. We can be sympathetic with those who are so afflicted just as we are sympathetic with any one who is the victim of a loathsome disease. But the College does not have to embrace them!

The open affront to [the college] by homosexuals on the faculty and in the student body should be denounced and all should be dismissed.

Despite the modest success in achieving some limited legal reforms in a few dozen cities, gay activists recognized that decriminalization and local civil-rights ordinances still left untouched the pervasive view of homosexuality as a form of mental illness—a "sickness" or "disease." Central to gay liberation is the conviction that homosexuals must create a new consciousness, a new sense of identity based on pride in being gay. "Redefinition for the homosexual, as for the black," argues gay activist Dennis Altman, "is a necessary part of liberation."[63] Thus the psychiatric and medical professions—the official custodians and proponents of the pathological view of homosexuality—have become a growing target of gay rage, especially such defenders of the illness perspective as psychoanalyst Irving Bieber:

The central question is: Is homosexuality a normal sexual variant, that develops like left-handedness does in some people, or does it represent some kind of disturbance in sexual development? There is no question in my mind: Every male homosexual goes through an initial stage of heterosexual development, and in all homosexuals, there has been a disturbance of normal heterosexual development, as a result of fears which produce anxieties and inhibitions of sexual function. His sexual adaptation is a substitutive adaptation.[64]

For Bieber, homosexuality is clearly an undesirable condition and a psychiatric disorder: "[W]hat you have in a homosexual adult is a person whose heterosexual function is crippled like the legs of a polio victim."[65] According to another influential supporter of Bieber, psychoanalyst Charles Socarides, "there is no obligatory homosexual who can be considered to be healthy. The very existence of this condition precludes it."[66] Socarides, in fact, has frequently provided expert witness in court cases on the "severely incapacitating problems" that allegedly afflict all committed homosexuals. In one case his views were used to support a decision by the government to fire a homosexual from his job. (Socarides, like Bieber, however, has recently disavowed such categorial discrimination and supports the civil rights of homosexuals, although still maintaining that persistent same-sex preferences are symptomatic of a serious psychiatric dysfunction.)[67] For many therapists who accept the view of homosexuality as a pathological affliction, there is a murky and mystical assumption of an inherent *heterosexual destiny* in humans. Any persistent adult departure from this mode of sexual development is prima facie evidence of an illness—a distorted and "unnatural," "abnormal" sexuality:

> The . . . male-female design . . . is anatomically determined, as it derives from cells which in evolutionary scale underwent changes into organ systems and finally into individuals reciprocally adapted to each other. This is the evolutionary development of man. The male-female design is thus perpetually maintained, and only overwhelming fear can disturb it.[68]

But as Erich Goode points out, "The anatomic equipment of men and women certainly *permits* heterosexual intercourse—but it does not dictate it."[69] The fact that homosexuals choose to use their hands, mouth, anus, and genitals for sexual stimulation and satisfaction is no more "unnatural" and "abnormal" than the decision by vast numbers—often a majority— of *heterosexuals* to enjoy nonreproductive oral-genital sex (fellatio and cunnilingus), to engage in anal intercourse, to undergo male or female sterilization, to choose not to bear any children, or to remain celibate for certain parts of their life. Rarely, however, do these psychiatrists who would condemn homosexuality as unnatural and pathological apply the same judgments to the more socially approved nondeviant sexual conduct of the dominant heterosexual population.

By the early 1970s gay activists began to retaliate against such absolutist psychiatric dogma, even disrupting the national conventions of the American Psychiatric Association and the American Medical Association. In one confrontation militants bitterly attacked the use of "aversion therapy" to "cure" homosexuals of their presumed illness (a form of behavior modification in which the patient is given drugs to induce vomiting immediately after viewing films of homosexuals making love). Finally, after intensive backstage lobbying by a gay task force, the American Psychiatric Association in 1973 issued an official declaration that homosexuality "by itself does not necessarily constitute a psychiatric disorder." The APA declaration, however, still retained the clinical psychiatric label of "sexual orientation disturbance" for homosexuals who are either "disturbed by, in conflict with, or wish to change their sexual orientation."[70] This official action by the APA touched off a major internal political battle within the association. And in a forced referendum on the issue placed before the eighteen thousand members, 42 percent of the ten thousand psychiatrists responding voted *against* the official APA declaration. The traditional perspective that views homosexuality as a kind of psychiatric disorder apparently is still widespread in the profession. As one campus psychiatrist commented: "Politically we said homosexuality was not a disorder . . . but privately most of us feel it is."[71]

Yet challenges to the view of homosexuality as an illness have continued. Social scientists have pointed out that the clinical experience of psychiatrists is based upon a highly selective and biased sample of homosexuals: persons who are overwhelmingly distressed and troubled by their sexual impulses. Homosexuals who are well-adjusted, contented, and relatively satisfied with their lives would have little reason to seek help from psychiatrists. (In response to the observation by one psychiatrist who insisted that all his homosexual patients were seriously disturbed, another psychiatrist replied: "Yes, and so are all my heterosexual patients!")

Critics have also marshaled evidence from a growing number of studies that casts serious doubt on the assumption that homosexuals must invariably suffer from "disordered personalities" simply because of their sexual preferences. Psychologist Evelyn Hooker, for example, presented a battery of personality tests to a sample of male homosexuals who were *not* in therapy and to a comparable heterosexual control group matched for age, education, and intelligence. She then had a panel of experienced psychiatrists and clinical psychologists attempt to select the sexual identities of the subjects simply on the basis of their test scores. The result: the panel of experts could do no better in picking out the homosexuals than if the therapists had flipped a coin. There were no significant differences in the ratings of the homosexuals and heterosexuals.[72]

Furthermore, self-admitted homosexuals are far more likely to have experimented with heterosexuality in their lives than heterosexuals have been willing to experiment with homosexuality. The majority of lesbians, for example, have at least tried intercourse with men but very few committed heterosexual women have had sex with women. From this perspective, it is perhaps the exclusive heterosexual who should be seen as suffering from an "obsessive-compulsive" orientation! In other words, the assumption that heterosexuality is the only desirable or normal life-style is a value *judgment* commonly masquerading as a scientifically proven medical fact.[73]

Recent studies suggest that despite the societal prejudice against homosexuality, self-admitted homosexuals who accept their sexual orientation and never try to change it appear to be remarkably well-adjusted—and may find their sexual life-style quite *gratifying*, a fact that is too often overlooked in studies that presume homosexuality to be a "psychiatric disorder." As one lesbian commented, interrupting her interviewer: "We've kept talking about emotional turmoil and male avoidance. But the truth is I go to bed with her because it's fun."[74] In 1978, the Kinsey Institute for Sex Research released a report of the most comprehensive study to date of homosexual

life-styles in America. Based on 4-hour interviews with about 1,500 homosexuals, the authors of the study, psychologist Alan Bell and sociologist
Martin Weinberg, conclude that homosexuals who have come to terms with
their homosexuality "are no more distressed psychologically than are heterosexual men and women."[75] For persons, however, who have more self-
doubts and regrets about their homosexual inclinations, and worries about
sexual adequacy, the strains from their typically more secretive (and often,
in practice, less exclusive) homosexual life-styles may cause considerable
personal stress and maladjustment.

By the mid-1970s, the pathological view of homosexuality was increasingly under attack not only by gay activists but by sociologists, psychologists, and growing numbers of younger psychiatrists, as reflected in the title
of psychotherapist George Weinberg's book *Society and the Healthy Homosexual.* In a reversal of the traditional psychiatric focus, Weinberg high-
lighted the particular psychiatric problems of the heterosexual person who
has a severe case of "homophobia"—an intense hostile reaction to homosexuality and fear of homosexuals—a common ailment in America, which,
the author suggested, is in need of a cure: "I would never consider a [hetero-
sexual] patient healthy unless he had overcome his prejudice against homosexuality. . . . his repugnance . . . is certain to be harmful to him."[76]

Despite significant changes by some psychotherapists in their views,
the widespread fear of homosexuals by large segments of the general public
continues to hamper the struggle for homosexual liberation. And in the late
1970s, a growing *backlash* threatened some of the hard-won legal victories
recently attained. In Oklahoma, for example, a proposal to permit school
districts to fire homosexual teachers was enacted into law in 1978. In California, efforts were underway to place a statewide initiative on the ballot
that would permit the firing of any person employed by the schools who is
even openly *supportive* of homosexuality. And not only in the Miami area,
but in several other cities such as Eugene, Oregon, and Wichita, Kansas,
voters have recently repealed antidiscrimination ordinances enacted by
city councils.

The campaign to rescind a 4-year-old ordinance prohibiting discrimination on the basis of "affectional or sexual preference" in St. Paul, Min-
nesota, in 1978 is perhaps indicative of the inflamed feelings that the issue
of gay civil rights still arouses in many parts of America. In a supercharged
atmosphere, which polarized much of the city, supporters of the repeal frequently quoted from biblical scriptures. For these anxious citizens, the
homosexual rights ordinance represented an attack on some of their most
fundamental values. Many of these voters saw the growing tolerance for
homosexuals as a threat to their children, family life, and religious beliefs—
and perhaps to their own repressed feelings of sexuality. For homosexuality clearly represents an anomaly: an expression of sex, love, and playful

eroticism divorced from procreation and religiously sanctified marriage, and, for some voters, perhaps, an anxiety-provoking reminder of their own homosexual impulses that could spill over into overt behavior.

Defenders of the ordinance drew upon the spirit of the Constitution and framed the issue in the context of fundamental human rights: not an attempt by gay teachers to convert the city's children to homosexuality but simply to give gay citizens a fair chance to find a job and a place to live and maintain their self-dignity.

In a heated campaign that saw opposing sides calling each other "perverts" and "fascists," voters turned out in larger numbers than usual for an off-year election to repeal the rights ordinance by a vote of 54,096 to 31,694. A pastor of a fundamentalist Baptist church who had directed the repeal campaign summed up his interpretation of the vote: it was, he said, a "victory for morality and the rights of parents to decide the moral caliber of persons coming into close contact with their children. . . . being a pervert is like being a thief, both are wrong and both can continue or repent." A dejected city council member who had supported the ordinance put the election results in a very different and more ominous light: "The human rights implications of the vote are frightening. . . . Who knows what rights they may seek to take away next."[77]

The moral and psychiatric status of homosexuality and the legal rights of gay men and women in America thus remained in a volatile flux at the end of the decade. Both gay liberation advocates and their moral adversaries marshalled their resources and allies as they prepared to do battle in communities across the nation during the 1980s.

THE END OF THE HOMOSEXUAL ROLE?

Looking beyond the contemporary strife over the rights of homosexuals, some writers envision the possibility of a very different kind of America developing in the distant future. The kind of society that would blur the conventional pink/blue sex-role prescriptions, erode the rigid hetero/homo categories, and accept, rather than merely tolerate, various kinds of sexual, affectional, and familial life-styles, ones that would transcend the narrow confines of the traditional, heterosexual, monogamous nuclear family. The possibilities for greater sexual freedom are already evident in a world where sex is being separated from reproduction and anatomy from role under the pressures of the women's movement, new birth-control technologies, and an overpopulated earth. With the emergence of a culture that imposed little stigma and few sanctions on sexual preferences, where most of the taboos were lifted, there probably would be less exclusive forms of sexuality, either heterosexual or homosexual, and more overt bisexuality. If America were to evolve in these directions, it would become a society in which the distinctions between heterosexuality and homosexuality might no longer be so necessary for the establishment of a satisfying and worthwhile human identity.

Yet the evolution of such a society would amount to a vast social revolution, a society "that is based on a 'new human' who is able to accept the multi-faceted and varied nature of his/her sexual identity."[78] And it would entail the social creation of a new vision of human nature, one less biologically constrained and fated. Writer Gore Vidal has observed that in such a radically different America, "homosexual" would be used as an adjective to describe *behavior* rather than a noun to describe the fundamental *identity* or essence of a person. (As several gay activists have pointed out, "homosexuality is a crucial part of our identity, not because of anything intrinsic about it but because social oppression has made it so.")[79]

Whether such a society is possible—or even desirable—is still conjecture and the source of continuing dispute. But whatever else might be required, the emergence of this kind of individual and collective consciousness would necessitate a radical change in the socialization of children—new definitions of manhood and womanhood—and a much greater acceptance of human diversity. *Both* homosexual and heterosexual orientations would have to be seen as equally valid and morally acceptable variants. Such a cataclysmic transformation would also require a much greater awareness of the polymorphous sexual potential that Freud and many contemporary behavioral scientists believe is inherent in all humans. The development of such a society, however, would witness the end of the special status for the homosexual in America—both as a target of oppression and as a source of shame or pride.

FOOTNOTES

1   Martin Duberman, "The Case of the Gay Sergeant," *The New York Times Magazine*, Nov. 9, 1975, pp. 16–17. © 1975 by The New York Times Company. Reprinted by permission.

2   *The New York Times*, Nov. 28, 1977, p. 7. See also Frank Rose, "Trouble in Paradise," *New Times*, April 15, 1977, pp. 44–53.

3   Thomas F. Coleman, "Sex and the Law," *The Humanist*, 38 (March/April 1978), p. 41.

4   "Playboy Interview: Anita Bryant," *Playboy* (May 1978), p. 89.

5   Coleman, "Sex and the Law," p. 41. Of the nineteen states that decriminalized private sexual acts, however, eighteen did so in the context of a general change in the penal code. Very few of these laws specifically mentioned homosexuality; most dealt with sexual acts that could be participated in by homosexuals or heterosexuals. California was the only state that unilaterally repealed the anti-homosexual laws.

6   Quoted in Erich Goode, *Deviant Behavior*, Prentice-Hall, Englewood Cliffs, N.J., 1978, p. 362.

7   Eugene E. Levitt and Albert D. Klassen, Jr., "Public Attitudes Toward Homo-
    sexuality," *Journal of Homosexuality*, 1 (Fall 1974), pp. 29–43.
8   Joseph Epstein, "Homo/Hetero: The Struggle for Sexual Identity," *Harper's*
    (September 1970), p. 51.
9   Laud Humphreys, *Tearoom Trade*, Aldine, Chicago, 1970, pp. 114–115.
10 Humphreys, *Tearoom Trade*, p. 112.
11 Humphreys, *Tearoom Trade*, p. 114.
12 Humphreys, *Tearoom Trade*, p. 117.
13 Albert J. Reiss, Jr., "The Social Integration of Queers and Peers," in William
    A. Rushing (ed.), *Deviant Behavior and Social Process*, Rand McNally, Chi-
    cago, 1975, p. 258.
14 Reiss, Jr., "The Social Integration of Queers and Peers," p. 265.
15 Reiss, Jr., "The Social Integration of Queers and Peers," pp. 266–267.
16 Barry M. Dank, "The Homosexual," in Don Spiegel and Patricia Keith-Spiegel
    (eds.), *Outsiders, USA*, Rinehart Press, San Francisco, 1973, p. 270.
17 For insightful perspectives on different homosexual life-styles, see Carol A. B.
    Warren, *Identity and Community in the Gay World*, Wiley, New York, 1974;
    Alan P. Bell and Martin S. Weinberg, *Homosexualities: A Study in Diversity
    Among Men and Women*, Simon and Schuster, New York, 1978; Howard
    Brown, *Familiar Faces, Hidden Lives*, Harcourt Brace Jovanovich, New York,
    1976; Karla Jay and Allen Young (eds.), *After You're Out*, Links Books, New
    York, 1975; Del Martin and Phyliss Lyon, *Lesbian/Woman*, Glide Publica-
    tions, San Francisco, 1972; Donna M. Tanner, *The Lesbian Couple*, Lexing-
    ton Books, Lexington, Mass., 1978; Edward William Delph, *The Silent Com-
    munity: Public Homosexual Encounters*, Sage, Beverly Hills, Calif., 1978.
18 Philip W. Blumstein and Pepper Schwartz, "Lesbianism and Bisexuality," in
    Erich Goode and Richard R. Troiden (eds.), *Sexual Deviance and Sexual Devi-
    ants*, William Morrow, New York, 1974, p. 289.
19 Marcel T. Saghir and Eli Robins, *Male and Female Homosexuality*, Williams
    & Wilkins, Baltimore, 1973, pp. 246, 250.
20 Goode and Troiden (eds.), *Sexual Deviance and Sexual Deviants*, p. 233.
21 Alfred C. Kinsey et al., *Sexual Behavior in the Human Male*, Saunders, Phila-
    delphia, 1948, p. 639.
22 Alfred C. Kinsey et al., *Sexual Behavior in the Human Female*, Saunders,
    Philadelphia, 1953.
23 Morton Hunt, *Sexual Behavior in the 1970s*, Dell, New York, 1975, Ch. 6.
24 Goode, *Deviant Behavior*, pp. 366–367.
25 Mary McIntosh, "The Homosexual Role," *Social Problems*, 16 (Fall 1968), pp.
    182–192.
26 Arno Karlen, *Sexuality and Homosexuality*, Norton, New York, 1971, p. 26.
27 Clellan S. Ford and Frank A. Beach, *Patterns of Sexual Behavior*, Harper &
    Row, New York, 1951. See also Vern L. Bullough, *Sexual Variance in Society
    and History*, Wiley, New York, 1976; Martin S. Weinberg and Colin J. Wil-
    liams, *Male Homosexuals: Their Problems and Adaptations*, Oxford Univer-
    sity Press, New York, 1974, Chs. 5–6.
28 Martin Duberman, "Homosexual Literature," *The New York Times Book Re-
    view*, Dec. 10, 1972, p. 7.

29   Ira Glasser, "The Yellow Star and the Pink Triangle," *The New York Times*, Sept. 10, 1975, p. 45.
30   John H. Gagnon and William Simon, *Sexual Conduct*, Aldine, Chicago, 1973, pp. 136, 189–190.
31   Goode, *Deviant Behavior*, p. 380.
32   Siegrid Schafer, "Sexual and Social Problems of Lesbians," *Journal of Sexual Research*, 12 (February 1976), p. 51; Gagnon and Simon, *Sexual Conduct*, p. 184.
33   Gagnon and Simon, *Sexual Conduct*, p. 185.
34   Goode, *Deviant Behavior*, p. 381.
35   Goode, *Deviant Behavior*, pp. 380–381.
36   Goode, *Deviant Behavior*, pp. 381–382.
37   Denise M. Cronin, "Coming Out Among Lesbians," in Goode and Troiden (eds.), *Sexual Deviance and Sexual Deviants*, p. 270.
38   Warren, *Identity and Community in the Gay World*, pp. 146–147.
39   Barry Dank, "Coming Out in the Gay World," *Psychiatry*, 34 (May 1971), p. 191.
40   Dank, "Coming Out in the Gay World," p. 190.
41   Kenneth Plummer, *Sexual Stigma*, Routledge & Kegan Paul, London, 1975, p. 148.
42   Dank, "Coming Out in the Gay World," p. 187.
43   Dank, "Coming Out in the Gay World," p. 183.
44   Plummer, *Sexual Stigma*, pp. 149–150.
45   Plummer, *Sexual Stigma*, p. 150.
46   Dennis Altman, *Homosexual: Oppression and Liberation*, Avon, New York, 1971, p. 13.
47   Weinberg and Williams, *Male Homosexuals*, p. 105.
48   Gagnon and Simon, *Sexual Conduct*, p. 205. See also Barbara Ponse, "Secrecy in the Lesbian World," *Urban Life*, 5 (October 1976), pp. 313–338.
49   Plummer, *Sexual Stigma*, p. 191.
50   Stanford M. Lyman and Marvin Scott, *A Sociology of the Absurd*, Appleton-Century-Crofts, New York, 1970, p. 60. For a general discussion of strategies of avoidance and information control, see Erving Goffman, *Stigma: Notes on the Management of Spoiled Identity*, Prentice-Hall, Englewood Cliffs, N.J., 1963.
51   Jerry L. Simmons, *Deviants*, Glendessary Press, Santa Barbara, Calif., 1969, p. 82.
52   Plummer, *Sexual Stigma*, p. 175.
53   Plummer, *Sexual Stigma*, pp. 177–179; Weinberg and Williams, *Male Homosexuals*, p. 272.
54   Quoted in Saul D. Feldman, *Deciphering Deviance*, Little, Brown, Boston, 1978, pp. 380–381.
55   Altman, *Homosexual*, p. 50.
56   Altman, *Homosexual*, p. 50.
57   Altman, *Homosexual*, pp. 50–51. Italics added.
58   Laud Humphreys, *Out of the Closets*, Prentice-Hall, Englewood Cliffs, N.J., 1972, pp. 5–6.

59 Quoted in John Gagnon and Bruce Henderson, *Human Sexuality*, Little, Brown, Boston, 1975, p. 49.

60 Carl Wittman, "Refugees from Amerika: A Gay Manifesto," in Joseph A. McCaffrey (ed.), *The Homosexual Dialectic*, Prentice-Hall, Englewood Cliffs, N.J., 1972, p. 160.

61 Humphreys, *Out of the Closets*, pp. 6–7; *The New York Times*, June 26, 1978, p. 1A.

62 Grace and Fred H. Hechinger, "Homosexuality on Campus," *The New York Times Magazine*, Mar. 12, 1978, p. 15.

63 Altman, *Homosexual*, p. 130.

64 "The A.P.A. Ruling on Homosexuality: The Issue is Subtle, The Debate Still On," *The New York Times*, Dec. 23, 1973, p. 5E.

65 "The A.P.A. Ruling on Homosexuality," p. 5E.

66 Charles W. Socarides, "Homosexuality and Medicine," *Journal of the American Medical Association*, 212 (May 18, 1970), p. 1201.

67 Malcolm Spector, "Legitimizing Homosexuality," *Society*, 14 (July/August 1977), p. 56.

68 Charles W. Socarides, *Beyond Sexual Freedom*, Quadrangle, Chicago, 1975, p. 99. See also Irving Bieber, "Homosexuality—An Adaptive Consequence of Disorder in Psychosexual Development," *American Journal of Psychiatry*, 130 (November 1973), pp. 1209–1211.

69 Goode, *Deviant Behavior*, p. 377.

70 Quoted in Spector, "Legitimizing Homosexuality," p. 53.

71 Quoted in Hechinger, "Homosexuality on Campus," p. 32.

72 Evelyn Hooker, "The Adjustment of the Male Overt Homosexual," *Journal of Projective Techniques*, 21 (March 1957), pp. 18–31; Evelyn Hooker, "Male Homosexuality in the Rorschach," *Journal of Projective Techniques*, 22 (March 1958), pp. 33–54. See also Saghir and Robins, *Male and Female Homosexuality*, Ch. 7.

73 Goode, *Deviant Behavior*, p. 377.

74 Simmons, *Deviants*, p. 63.

75 Quoted in "Charting the Gay Life," *Newsweek*, March 27, 1978, p. 100. See Bell and Weinberg, *Homosexualities*; Mark Freedman, "Homosexuals May Be Healthier Than Straights," *Psychology Today*, 8 (March 1975), pp. 28–32; Weinberg and Williams, *Male Homosexuals*, pp. 276–278.

76 George Weinberg, *Society and the Healthy Homosexual*, Anchor, Doubleday, Garden City, N.Y., 1973, p. 1. See also Robert E. Gould, "What We Don't Know About Homosexuality," *The New York Times Magazine*, Feb. 24, 1974, pp. 13, 51–63; Thomas S. Szasz, *The Manufacture of Madness*, Harper & Row, New York, 1970.

77 Grace Lichtenstein, "Laws Aiding Homosexuals Face Rising Opposition Around Nation," *The New York Times*, Apr. 27, 1978, p. 20.

78 Altman, *Homosexual*, p. 231.

79 Altman, *Homosexual*, p. 230.

Epilogue

From the perspective of the dominant social groups, socialization is considered successful in a society when its members come to accept the "noble lie" that the limited range of options available in the dominant culture are the only real, proper, and natural ways of acting, thinking, and feeling and that they constitute the full range of human freedom. Part of this process involves instilling in neophyte members the belief that the traditional social rules and institutionalized social practices are inevitable and binding. To depart from these culturally approved moral paths is to court danger and disaster.

Such reality-constricting propaganda and social controls tend to *alienate* a person from the many potential selves and life-styles possible, from what a person might become were he or she more aware of the arbitrariness and narrowness inherent in the conventional social rules and behavioral roles and were he or she accorded a wider range of options.[1] During the last two decades, however, hippie and communal countercultures, new mystical religious cults, gay and women's liberation movements, sexual freedom organizations, and other activist groups have emerged to challenge these collective fictions—this ideological and moral monopoly—of the traditional and conventional social order. From bisexuality to satan worship, from group sex in the suburbs to people preparing to receive the divine light, a vast proliferation of divergent subcultures and life-styles is slowly eroding the moral certitudes and normalized repressions of the dominant cultures of many Western societies.

The beginning of the 1980s thus witnesses an abundance of life-style choices in a rapidly changing and pluralistic America. As the stigmatizing imagery fades from many kinds of behavior and identities once considered deviant, a broader tolerance for *diversity* appears to be emerging, reflected in the burgeoning popular movements labeled in the mass media as "alternative life-styles," "self-actualization," and "human potential." Yet the likelihood is very great that the current self-centered thrust of such expressive movements (whether it be "open marriage," "swinging," "primal screams," sensitivity encounter groups, or religious cults) will divert concern and effective social action away from any meaningful challenges to the more repressive features of the larger political and economic structures commanded by the dominant groups of the society. Although involvement in self-actualization movements may heighten personal feelings of happiness and satisfaction, perhaps eventually helping to galvanize some groups into political action, it may just as easily stagnate into a narcissistic self-absorption.[2] "Sensory awakening," "cultivation of inner experience," sentiments of authenticity, and other individual psychological mood changes will not necessarily mitigate the social oppression from those societal power structures that restrict basic life chances for the disadvantaged and socially marginal. Clearly, freedom presupposes a certain liberation of consciousness; yet it is a double-edged sword.

Whatever the future quality of American life, its shape and contours—as well as its deviants—will be in large measure the social product of our collective choices. A major challenge of this decade will be to devise social policies that will enable the society not only to manage diversity—and the social conflict that it will generate—but to accept it as an important social value in postindustrial America. That our nation is still some distance from the achievement of such policies is evident in the recurrence of absolutist moral crusades stimulating new legislation and political acts which millions of Americans experience as repressive (for example, abortion restrictions, confiscation of sexually erotic films, denial of homosexual civil rights, and suppression of antinuclear demonstrations).

Although a relativistic perspective on deviance is an antidote to the kind of rigid moral absolutism that oppresses humans and constricts human potentiality, such a relativistic stance does not mean that humanistically oriented sociologists should give up the attempt to discover those social arrangements that foster human freedom, social justice and individual dignity, that facilitate growth and self-fulfillment, and that encourage other human values. Quite the contrary. The awareness of the socially created character of deviance precludes neither the search for intrinsic human values that transcend particular cultures nor the design of social institutions that facilitate the "good society."[3] And if we discover such values and identify the kinds of social structures that contribute to the liberation of the human mind and spirit, then humanistic sociologists may indeed choose to articulate a more "absolutist" perspective.

FOOTNOTES

1 See Peter L. Berger, *The Sacred Canopy*, Doubleday, Garden City, N.Y., 1969, pp. 24, 81–96; Erich Goode, *Drugs in America*, Knopf, New York, 1972, p. 232.

2 See Edwin Schur, *The Awareness Trap*, Quadrangle, New York, 1976; John Irwin, *Scenes*, Sage, Beverly Hills, Calif., 1977; Charles Y. Glock and Robert N. Bellah (eds.), *The New Religious Consciousness*, University of California Press, Berkeley, Calif., 1976.

3 See John F. Glass, "The Humanistic Challenge to Sociology," in John F. Glass and John R. Staude (eds.), *Humanistic Society*, Goodyear, Pacific Palisades, Calif., 1972, pp. 1–12; Alfred McClung Lee, *Sociology For Whom?* Oxford University Press, New York, 1978; Graeme Newman, *Comparative Deviance*, Elsevier, New York, 1976.

Name Index

Subject Index